WORDPLAYS 5

LSCA TITLE I

JAN 24 1990

Library of Congress Cataloging in Publication Data
Wordplays 5
CONTENTS: *North Atlantic, Sunday in the Park with George, The Death of von Richthofen as Witness-
ed from Earth, Deep Sleep, The Birth of the Poet*
Library of Congress Catalog Card No.: 86-63190
ISBN: 1-55554-006-6 (cloth)
ISBN: 1-55554-007-4 (paper)

Printed in the United States of America

Publication of this book has been made possible in part by a grant from the National Endowment
for the Arts, Washington, D.C., a federal agency, and public funds received from the New York
State Council on the Arts.

General Editors of the DramaContemporary Series:
    Bonnie Marranca and Gautam Dasgupta

WORDPLAYS 5

an anthology of
New American Drama

---

plays by

James Strahs
James Lapine-Stephen Sondheim
Des McAnuff
John Jesurun
Kathy Acker

PAJ Publications
[a division of Performing Arts Journal, Inc.]
New York

THE WORDPLAYS SERIES

We published the first volume of WORDPLAYS in 1980, and the book's reception, both in the theatre and in places where theatre is taught, was so positive that we decided to expand the concept into a series. *Wordplays 2*, *Wordplays 3*, and *Wordplays 4* followed, and now we have *Wordplays 5*.

WORDPLAYS is about new approaches to writing for the theatre by American playwrights. We choose plays that we think audiences should know about, hoping that this will give the plays a longer life in the theatre through productions. Sometimes we include writers who have never been published before, others who are not known throughout the country but we feel they should be, and we always want to publish writers who already have a history in the theatre.

For us, the most important thing is that the writing go beyond the cliché into something more provocative, even more difficult at times, to bring us closer to the kind of characters, the feeling of communication, of time, and of space, and the processes of thinking that outline the contemporary experience of living. Our hope is that this ongoing WORDPLAYS series embraces the panorama of styles and temperaments reflected in contemporary American plays.

The Publishers

Contents

North Atlantic

James Strahs

North Atlantic was first performed in its final version by the Wooster Group at the Performing Garage in New York City in January 1984 with the following cast:

Willem Dafoe	*Colonel Lloyd "Ned" Lud (A. A.)*
Spalding Gray	*General Lance "Rod" Benders*
Anna Köhler	*Nurse Private Wendy-Gwen Clark*
Nancy Reilly	*Corporal Nurse Jane Babcock*
Peyton Smith	*Master Sergeant Mary Bryzynsky*
Michael Stumm	*Marine Private Guy Doberman*
Kate Valk	*Ensign Word Processor Ann Pusey*
Ron Vawter	*Captain N. I. Roscoe Chizzum*
Jeff Webster	*General Understudy*

Director: Elizabeth LeCompte
Original Music: Eddy Dixon
Set: Jim Clayburgh
Technical Direction: Jeff Webster and Michael Nishball

The initial development of the *North Atlantic* text and mise-en-scène was done by the Wooster Group and James Strahs in collaboration with members of The Globe Theatre, Eindhoven, Netherlands, and the Mickery, Amsterdam in June 1983.

In 1983, over forty years after the middle of the second great war, the allied powers continued to maintain a military presence in the center of Europe. These are but a few of the men and women in uniform who served their country in the cause of peace. The scene is a ship of the United States on an intelligence cruise off the coast of Europe.

CHARACTERS

(*Author's note: The armed-service characters in this play are all continental Americans of European lineage though they need not be played by such.*)

Ensign Word-Processor Ann Pusey
Corporal Nurse Jane Babcock
Nurse Private Wendy-Gwen Clark
Cadet Word-Processor Gretchen Handcock
PFC Med-Tech Kim Buttersworth
Master Sergeant Mary Bryzynsky
PFC Word-Processor Alice Buckingham
PFC Word-Processor Crystal Gale Mumford
Captain N. I. Roscoe Chizzum
Colonel Lloyd "Ned" Lud (A. A.)
General Lance "Rod" Benders
Marine Private Bernard "Gregory" Houlihan
Marine Private Walter "Raj" Doberman
Dutch Mother
German Priest
French Schoolgirl
Dutch People (ensemble)
South Korean Judge (voice)

SCENE 1

(*Female Quarters.*)

KIM: Look, you're in this up to your wrinkly neck so you'd better keep your mouth shut.

CRYSTAL: Look who's throwin' her weight around.

KIM: I'm telling you, sister, you queer this for us an' I'll . . .

CRYSTAL: Naw, naw, you got me wrong. It's just that they're all such stinkin' cheats, no goods, rotten to the core. They're a disgrace to the service.

KIM: Aw, cut the grousin' and the gripin'. How we supposed to get by 'cept we go along?

CRYSTAL: Cheezit! Who comin'?

WENDY-GWEN: 'Smee, Wendy-Gwen. I got it! I got the stuff. Look, manifolds and solenoids, loop tubing, floppy disks, daisy wheels. We're rich!

KIM: 'Atta girl, Wendy-Gwen, doomsday! We'll fence it in Finland. S'off his plane?

WENDY-GWEN: Yeah. They never saw me coming. Ole Gwendy knows her stuff.

KIM: Hot damn. Spanish gold as easy as cuttin' rings off a corpse . . .

CRYSTAL: Okay, can it. Let's stash it then splitski down the chowstroy for hash. It'll look like we live there, never been up for air. They'll never know a thing.

KIM: Good thinking, Crystal Gale, you just stick with little Kimmy, you hear . . .

MARY: (*On bullhorn.*) Good work, girls, bring it up top side. I got containerized cargo's got false bottoms. Good girls, good girls.

WENDY-GWEN: Quick, they 're coming back! (*Exit. Enter Jane and Ann.*)

JANE: So, Ann, give that to me again, wouldja? Whoja say?

ANN: I didn't say anybody, Jane. And watch out, you start up with me.

JANE: I just asked you who. I really wanna know.

ANN: Well, nobody. Another nobody from the department of defense. Not even the same guy.

JANE: But a guy, huh? There ain't nothin' like a guy. D'ya lettum snake?

ANN: Snake! That's repulsive. Are you crazy?

JANE: Well, what do you do? Do you do anything?

ANN: Now listen, Corporal, you shut up if you want to talk to me. I've got a lot better things to do than listen to you play the radio. Believe you me!

JANE: Well, excuse me! Can I help it if some of us are a little more physical than others of us. So I like what you can do, what people do. Can I help it? What are you going to do, execute me?

ANN: You are excused, I'm sure.

JANE: Come on, Ann. Tell me about him. I mean, is he blond?

ANN: Is he blond?

JANE: I mean, is he light? You know what I mean.

ANN: Is he light! You're too much, Jane.

JANE: Well, what's he do? Does he do electronics?

ANN: Oh, God, Jane, you are such a drone!

JANE: Well, can he spit?

ANN: Spit! I can't believe you said that. I'll tell you this much and no more.

JANE: Oh, goody.

ANN: He's a colonel. His name is Lud. But I call him Luddy. And his first name is Ned. Neddy. I'll have to admit he's cute.

JANE: Yeah, and then what?

ANN: And then nothing. He just came on board. I hardly know him.

JANE: Oh no, he's a dirty dick from the D.O.D.!

ANN: Yes, Jane, and he's here to get a tape. Well, we'll see who gets that tape, won't we, Jane.

JANE: Yeah, Ann, and I'll bet it's you!

ANN: Yeah, because that's the kind of gal I am!

JANE: How'd he come in.

ANN: Private plane.

JANE: Wow, that's class. I hope it don't get stripped.

ANN: Oh, I know, aren't those girls a sketch the way they steal. Call them up here, Jane. There's something I've got to say to them. (*Air raid alert siren.*) Girls! Girls! Listen to me. (*Enter Alice, Wendy-Gwen, Crystal and Kim.*) There's something special tonight, girls. A contest! Miss G. I. Dream Girl Wet Uniform Contest.

GIRLS: Ugh!

ANN: Don't say that.

CRYSTAL: Whose idea is this, Ann?

KIM: Yeah, let's see you mork your way out of this.

ANN: Don't say that! There's a prize. The winner gets to be in Mike Smith's new movie!

GIRLS: Ugh.

ANN: Don't say that! It's a good idea. It's good for the soldiers' morale. So be there and look good. Wear your best. At the officer's club, tonight!

CRYSTAL: Is this like your last one, Ann, where we all wound up without our panties?

GIRLS: Yeah!

ANN: No, no. You don't understand. This is on the up and up.

KIM: Oh, God, pass the grease.

ANN: No, it's for the boys. Our fighting boys. The boys who are going to give their lives for us.

GIRLS: All right!

ANN: And look, as a special treat I'll let you come early with Jane and I. They're going to grill some natives and I know how much you love to watch.

GIRLS: Yippee! Whoppee!

ANN: Look, girls. In my secret life, my real life, the one I live in dreams, I love you all. But I can't give you everything you want!

Listen, you girls. I don't think anyone ought to complain.

I want to say this to you girls and I only want to say it once and with no mincing words so you might think you understand.

Loose lips sink ships!

As far as I'm concerned all this thievery and all your negativity are all in the nature of aid to the enemy and treason with a capital T. You're a disgrace to the service.

I'm going to tell you this so you know: if things ever come around to my way of thinking, I'm going to show you. First, I'm going to have you brought up on charges and then I'm going to have you broken on the rack of public scrutiny. I'm going to throw you in the lock-up and watch the jailers have their way. I want to see them break through to the you in you that's just like me. And all the time I'm going to enjoy. Enjoy. Enjoy. (Ann sings "Did I Throw My Life Away.")

JANE: I think they like you better than they like me.

ANN: Don't be silly, Jane. I want you to come tonight. General Benders wants to see some local color.

JANE: Do you think he likes me?

ANN: Oh, don't be silly, Jane. You just be sure we get that tape. (Exit Ann.)

CRYSTAL: Who's she? Queen of the Pantry?

KIM: Man, I just cannot stand her private world.

WENDY-GWEN: What's happening? We working beach blankets or what?

JANE: The usual.

KIM: Yeah, gravy boat and deviled weenies.

WENDY-GWEN: Hey, where's Gretchen and Mary?

ALICE: Yeah, and Bernice? Where's she?

KIM: Hey, Alice, you know who's gonna win the wet uniform contest, don't ya. You're looking at her.

ALICE: Oh, really, I thought that was up to the judges.

KIM: The judges! Forget it! I'm gonna be Miss G. I. Dream Girl and be in Mike Smith's movie. So stay outta my way. You understand?

ALICE: That's not fair. And anyway, what kind of a prize is that?

JANE: You kiddin'? He's the guy they call Mr. Pogo.

ALICE: And anyway, Kim, you are about the ugliest whack I have ever seen.

KIM: I don't know what game you're playing, sweetheart, but whatever it is, little Kim is gonna find out all about it.

JANE: Aw, leave her alone. She's in over her head.

KIM: Over your head, you mean.

JANE: Look, you're in this up to your wrinkly neck, so you can keep your mouth shut.

ALICE: And anyway, Ann said this time there's no fix. It's going to be totally legit. You're not going to believe it.

JANE: Come on, Al, I'll show you the new shower head I got.

ALICE: Oh, great, never used one of them. Is it a Water Pik?

JANE: For sure. (*Exit Jane and Alice.*)

KIM: If they think they can cross little Kimmy they got another thought comin'.

CRYSTAL: Aw, come on, Kim, you're just talking a lot of hooey. (*Exit Kim, Crystal and Wendy-Glen.*)

SCENE 2

(*Operations Room.*)

ROSCOE: The name's Chizzum. Roscoe, navy intelligence. Mother's name was Guidry but the old man was a Chizzum. That's the handle. So the less said the better.

I thought I'd let you know who I am before anything comes up. Not that anything's gonna come up. We'll just sit tight and watch and see what happens, see which way the wind blows. So to speak. Obviously we're on the inside here . . .

You know the score. You'll figure it out for yourself. That's why we're all here. Okay. I can hear them coming. (*Enter Benders, Houlihan, Doberman and one or two other "listeners." The "listeners" wear headsets like stethoscopes.*)

BENDERS: Okay, men, attention up now. I want you to spread yourselves out over there. That's right, by the console. Make a semi-circle as best you can. Now men, Captain Chizzum, navy intelligence, is going to run some stuff by you all to see what you can make out of it. Captain, you want to run by them what you were running by me this morning?

ROSCOE: Whatever you say, General Benders, sir.

BENDERS: Now remember men, Doberman and you, Houlihan, and this is real important, this is the meat that is going to make us or break us so listen up and listen good.

ROSCOE: Okay. At ease you guys. Okay, as I see it there's two things I want to say and this is what I was saying before to the General here in his office. I'm going to tell you I've been down to the Pentagon and it's the latest way of thinking and he thought you should hear it.

Okay. The first point is basic to all this kind of work. This is like a theorem or a proposition.

No, no, not like you guys are thinking. There'll be plenty of time for that when the time comes. Okay.

You know, we used to have a saying over at Shape command that such and such or something or other was axiomatic, meaning, well, meaning what I'm talking about. So okay. It's this: you have to face the fact that all these code things are created after the fact of the production of the material to be encoded. Or put out. That's the meat of it.

BENDERS: Yes, I see, the meat.

ROSCOE: You want to take off the headset, Doberman, so you can hear me? Thanks?

DOBERMAN: Sorry, Captain, I thought I was hearing something . . . Sorry.

ROSCOE: Okay. So . . . So, in fact, you can operate a pretty good size encoding works, even a major operation, without anyone in the operation being aware, in any direct manner or fact of what exactly it is that he or she is doing insofar as he or she won't know she or he's working on the raw material for a future encodement effort or operation. Any questions?

DOBERMAN: Let me see if I got this straight, sir. Do you mean the newspapers and magazines, radio/television, things like that there?

ROSCOE: Major media of propaganda. Yes, I follow you there, Boberman.

DOBERMAN: Doberman, sir.

ROSCOE: Yes, okay. No. About what you were saying, no. Not exactly. Listen to this. You've got your guy working in a specific industrial or service occupation. He's out on the line or in the back or up in the office pushing a pencil or puttin' out product or makin' rounds or maybe he's just killing time. How am I supposed to know? Or so he thinks! And it turns out he's in some covert operation or even something like Radio Free Europe. It's all potentially collaborational and, on the bottom line, synergistic.

BENDERS: That's a tough one. But go ahead, Captain.

ROSCOE: Okay. Well, in so many words what I'm saying is you may individually think you're in sales or administration or analysis or some special promotion but it's often not what it seems and that's a command decision from the top. A soft drink war, for instance, we've found a few of these very useful.

HOULIHAN: I wish I could follow you better, Captain, but this thing beats me cold. Are you talking about them or us?

ROSCOE: I appreciate your situation, Doberman.

HOULIHAN: Houlihan, sir.

ROSCOE: Right, Houlihan. I appreciate your situation. I've been there myself, believe me. Let me put it to you like this. I just want to say that the whole thing can be going on nationwide and you may feel small and alone and isolated inside yourselves and maybe you are. Sometimes there's no substitute for what we call a sanitary cordon. So, it pays to check your information through channels three or four times a day. Myself, I do it after meals. You only need to pick up the phone to get yourself back in the start mode. And I don't think I need remind you men that we have in our possession a communications network the likes of which'll never be seen again.

And don't think that I mean to suggest here some sort of absolute equation of all mental activity. But after we swallow our pride and swallow hard it's something to think about. Okay.

Point two is straight and to the point. Men, you've got the right stuff to do this job and to do it good. There's been a lot of talk about right stuff and what it is and who's really got it but let's just say it's the stuff you need to do the job, get it done come whiskey or water and be proud you did it. And you guys have got it and you got it in spades and to a man, believe you me.

Okay, that's about it, General.

BENDERS: Just great, Chizzum, that's A-1 stuff!

ROSCOE: Just part of my job, General, believe me, sir.

BENDERS: Well, I hope you men took all this in. Remember, we're headed for war so this is no time to shilly-shally. Thanks again, Chizzum, I'm sure we'll be coming back to that. That was a first class breakdown of some fine points. I can't say I follow every strand of them but that's why we're here.

DOBERMAN: Like you always say, General, sir, intelligence is a twenty-four-hour, seven day a week job. It's a challenge and we're here to take it.

BENDERS: Now you're talking, Doberman. Esprit de corp is worth three divisions.

HOULIHAN: If we could get this code we could break them, break them wide open, split 'em, crack 'em, I just know it.

ROSCOE: Not so fast with the rough stuff, Houlihan. This is a subtle business. Push too far one way or the other and you're talking broken English. Get it?

BENDERS: The Captain is right, men. Now back to work. Keep your eyes peeled and your ears on the track.

Chizzum, come here. Chizzum, you don't mind I call you Roscoe, do you?

ROSCOE: Hell, no, chief. Let's roll up our sleeves.

BENDERS: What time are the interrogations, Roscoe?

ROSCOE: Fifteen-hundred, if I'm not mistaken, sir.

BENDERS: And my address to the men?

ROSCOE: Twenty-two hundred is how I figure it.

BENDERS: Roger.

ROSCOE: Yes, sir?

BENDERS: Good.

ROSCOE: General, sir?

BENDERS: Come over here for a minute, will you, Roscoe. Look, we've got a problem.

ROSCOE: Yes sir. What problem, sir?

BENDERS: It's got to do with this guy Lud. We're bringing him on board on a hunch it could pan out for us but to say the least it's . . . chancey.

ROSCOE: You mean he's a gambler, sir?

BENDERS: No, no, it's that he's weird . . .

ROSCOE: You mean queer, sir, 'cause if he is . . .

BENDERS: No, no, nothing like that. Well, you'll see in a minute because I'm bringing him in on this thing.

ROSCOE: Yes, sir, anything you want, sir, we got nothing to hide here, sir.

BENDERS: Right. We need a break on this thing, Jim, and I don't mind sticking my neck out to get it. Do me a favor and do what you can to easy this thing on as much as you can, will you? Of course we'll debrief him . . .

ROSCOE: I'll do what I can, sir. That's what I'm here for.

BENDERS: I knew I could count on you, Chizzum.

ROSCOE: Thank you, sir, I'll take care of him myself personally.

BENDERS: Good. I don't know what he knows. He's sitting on something I don't quite understand. He's one of these whiz kids, all wrapped up in this information technology thing. Lot of hooey, as far as I can see.

ROSCOE: If you don't mind my saying so, sir, I feel like this whole thing is a can of worms.

BENDERS: Gotcha. Fore-armed is fore-warned. Nothing's more important than that old human element. Right, Roscoe. Ha, ha.

One more thing, Captain Chizzum.

ROSCOE: Yes, sir?

BENDERS: What's it like to give it to that Ann Pusey? I mean in the tail. Is it all it's cracked up to be?

ROSCOE: Come on, General, get serious. You never felt a surge like that. Just knowing you're in there, makes your knees give.

BENDERS: Better than Argentina, huh?

ROSCOE: Are you kidding? There's no comparison. Look, General, are you interested? I can make some discrete inquiry . . .

BENDERS: Jeez, I don't know if I could take it. You know Potter, don't you? He kicked while he was down the tube. Girl freaked, went morbid. Couldn't get him dressed. It was a horror show.

ROSCOE: He was wearing her things, right?

BENDERS: Right.

ROSCOE: Hey, don't worry. What you want is what you want, right? Nothing you can do about it. Let's face it.

BENDERS: Somebody has to, right? It's like a burden, right?

ROSCOE: Right, sir. Sir, if I might?

BENDERS: Go ahead, Roscoe.

ROSCOE: If you don't mind my asking, sir, who is this guy Lud? He's not the foreigner, is he, sir?

BENDERS: What makes you ask, Roscoe?

ROSCOE: Well, maybe he wasn't born here. I mean over there. I mean, maybe there's some foreign influence at work here.

BENDERS: Oh, I don't think so, Chizzum. He talks perfectly good.

ROSCOE: Well, I don't know, sir. Maybe too good. There's something fishy here for my money.

BENDERS: Don't worry, Roscoe. From what I hear his cover's special services.

ROSCOE: Begging your pardon, sir, from what I've heard it looks like more than that to me.

BENDERS: Yes, well, I've heard rumor he's more, maybe the mid-Atlantic man. I'm sure it's all very normal. But, of course, you never know.

ROSCOE: No, sir, if you don't mind my saying so, you never know.

BENDERS: Oh, here's Colonel Pusey. You're just in time, Ann. (*Enter Ann.*)

ANN: I'm so sorry I'm late, General. We were having some discipline problems down in the women's compound and I had to step into a very tense situation.

BENDERS: Oh, Ann, I hope it's nothing serious.

ANN: Oh, no sir. Nothing I can't handle, General, really. Please proceed. I apologize again.

BENDERS: Well, all right, Ann, if you say so. Wait here just a minute, will you, Ann.

All right, you men, go back to your work. And see if you can come up with anything. We need a break on this thing and we're going to go for it. And when we get it you'd better believe Charlie's going to shit pajama!

Ann, come over here for a minute, will you. Have you got it set up for tonight? With the stenographers and everybody?

ANN: Oh, General, I told you I'd take care of everything, didn't I?

BENDERS: Yes, yes, good. Now about the redhead, what's her name? Is she coming?

ANN: Try brunette, General. She's hardly a redhead!

BENDERS: Well, all right. But it is streaked. You can see a hint of copper in it. Is she coming?

ANN: Oh, you mean Jane! Why, yes, she's coming. Every chance she gets!

BENDERS: Now, don't tease me, Ann. Is she really that way? Is she really that loose?

ANN: Loose! Why my goodness, General, you could drive a dump-truck down that alley and K-turn without even using the rear-view mirror.

BENDERS: Ann, you're just too much. You make me feel like a boy again!

ANN: A boy! General, that's absurd!

BENDERS: Oh, Ann, come on down to the canteen with me and I'll get you something to warm us up.

ANN: Why, General, so early?

BENDERS: Will she do it, Ann? Did you ask her?

ANN: Why General Benders, I have no idea what you are talking about. (*Exit Ann and Benders.*)

ROSCOE: Okay, you guys, take a break.

What a can of garbage that guy is! Pwheww. Talk about air heads.

DOBERMAN: Shut it down, sir? Regular duty-day?

ROSCOE: Keep it on standby. Nobody knows how long he'll be down there.

HOULIHAN: Captain, sir? Begging your pardon for asking, sir, but could you give us the straight dope on this operation? Is there anything in this whole thing? All this listening.

DOBERMAN: Yeah, Captain, are they just blowing it up our assholes or is this the real thing, the way it is. . . ?

ROSCOE: Okay. Look, I'm going to give you guys the low down but I'm going to be real careful about the way I give it to you. You understand? I'll give you guys this much and then you keep it shut how I blow steam when we're in port.

DOBERMAN: That sounds like a fair deal to me. But, honest, Captain, I never gave it a thought to say anything anyway.

ROSCOE: And I knew you didn't, Doberman, that's why I trust you enough to make a deal. How 'bout you, Houlihan, you want to know?

HOULIHAN: Well, I don't know, that don't sound like much of a deal to me . . .

ROSCOE: What's your first name, Houlihan?

HOULIHAN: Gregory, sir.

ROSCOE: And is that what you think, Gregory, think I'm not givin' you much of a deal? You know what'd happen if I started messing with your entitlements? Like if the computer changed your name and shipped you out to Saudi Arabia?

HOULIHAN: Okay, okay, I'll go along. What's in this shit, Captain?

DOBERMAN: Gee, I didn't know we had troops in Saudi fucking Arabia!

ROSCOE: Pipe down, okay, Doberman. Okay, Gregory. And I told you I'm going to be careful the way I tell you this and I'm gonna be. Okay, this is it. As far as I'm concerned this whole operation is just so much piss in a splatter pan.

HOULIHAN: Piss in a splatter pan, sir?

DOBERMAN: That's it?

HOULIHAN: Come on, Captain, tell us what you mean. Are you putting the whole thing down, intelligence and the national security and all, the whole thing?

ROSCOE: Now don't be going back on your deal, you guys! I told you I was going to be careful about what I told you and I was.

DOBERMAN: But I don't even know what that means.

ROSCOE: Okay. Okay. I'll spell it out for you but you guys'll owe me for this one. Now listen and listen good. 'Cause this is cabbage I just ain't chewin' twice! The whole place is a fake. It's a dummy, a pilotless airplane. It's a drone, it's all make believe.

HOULIHAN: Wha. . . ?

ROSCOE: It's the old statue of liberty! The entire operation is set up to throw them off the scent. Dis . . . mis . . . information, get it? The real operation is five hundred miles south a here.

HOULIHAN: No shit!

DOBERMAN: You mean we don't do shit here, we're just making patterns and somebody else is making the plays. . . ?

ROSCOE: You got it, baby. That, at the moment, is the sad, sad truth. You're not even backup. It's all as useless as a nun sucking on a lizard head. But one word a this to flap-face and I'll see you fuckers busted off the surface a the earth, you follow?

HOULIHAN: Yeah, sure, but the shit is I thought we were doing something out here, I thought we had action . . .

DOBERMAN: Yeah, it felt just like it . . .

ROSCOE: The hell! You never get anywhere near action in the studio, this inside stuff. It's got to do with getting out on the street and making some moves, making some moves and then seeing what shakes out of the mattress . . . After you get up and shake off your snake and stand down there at the end of the bed. Just standing down there and looking at what you just done, what's lying there after you had your way . . . You guys know what I'm talking about?

DOBERMAN; I guess so . . .

HOULIHAN: Yeah, sure we do . . .

ROSCOE: You're good guys. Hang tough, you hear. And remember, a couple a false moves and the whole damned North Atlantic is another stinkin' bowl of muscleman soup. Okay, stations, I hear them coming back. (*Enter Lud.*) Hey there, buddy. S'Roscoe, navy intelligence.

LUD: Lud. Ned Lud.

ROSCOE: Okay. Welcome aboard, Lud. General Benders mentioned you were due.

LUD: This operations, this place here?

ROSCOE: Right. Operations room. Nerve center. We got everything here. Take a look around.

LUD: Those guys readers?

ROSCOE: Right. They're good boys. Good ears. What can I do for you, Lud?

LUD: Nothing.

ROSCOE: Okay. Okay, we got all the services here. You're regular army, right?

LUD: Right.

ROSCOE: Where you been stationed?

LUD: Jersey. Mendocino.

ROSCOE: That's weird.

LUD: Why?

ROSCOE: Uh, nothin', just not a lot of guys pull those slots.

LUD: Dumb luck.

ROSCOE: What's that again, Lud? You talkin' fortune cookie?

LUD: S'name a my plane. I'm army air.

ROSCOE: S'that so, Lud? No kiddin'. You with the I-corps then, huh?

LUD: I-corps, yeah. I-corps. How'd you know?

ROSCOE: We had I-corps through here before. I-corps guys. You know Eddie Slovik? He was I-corps.

LUD: Yeah? Never heard a him.

ROSCOE: Never heard a him, huh? Well, he was I-corps. Or D-corps.
  Okay. I think it's great we all work together. I don't even think the services should be separate. Unified command, that's the watchword with me. Get rid of this loose configuration a rigid bureaucratics, put an end to the competition. That's what I say. No branches at all, just one massive and vicious fighting machine. You follow?

LUD: That's weird, Chizzum.

ROSCOE: What'd'you mean?

LUD: Just is. We always been separate and you know it. As I understand it we was just gonna work out a little common logic, put it in a language we could insert . . . Make a tape. You follow me at all?

ROSCOE: Lud, that may be your fraulein's opinion a what's goin' on, but what I want's a real fightin' force, no namby-pampy ad-min flag staffers, fat ass fly boys jackin' off over Virginia. I wanna crack rifle-man, a hawk-eye sucker take the whole thing, the whole shootin' match no matter where it takes place, any kin'a terrain, mud, water, fire-storm, twenty-thou, outta space. You name it! I'm talkin' about something made outta blood and guts. Shit, major force ain't took nothin' fo' forty years. Don't talk to me about containment, sanitary shit, paper shufflers, desk jocks. I wanna victory with a capital V. I wanna force fight all day party half a night, move in a territory, take it an' keepsies. Never move out, change names, nationalize the women an' settle. Like days a old. Like god-damn Jesus H. Caesar.

LUD: Let me see if I follow you. I think I see what you're saying.

ROSCOE: Naw, I'm not saying nothing. Mercenaries are just fine by me. Turks the best god-damned mercenary you can buy. We get five times as much soldier for our money there than we do at home. Give 'em a couple a uniforms, a little food, tell 'em stay in a hole an' they will till somebody comes along an' kills 'em.

LUD: You're crazy, Chizzum, we've got no place for that kind a soldier, cannon fodder . . .

ROSCOE: Yeah, yeah, I know what you're gonna say, s'all mechanized infantry now, s'lot a good work bein' done there by the big boys, Kenner, Marx, Hasbro . . .

LUD: All right. You're a funny guy, Roscoe. That's real amusing. I think we're gonna get along just fine. Reminds me a this joke. You see, this guy has a girl he wants to make so he tells her to wear thin clothes. She shows up in a tin suit and he says, what do you think, my pecker's a can opener.

ROSCOE: That's a good one, Lud. You got a real good sense a humor. Real good one. I can see that. Only one thing . . . you know, things can get real unpleasant when you're forced into not doing things you're used to doing. You know the Tech House story, don't you? About the family forced to live in a house where the bulbs don't blow? A solid year and they only changed one light. And you know where it was? In the fridge. I'm telling you it was a nightmare.

LUD: Is zat so?

ROSCOE: Yeah, you wanna stick around, I'll tell you the thermodactyl story. It's about how ya store your body heat in the empty spaces in a polyestrous fabric. But it'd be a terrible punishment just for being who you are.

LUD: Look, I know why you're talking to me like this.

ROSCOE: Talking like what, I'm not talking like anything . . .

LUD: Look, I know you think I'm stupid . . .

ROSCOE: You're crazy, Lud, I got no idea who you are. You had a few too many those Pasadena pretzels, Lud, they took you off the beam.

LUD: Lemme be real straight witcha here, Chizzum, you're talking to me like this 'cause you think I'm stupid, isn't that so?

ROSCOE: Naw, naw, you been smoking too much a that san familia . . . What I'm saying is maybe you're too smart. Maybe you know a few too many things an' wanna know more, more an' you should wanna know. Naw, I can see you're real smart, maybe an intellectual . . .

LUD: You take that back, you hear, nobody smears me with that paint brush . . .

ROSCOE: Yeah, well who you callin' tin prick . . . (*Enter Ann and Benders.*)

BENDERS: It's in an envelope in my center drawer, Ann, if you want any more. I screen their mail at random and take what I want.

ANN: Oh, General, is there a pie without your finger in it. Oh, look, it's Captain Chizzum and . . .

BENDERS: Oh, it's Colonel Lud. I see you boys have met. That's very good. Lud, this is Colonel Ann Pusey, one of our top word processor girls.

LUD: It's my pleasure, mam.

ANN: I'm very pleased to meet you, Colonel Lud.

BENDERS: Easy now, Lud, we've got a lot of work to do here.

ROSCOE: General, sir, could I talk to you for a minute over here. It's top priority.

BENDERS: What is it, Chizzum?

ROSCOE: 'Scuse me, sir, but I'm not at all sure this is going to work with this guy Lud.

BENDERS: Don't be silly, Roscoe, of course it's going to work. I think he shows tons of personality. I hear he's a real dynamo, just bubbling over with juice . . .

ROSCOE: But, sir, I'm not even sure he's who he's supposed to be.

BENDERS: That's absurd, Captain. Of course he's who he is!

ROSCOE: If you say so sir.

ANN: Oh, Colonel, I watched you land your plane. It was so smooth.

LUD: Ah, it's nothing. I've done it thousands of times.

ANN: Thousands of times! Oooh, that's exciting.

BENDERS: All right, attention up and gather 'round! Now, Lud, let me run a few things by you before we start. First, let's synchronize our watches. What time you got?

LUD: I got 19:34.

ROSCOE: Shit, I'm a minute behind.

LUD: S'nice watch, Roscoe. Z'at a spidel?

ROSCOE: What d'ya mean by that. You getting at something, Lud?

BENDERS: All right. Now about the program. Lud, I want everything we've got here processed and processed good. Look at the size of this stuff, we got more K's here than we know what to do with. I want everything we got here on a tape I can take out in my pants' pocket. And I don't much care how you get it. We got a crack crew of nurse/word processor girls at your service and ready to go whenever and wherever you need them.

LUD: Well, it's a complex process, sir, it requires a minute examination of first the raw data . . .

BENDERS: Well, keep it to yourself, I always say. Technical detail's never been my thing. How we going to go, Roscoe?

ROSCOE: We'll clear it two ways and then bring in the hostages, that's the way I see it, sir.

BENDERS: Sounds good to me. Now, you want to show me some of that fancy software you're packing, Lud?

LUD: You mean my kit, sir?

BENDERS: Well, I don't care. What have you got for the layman, your ordinary line officer, something that lights up and talks back . . .

LUD: Well, I guess I could show you . . .

ROSCOE: Ann! Ann! C'mere. Where the hell were you. I almost crapped when I didn't see you.

ANN: Oh, it was nothing, Roscoe. It just took me longer than usual to do my hair.

ROSCOE: What was that about the girls? What was it, Ann? Are the girls going to balk?

ANN: No, no. Don't worry. Everything is under control. It's all right.

ROSCOE: What is it, they won't come across. Is that it? Won't play ball?

ANN: It's nothing like that, Roscoe. Wake up!

ROSCOE: You're right. I'm tense. I probably got it wrong. You're gonna have to help me here, Ann, I'm a little lost.

ANN: Now stop worrying. It's nothing like what I said. There's no problem with the girls. I just say that to him because it turns him on.

ROSCOE: Okay. No trouble. You understand?

ANN: Yes, Roscoe. I do understand. It's unbelievable the way you worry. You're like an old woman.

ROSCOE: Yeah, well, you hoover more dick'n a South Carolina hausfrau . . .

ANN: Don't you dare talk like that in front of me! (*Ann slaps Roscoe. Exit Ann.*)

BENDERS: Oh, sure, I understand. Well, like I say, I don't much care how we get this jump done.

LUD: Oh, you were in paratroops, sir?

ROSCOE: No, he wasn't in paratroops, Lud.

BENDERS: Ha, ha, every man to his own pleasure, that's what I always say. Go stow your gear, Lud, I got a piece of business with Captain Chizzum. (*Exit Lud.*) Did you talk to her, Roscoe?

ROSCOE: I did, sir. As far as I can tell she's real excited but wants to think about it.

BENDERS: Oh, god, my knees, already . . .

ROSCOE: It may take some time, sir, so don't go getting too worked up right off . . .

BENDERS: Oh, my god, that girl. She can't be as bad as she seems.

ROSCOE: Are you kidding? Ann'll drive you nuts, make you crazy, like in a jacket in the asylum. You gotta be outta your mind. She'll blow you away, leave you snivelling and drooling and drippin' off your stick, suckin' off an old rusty bottle a gin, toothless, sclerotic, diabetic, amoebic, bummin' a dime for a fix a menthadone or whatever it is you junkies want.

BENDERS: Oh, Roscoe, I don't know if I can take much more.

ROSCOE: You gotta realize, sir, it's a ripe banana, the whole thing could explode right in your hand while you're still holding it!

BENDERS: Oh, no!

ROSCOE: Did you ever hear a the Chinese horse, sir, it's a little thing people do . . .

BENDERS: Oh, god, Roscoe, I hear that sort of blonde, the really light ones, the platinums, they can't stop doing it once they get started. Is that true. . . ?

ROSCOE: Yes siree bob. They get goin' like machines sometimes.

BENDERS: Oh, that's no good. That scares me. I'm just not that vigorous anymore.

ROSCOE: Oh, no, no, I've got it wrong. They're actually undersexed. They go passive and let you do anything you want.

BENDERS: Are you sure?

ROSCOE: Yes sir.

BENDERS: And when she drops a load. . . ?

ROSCOE: Yes sir, she shits white, sir. They're small and white, sir, and taste, from all reports, like toasted almond. You may find this difficult to believe, sir.

BENDERS: Oooh, weisse heisse scheisse!

ROSCOE: Yes sir, Maude Gone, no work-shy army mattress lazy-lay but a real fish-fanny. Many a man'd eat a yard a her sausage for a lick at her hole. It's what Fritz here calls your barsch arsch . . .

BENDERS: Oh, no, what about the smell?

ROSCOE: Heather and rosewater, sir.

BENDERS: Oh, thank god, at least she's not old and haggy like all the rest. I like that. I need that. I don't know where these urges come from, do you Chizzum?

ROSCOE: Yes, sir, I do. They come from God, sir.

BENDERS: That's good, Roscoe, I'm going to use that myself.

ROSCOE: If I might suggest something, sir, did you ever hear the one about the little witch over in Dusseldorf who can play your mother's corpse at the age of twenty-five just after she's been successfully violated by your father or the milkman or by an International Harvester for that matter. Anything. Quite spectacular. She's got a little thing she calls her cheviot noir that'll just tear your nuts off . . .

BENDERS: Oh, Chizzum, you are too much. You are the best god-damned whore-monger in this man's army . . . (*Benders dances. "Bitchin'."*)

SCENE 3

(*Female Quarters.*)

ANN: Don't be silly, Jane. You're in the service now. It's a terrible burden.

JANE: Well, do you think he likes me?

ANN: Oh don't be silly, Jane.

JANE: Yeah, well, I may be dark, but I've had some blonds.

ANN: Oh, don't be silly. Of course you have. We've all had blonds . . .

JANE: And they're all very fucked up. I remember one who'd call it all "inappropriate desire." He'd call it "she" and she'd come when he called. So I said, well, call me anytime. But I wasn't blond and he never called. So I said "the hell." Blonds are hard to handle. They never do what you tell them. You got a decent nail file, Ann?

ANN: Yeah, sure, here.

JANE: Thanks, hon.

ANN: Oh, don't be silly.

JANE: So I got to sort of going out with French boys. Though there's only one thing they really like. You know what it is? It's the bigger brown circle around the nipple, the part that's flat but colored.

ANN: Oh, don't be silly, Jane. Nobody likes that. But I can't believe you date Gauls.

JANE: Well, he's not really. I mean he's American. I mean he was born there. An' his father was Welsh. But then I had a grandmother from Albania so it just kind of follows . . .

ANN: Ooh, Welsh, they're dark . . .

MARY: (*On bullhorn.*) The Sikorski parts! Where are they? The props and the housings for the prototype? Get 'em ona skids pronto!

JANE: What's she talking about?

ANN: I don't know. I never listen to her. (*Enter Wendy-Gwen and Alice.*)

WENDY-GWEN: Hi, girls, what are you talking about?

JANE: Oh, Ann here has got a blond does electronics.

ANN: He doesn't do electronics, Jane, but he's not exactly an eyebrow pencil.

ALICE: Oh, Ann, another hook on your fish, how selfish.

JANE: Oh, yes, and you know what he said, he said there is no smell on earth worse than your sort of dishwater snatch.

ANN: Jane, don't talk like that! The way you girls talk, I just can't believe it. (*Enter Gretchen.*)

GRETCHEN: I heard you talking. What can't you believe?

ANN: Oh, Gretchen, hi. I was just thinking about you.

GRETCHEN: Oh, really, what were you thinking?

ANN: Oh, nothing.

JANE: That's not true, Ann, we heard you crimped your boyfriend's hose and now he don't know how to spit.

WENDY-GWEN: Spit, what's spit?

JANE: Spit, hell. What's a hose?

GRETCHEN: Oh, spit's nothing. It's just that glue keeps our Miss Ann's knees stuck together.

WENDY-GWEN: Glue? What does that mean?

ANN: Oh, don't worry about it, Wendy-Gwen, it's just these girls are so mental.

JANE: Yeah, honey, stop worrying, it'll make you look years older and you'll have to work twice as hard for your spit.

WENDY-GWEN: What's that mean?

GRETCHEN: Oh, nothing, it's the ink that comes out a boy's fountain pen . . .

JANE: Yeah, 'cept every time you look down you see something like "Duane" slobbered on your thigh.

ANN: Oooh, Gretchy, I think she's saying you date illiterates who make gobs for guys.

ALICE: Oh, god, what are you girls talking about? What's in those little heads of yours?

JANE: Oh, I know there's nothing in little Gretchy's head, I mean she's not even a real American.

GRETCHEN: I am so! I'm as American as you!

ANN: Oh, come on, Gretchy, take a look in the mirror some morning.

JANE: Ann is right, Gretch, you're not even off the boat, you needed a green card to get in the service.

ANN: So there.

MARY: (*On bullhorn.*) The gross a Stratney A harbormasters, where are they? I got 'em going to the Lebanon special. I need 'em now! (Enter Kim and

Crystal.)

KIM: Hi, guys, what are you talking about?

JANE: Oh, we were talking about that horrible venereal disease you've got and just can't get rid of . . .

KIM: Yeah, and you know where I got it, the same place you got that hideous dark complexion of yours.

ANN: Oooh, look who's claiming to be light!

KIM: Oh, there's Miss Ann, down there stuffing trash into her plastic bag . . .

ANN: But you do have quite a tan, dear, and here it is the middle of the winter.

KIM: But you must use so much bleach to get like that, darling, it's such a wonderful unnatural effect. But I bet from your point of view it looks like it makes perfect sense.

GRETCHEN: You'll even catch a whiff of it if you get too close.

ANN: Well, share the fantasy! You should know about smells, shouldn't you. I mean, I know how you girls get a guy. You just sit him down on a whooppee cushion and blow a little up his nose.

WENDY-GWEN: Blow what up his nose?

CRYSTAL: Oh, cripes, Gwendy, what are you, a smurf? You know what she means.

KIM: Well, it's not toilet water, that's for sure, or that stuff you feed 'em when you make 'em dig.

MARY: (*On bullhorn.*) All right, we'll have none of that stuff around here. I don't care what you girls do with each other after I turn off the lights but when you're in uniform you'll do what I tell you. Kimmy, you better learn a little respect for a superior officer.

KIM: And who says she's superior to me?

MARY: (*On bullhorn.*) I do! You want me to bust you back to pay-grade. You'll go along, and you'll go along with grace and good humor!

ANN: If I looked like you, Kimmy, I wouldn't risk being quite so lewd and disrespectful!

CRYSTAL: I'm getting so excited! Let's go down the poop and light a fire. Maybe some of the James gang'll be down there.

MARY: (*On bullhorn.*) Forget it! I don't get those Stratneys in two minutes I'm gonna come in there with a cattle prod and make you whump over and load your panties with shit-balls! So move! (*All girls exit double-time except Ann.*)

ANN: I just hate to pull rank! But when a girl's a girl like me, a girl gets what she wants. And when what she want's a boy, she goes out and gets that boy. (*Lud enters. Ann and Lud sing duet.*)

SCENE 4

(*Operations Room.*)

ROSCOE: Who's he think he is, Admiral Cipher?

LUD: Who you talking about?

ROSCOE: Him. Pearhead. Guy comes on like a señor dog.

LUD: Whatd'ya mean. He's a hero. He'd been through thirty-seven major engagements before the age a forty. That's an amazing record, almost one a year.

ROSCOE: I'd like to know where he's from. Guy like that'd nuke his home town. I know the type.

LUD: What do you figure him for, Roscoe? Cincinnati Society? Front for Progress? ABC?

ROSCOE: Ah, ABCD goldfish. I don't know how to figure him. Another Norstad he ain't. Another Bendetsen.

LUD: Those guys were before your time, weren't they?

ROSCOE: Yeah, that was another time. Those were guys with—what'd'y call it— foresight. Right. Could hear the grass grow. Wouldn't be no goddamn Rooskies in Dubrovnik today if . . .

LUD: Yeah, I see what you mean, about the masters of Bohemia. So the element's still pretty active around here?

ROSCOE: I don't know what you're talking about, kid. D'jyou get yer gear stowed?

LUD: So you never heard of the element, right? You heard what the general said.

ROSCOE: General! Some general. One star. And not rising. I'll tell you, Lud, I don't get involved in these petty internecine disputes. I stay above all that.

LUD: What about Ridgeway?

ROSCOE: Ridgeway. Yeah, he's a bomber from way back.

LUD: You know about the Ratford Plan then?

ROSCOE: You mean the TV show? Naw, I never watch TV.

LUD: You like playing dumb, don't you, Chizzum? That's smart.

ROSCOE: Yeah, smart. Don't lord it over me. You're looking at Michigan State.

LUD: Oh, yeah, Michigan? I'm Purdue.

ROSCOE: That's great, kid, send me a chicken for X-mas. I got to tell you, Lud, you're a hard guy to have a conversation with.

LUD: Look, here's an old joke for you, maybe get us off on the right foot. You see there's this guy with a wife and a parrot. The parrot starts squawkin' so he cuts its throat and throws it down the crap hole. So the parrot's lying down there dying and sayin' to himself something like, oh shit, and in comes the wife who's got her monthly and squats down over the hole, it's like a French toilet. Then the parrot looks up and he's wiping it off his face and says, I thought I had it bad.

ROSCOE: That's a chemical toilet, Lud, don't shit me.

LUD: You're getting a little hot there, aren't you, Roscoe? I'm just asking a few questions. So, tell me, I suppose you never heard of Swirling Clouds of Dust? Acres of Diamonds?

ROSCOE: What is this, Lud, piano lessons?

LUD: So what's a Bud Light?

ROSCOE: I'll tell you where I stand, Lud, I'm for America first. If King George doesn't keep his nose out a American affairs, I'll bust him in the snout.

HOULIHAN: Excuse me, sir, can we take a break?

ROSCOE: Yeah, sure. You guys depressed? Okay, let's shut it down. Benders'll be back but we'll just tell him it's night. Safe locked? Carbons and message scraps in the burn bag?

DOBERMAN: Most of them, anyway.

ROSCOE: What about the tape?

HOULIHAN: What tape?

ROSCOE: What tape? The tape for the automatic typewriter.

HOULIHAN: Oh, that tape.

DOBERMAN: I'm sorry, sir, we were thinking about that little corporal from the control tower.

ROSCOE: Oh yeah, what were you thinking?

HOULIHAN: Oh, nothing.

LUD: The captain's being nice, you guys. This is when security troubles start. When you work alone, when you clean up for everybody else, when you're tired after a long day. That's when you forget. Keep a check list and use it at closing time!

ROSCOE: Oh, I'm sorry. You guys, this is Lud. Lud, Doberman and Houlihan.

LUD: How are you, boys.

HOULIHAN & DOBERMAN: Pleased to meet you, sir.

LUD: Just checking, you guys, are there sentries set?

DOBERMAN: Where?

HOULIHAN: Outside, sir?

DOBERMAN: Oh, yeah, I think there's somebody out there.

LUD: What do you mean I think! Think is not good enough for me!

HOULIHAN: Sorry, sir.

DOBERMAN: I was just gonna do it. My hand was reachin' for the phone . . .

LUD: Well, you see they're set and they stay set!

ROSCOE: Lud's right, guys. Get on the blower and get Borden, Kraft, Mahoney, Nettleson, Raffles. Who's that other guy, McDermott. Get 'em all out there on this and tell 'em to be armed to the teeth.

HOULIHAN: Yes sir.

ROSCOE: Okay. No harm. Lud here's special services, right, Lud. Tell us why they got you in here on an intelligence operation?

LUD: Continuity. You follow, Roscoe. We're here for morale. You never heard about political commissars?

ROSCOE: You're shitting me, I like that.

DOBERMAN: Begging your pardon, sir, we don't have those, do we?

LUD: That's right, Doberman. I'm here to entertain the troops. That's it. Call it liaison, whatever.

ROSCOE: That's a good one. These guys aren't under cover, Lud.

HOULIHAN: That's right, sir, we can listen to anything we want to listen to!

LUD: Okay then, let me get back to where I was. Roscoe. You guys. I'm going to say one thing to you. This is like a test. At least I got to know if we're serving in the same army.

ROSCOE: No, we're not, Lud, we're navy. That's different.

HOULIHAN: Begging your pardon, sir, we're navy army. We're marines.

LUD: Okay. Whatever. I got to say this one thing to you. I got to know what's up. Okay, this is it: Charnel House of Desire?

DOBERMAN: Yes sir?

LUD: Don't play dumb with me. You know full well what I'm talking about.

ROSCOE: Nice try, Lud. As far as I can see you're just rollin' cigars outta toilet paper.

LUD: Christ, you guys are so ignorant you probably think I'm talking about something like the college of hard knocks.

HOULIHAN: I've heard of that, sir.

ROSCOE: I got no idea what you are talking about. That must be some sort of inter-office smack-book. Out here in the real world, Jim, that don't mean the words it's written outta.

LUD: And I suppose you guys don't know about Streets of Fire?

DOBERMAN: We're non-coms, sir, we never heard of any of that.

ROSCOE: Come off it. What are those supposed to be, code words? That shit don't cross our lips. We speak English. And anyway, who gives a crap?

LUD: Who gives a crap what you speak.

ROSCOE: Yeah, maybe you don't, Lud, but there's those who do. Because what we speak is American. And you can say what you want to in American and nobody gives a good goddamn.

LUD: Listen. I'm going to give you one more. And then that's it. Valley of the Dolls. Tell me you never heard of that. Or Operation Grass Shack.

ROSCOE: Nope, nothing. You strike out, Lud. You know the story about Snoopy and the Red Baron, don't you. You don't want something like that should happen to you?

LUD: NARFE? FICA? Main Street, Secaucus?

ROSCOE: Okay, I feel bad for you, Lud, seein' you stuck with all that smoke-stack stuff. Lemme give you a tip. You wanna know where to start?

LUD: Where? Politics? Don't try and tell me . . .

ROSCOE: Forget it. Sunspots. They're in cycles. Little ones all the time, big ones every 22.75 years. You laugh. Wait'll the blast from a double cycle solar storm hits you. You lose cable traffic even. Nobody knows what the other guy is doin'. Not only that, but rainfall. They done cores from Lake Victoria an' Lake Huron an' they're the same.

HOULIHAN: The same! That's incredible.

LUD: You're over the edge, Chizzum, I respect that.

ROSCOE: Like I say, I'm a scientist. You get eight hunert an' one rounds a peri-helion an' the spots go outta phase. Ya fall down an' crack your head on the toilet. Next one's due in the year two thousan'. Then you'll get it!

DOBERMAN: Armageddon? Sixteen-sixteen?

ROSCOE: No, overdone TV dinners, asshole. The second coming.

HOULIHAN: Ha, ha. He means a repeater.

DOBERMAN: Hey, Captain, I don't know how to ask this but any chance a gettin' near female quarters to have a little look-see?

ROSCOE: Hold it right there. Forget it. You ever see the way they lock up a bunny hutch? With the barbed wire an' the chain link, the starvin' dogs, high-voltage doorknobs, first alert sirens and anti-intruder devices? Just forget it. You're lucky to be alive.

HOULIHAN: Okay, Captain. We just thought we'd ask.

ROSCOE: So, you guys are into real beef satisfaction, huh? You know what I mean?

DOBERMAN: Sort of . . .

ROSCOE: Look, there's some high class stuff coming by later, real sharp, some-thin' else. You guys want a taste?

HOULIHAN: No kidding, on duty?

ROSCOE: Where else? Now look, you guys play your cards right and I may be able to set you up with a little something. You may have to share a single piece-o-tail but that ain't so bad is it? Matter of fact, I kin'a go for it in a fun-ny kin'a way. Maybe I'll go in with you guys on a red-ball special. Ya ever hear a that? Gotta be careful though, they get a little crazy on the third go round.

HOULIHAN: Christ, Captain, that is wild shit. I cannot believe it.

ROSCOE: Believe it, buster. You can't beat pussy.

DOBERMAN: But how do you make them do it? Why would they do it with us?

ROSCOE: The hell, what d'you mean. We got pictures of them eating it right off the tip of the tube. And in the raw, too. They'll do what I tell them.

HOULIHAN: Jeeze-o-man, that is dis-gusting.

ROSCOE: I'll tell you it's disgusting. And that's not all. But that's not what I want to say. There's more but I won't tell you about it. Let's just say I'm witholding for the purpose of internal security. But you fuckers make one false move and I'll hit you with it so hard you'll really get disgusted, believe you me.

HOULIHAN: Yes, sir, Captain.

DOBERMAN: We won't make any trouble, sir.

ROSCOE: That's good. There's times to be proud and times to be humble . . . (*Lud Overture begins.*) . . . times to stand up for what you believe . . . and times to go down on your knees, if what you want is down there.

Hey, you guys ever been over to Snitzelhoven or whatever the hell they call it over there? Cool it, I hear brass.

And one more thing, you guys. It may get hot in here, so be ready for ac-tion.

DOBERMAN: Jeeze, Captain, you're just like enlisted . . .

HOULIHAN: Yeah, just like real people . . .

ROSCOE: Thanks for the compliment, Doberman, Houlihan, I 'preciate it. I come up through the ranks. Keep it up and I'll see you get ski jackets at the end a the cruise. (*Exit Roscoe, Houlihan and Doberman.*)

LUD: Sometimes I wonder what it's like being who I am, wonder if it's worth it being me.

I'm just a guy, a guy on a physical beat, two feet on the floor, searching, searching, I just keep looking . . .

And there is a soul to every search, and every look, a heart and a soul and a reason why, why in the face of every thing I know, I go where I go . . .

. . . to live and breathe in the open air of my full wits, casting fortune to the wind, on the wing of a dove, walking on toward a new horizon, with a prayer in my heart . . .

. . . with a song on my mind. (*Enter Ann in fantasy gown. Enter non-com girls in chorus.*)

ANN: There's a little song I know. Maybe you know it too.

LUD: I do know it. I do. (*Lud sings.*)

There's a place in France
Where the women wear no pants.
And the men walk around
With their bananas hanging down.

There's a place in Wales
Where the women all have tails
All the men knock them down
And they really go to town.

There's a place in Spain
Where the women feel no pain,
And the girls walk around
With their pants falling down.

There's a place in Ghent
Where there's money to be spent
And when your nuts start to squeeze,
The women do what they please.

There's a place right here
Where the women give me beer
And I give it to them good
Just like they knew I would.

SCENE 5

(*Female Quarters.*)

JANE: I wanna find a Dutch sailor take me down a canal, forget what I look like, make a windmill outta me . . .

CRYSTAL: Dream on.

WENDY-GWEN: I can't do it. I just can't do it.

ALICE: What can't you do?

WENDY-GWEN: I can't do it.

KIM: So then whatcha do?

GRETCHEN: I went to work for an agency and you should have seen what that was about. And then two years on the road with some guy an' his ideas. Sort of a perv-meat sort a thing. It's been a good life on the whole.

ALICE: Who you think's gonna win tonight? I know I don't stand a chance.

MARY: Me, hell, I am. Looka these jugs, wouldja? Guys go crazy for these. They don't know nothing about pussy. I got it won upside down and backwards. They'd have to color code a snatch t'get a guy ta notice. An the drunker they get the more they need 'em. Poor dumb sucks.

KIM: The hell! I know one of the guys judging. He said he'd throw it to me.

JANE: Oh, him, I know him.

CRYSTAL: What'd you do for him? Something immoral, I'm sure.

GRETCHEN: Oh, him! He's a snerd.

JANE: Worse an a snerd, believe me.

CRYSTAL: Oh, there's nothing worse than that.

KIM: Yeah, well, he's not a stiff. He pays cash!

JANE: He pays playdough an' you know it. You get him to do anything you just butter his buns.

CRYSTAL: Guy eats fudge, I know it.

KIM: Oh, look out, honey, your bird just shit on your shoulder.

JANE: Oh, yeah, and look at the nasty doo coming out of your pony.

GRETCHEN: Look, he's just another beer head.

MARY: Hey, career girl, they're all beer heads. They drink beer right from the tap. All I've got to do is press the lever and they take it right down the throat. I can put it in a coke bottle I'm holding between my boots.

GRETCHEN: Yeah, well, I want a guy to love so when he comes home to me after a hard day's work I can make him eat a big cow pie.

KIM: Yeah, well, I want a guy's so grim a full moon'll come out when he sticks out his tongue.

MARY: That'll make him squirt. You got to make them squirt.

ANN: Girls, girls, please, they're all the same, really! You're just doing your hair in the rear-view mirror.

KIM: Yeah, when they're on their knees.

ALICE: Aren't you the crowd pleaser, honey.

WENDY-GWEN: So, I can't do it, what's that make me, a soft-shelled crab?

GRETCHEN: You think you could make a living stuffing dumplings in the back seat of a car.

KIM: I know you boy turned yellow 'cause you mess with his kidneys.

CRYSTAL: Say what you want my guy has got to be a spellbinder and not a crook, there can't be anything he can't make me believe.

ALICE: Dream on . . .

GRETCHEN: You're driving with two feet, baby.

KIM: Yeah, you'd better find the owner, sweetheart, and quit shakin' your napkin in the grass.

WENDY-GWEN: I can't do it! I can't do it! Can't anybody hear me?

KIM: Ah shit, it's her first time and she's gonna balk.

GRETCHEN: Easy, Gwendy, it's real easy once you learn to relax and keep your feelings to yourself.

ALICE: What is it, honey? You wanna talk? Maybe there's something we can help you with.

WENDY-GWEN: No, no. I just know I'm going to freak when the time comes, when I see the heads, and the stalls and I hear the drains and the pumps and . . . and . . . the plumbing!

CRYSTAL: Naw, it's real easy. You just step into the stall and swish—you're all wet and everybody can see.

KIM: And don't worry, doll, nobody's gonna be lookin' at you.

JANE: Go easy on her.

KIM: Hey, Wendy-Gwen, you know what a guy wants, don't you, when a guy wants to debrief you?

WENDY-GWEN: No, does it have to do with intelligence?

KIM: Does it have to do with intelligence! How'd she get in this outfit?

JANE: I said go easy.

WENDY-GWEN: Well, you see, I'm very intelligent. Everyone has always told me that. Even the boys, the boys have told me that.

KIM: Honey, you're so dumb you couldn't squeeze oatmeal outta a paper bag!

JANE: I said go easy and I mean it! You may not know this, Kimmy, but not everybody lives down in the sewer with you. I mean, an' this may be hard for you to believe, but some people don't even like to hear said the kind of thing you say. I mean, you suck garbage because you like it. You like it, you hear. You suck sewer gas off some john's asshole and you like it. You come off on that rotten cob you got shoved down in your drawers every time he blows one into your mouth and you like it. You taste it and you like it. I've seen you. You're livin' in a cloud a poison gas an' you like it.

KIM: So?

ANN: Jane, I've never heard you talk like that! Now you apologize right now. What is this, a witch hunt?

KIM: And don't you think you're superior cause you seen it on TV? I'll tell you, sister, that is the only place you've ever seen it.

ALICE: Oh, come on, you guys, so you throw a few fucks. Come off the tough talk.

CRYSTAL: Well, aren't you bucking for promotion!

ANN: No, no, she's right. I don't think anyone should complain.

MARY: Sit down, Ann. Okay. Thanks, honey.

ANN: I always get nervous before I go into action. I want to throw up the sponge.

GRETCHEN: Benders'd like that.

ANN: Oh, god, I think I will throw up if he gets any closer. I can't ever remember having a lower opinion of a superior officer.

JANE: Oh, Christ, Ann, I don't see how you can do it. I got to hand it to you!

ANN: I forgot to tell you, Jane. Tonight he wants you.

JANE: Oh my god!

ANN: Oh, don't worry, Jane, it's for a good cause. We need it. Especially now. We're so isolated. I am worried. And the GI is terribly worried. They are as worried as I am. Gee I'm worried. We are worried together. I am worried as they are worried and they are worried as I am worried. I am trying to get my worried down. I want it to be simple. My worried. Their worried. I know them well and what goes on in their minds.

I am completely drowned in the Army. I eat, think and sleep army so my friends are disgusted with me. I am almost the only woman these boys see and many of them talk to me as if I were their mother. I pick them up in the street and bring them home to talk.

KIM: When I get back, I'm gonna be from Miami Beach. I'm gonna have friends there. I'm gonna take everything off an' just be me. I'm gonna have clothes like nobody's ever seen. I'm gonna go to the beach dressed up in band-aids and take cool drinks a water every night. Everything I need I'm gonna have, have it good, extra good. I'm gonna own Miami Beach.

ANN: The GIs are worried. Their minds are being deadened. They lack spiritual courage. They lack interest in politics. They don't believe anything is true. It is kind of a dark picture. They don't take any active interest in anything. They have a leadership complex. I say to them: "Can any of you lead yourselves? Do you all have to be told?"

ALICE: Oh, no, not me. When I get back I'm going up to the country. I'm going to get an old farm and a couple of hundred acres. And the old farm house is going to have a front porch. And on this front porch there is going to be a rocker. And I'm going to sit on this rocker and I'm just going to sit there. I'm going to sit there and just watch the whole thing go to seed and weed and trees. It's going to go wild right before my eyes. The deer and the bear'll come back and live with me. I'll be cosy—nothing will every happen.

JANE: And how do you think you'll afford that, sweetheart, on a word-processor's pay?

KIM: Yeah, Alice, money don't grow on trees, you know.

ALICE: I'll scrimp and I'll save and I'll live right. I just know it'll all come true. Maybe I'll even have a baby.

KIM: Have a baby, have an abortion, you mean!

JANE: Boy, oh boy, talk about being out of touch with reality!

KIM: Man, I just cannot stand her private world!

ANN: They are beginning to feel this thing in themselves but they haven't any religion any more. You don't see the Bible any more. They know that Europe has gone west. These days it's all mechanical. What has god got to do with it, they say to me. They feel these things, subconsciously, and it makes them sad. People say, why are they so sad. I say, they've been away so long and they're homesick and they're young. And then they say to me, they don't look young. And underneath it all they're so conservative. And they know there's something wrong with this, all this.

And now ruthless men, ruthless gangs, who know what they want, are beginning to take over or are waiting in the wings.

MARY: Sit down, will you, Gertrude? That's about enough synthetic for one night.

ANN: The goody-goody pacifism of the English and the Dutch does not advance international action a single step. And these crass maneuvers by double-agent Hollywood freezeniks, flexing muscles of provocation . . .

MARY: Ann, get your panties off the line, will ya, they're starting to smoke.

Girls! Women! I know I don't have to tell you how important this moment is to everything we're going to try and be doing from now on out. Believe me, now it's do or die. And let's hope that's true. I mean, let's hope we do it and we die. I mean it! Don't be afraid of it. It's like going to sleep. You step in the shower stalls and swish — you're all wet.

WENDY-GWEN: Are you sure that going to sleep is the right way to do it, Mary?

ANN: That's not what she means and you know it! I think we've had enough willful misunderstanding for one night.

KIM: Are you kidding? I'm just getting started.

CRYSTAL: Oh, god, not another discourse on death, I just can't take it.

MARY: You'll take it and you'll take it the way I give it to you and you know why. Because you all just might get your little twats blown out of the water on this one, that's why. And then you're all shittin' sand dollars for the next thirty-five years and you know it. So dummy up. Y'all look like so many whiplash victims off some prototype roller coaster. You know the routines. It's the same one's we've been working from day one. The stakes don't change the game, remember that. So work 'em and work 'em good or don't come back. And you won't come back, believe me. (*Girls sing. "Did I Throw My Love Away."*)

SCENE 6

(Operations Room. Company dances. "There's a Place in France.")

ROSCOE: I hope you don't mind a few questions, Lud. We need some different
kind a clearances now.

LUD: Shoot, Chizzum, I told you, I'm totally clear, right up to the top.

ROSCOE: Oh, yeah? We'll see about that. I don't know if you know it, Lud, but
we took over the entire north-eastern theatre. They're thinking of centering
the whole thing right here.

LUD: Here, twelve miles off the Dutch coast?

ROSCOE: We're moving, Lud, that may seem weird to you. Pretty soon we're
going to be in a different place. We're headed into German waters.

HOULIHAN: Begging your pardon, sir, that's French.

ROSCOE: French what?

HOULIHAN: French waters, sir.

ROSCOE: Oh, yeah, then you tell me why the sun come up on my right side.
You better check your facts with the bo's'n, mister. You got to get your sea-
legs, Lud, so you can get your bearings.

LUD: You know, Chizzum, you talk the way people talk when they want to stop
barking.

ROSCOE: You calling me a dog, mister. 'Cause if you are I am going to bring you
up on charges!

LUD: Look, Roscoe, intelligence is not a question of rank . . .

ROSCOE: I'm asking the questions here, Lud.

BENDERS: Boys, boys, please! Let's get back to the questioning. Just a few more,
Roscoe, and don't make them too difficult.

ROSCOE: Yes, sir. Okay. Now, Lud, you want to give us some idea about how
you were treated when you were on the outside.

LUD: Well, I don't really like to talk about it.

ROSCOE: Aw, bullshit. Sir, we can't get anywhere with this guy . . .

BENDERS: Oh, yes, come on, Lud. You're theatrical. We know you don't hesi-
tate to explore the seamy side of existence, why should you demure at its exposition?

JANE: Oh, god, Ann, he's mixed his chemicals. Listen to him, he's totally over
the edge.

ANN: Oh, gee, and the party hasn't even started.

MARY: Don't worry, kids, I know the whole script by heart. Nobody has anything to worry about.

ANN: Oh, Mary, it makes me feel so good when you say things like that!

GRETCHEN: Oh, god, Ann, don't start up with that stuff. It makes me want to
throw up.

ANN: Oh, I know, I always get nervous before I go into action.

JANE: Oh, Christ, Ann, shut up and listen to him. He won't stay up long enough to read his speech.

ANN: I know! But Mary said not to worry. Here, hold my hand. Maybe we'll all feel better.

LUD: By the way, Roscoe, I'm not saying you're a dog, okay? I'm just saying you shit on the lawn.

ROSCOE: You're fast, Lud, I gave you that opening five minutes ago.

BENDERS: Officers, men, please. Act like men. Now, Lud, how exactly did they treat you? And be brief, if you would. I want to bring on the German priest before I lose interest in the whole thing.

LUD: Yes, sir, well, they treated me the way you treat women. They wouldn't let me telephone in private.

BENDERS: Surely you're joking.

LUD: It's no joke, sir, that sort of thought is operative in the civilian population. They are in no way on the sort of wartime footing that would demand equality . . .

BENDERS: Oh, I know them, those civilians. So soft, so sloppy, so sentimental. So hidebound. Well, don't worry about how they treated you, Lud. It doesn't matter in this man's army if you're a man or a woman as long as you're good.

ROSCOE: Or if you're good or you're bad as long as you act like a man . . .

GIRLS IN CHORUS: What does that mean, Ann? Can you explain that?

LUD: You're right, I was getting subjective . . .

BENDERS: Ann, about this next one. You and the girls can sit this one out if you want and no one will think the less of you for it.

ANN: Oh, no, General. That's all right. Really.

BENDERS: It's rough language.

GIRLS: We know and we can take it.

BENDERS: I'm warning you. It just may curl your toes!

GIRLS: Oh, no, no, no. And thank you, General Benders, for your kind consideration. But we'll take our licks with the rest of you.

ROSCOE: Atta girls, girls.

BENDERS: More power to you. Here's to the ladies.

LUD: Atta girl, Ann. I knew when I first saw you peeping out of the hangar that you'd be something else when it came to taking it.

ANN: Oh, please, Lud, save it for later.

LUD: I can hardly hold on to it, Ann, I got it so bad for you.

ANN: Oh, Luddy, just think about your work and coming home safe and sound to me, think about the dangers and years in a prison camp.

LUD: Okay, Ann.

BENDERS: Roscoe, what's that noise?

ROSCOE: That's just drunken firing, sir.

BENDERS: Oh, I didn't realize . . . You know that little intramural scrap outside

Putztown cost us forty GIs.

ROSCOE: There's gonna be excesses. Some of the boys are bound to get enthusiastic and go animal, exceed some of the limits. If you're worried about it, sir, I could put it on shock watch and then have some media recovery done on it in the morning . . .

BENDERS: Well, all right, we'll schnaus it in the morning with that guy down there at the whatchamacallit . . .

ROSCOE: Gigolo Joe Schmitt at the transit camp.

BENDERS: Ah, yes, the transit camp. Only a boche could eat that garbage.

ROSCOE: That was Operation Torch, wasn't it?

BENDERS: No, that was called Eat Nimrod. Ah, those were the days. It reminds me of this new one, the Pac Man Scat series.

ROSCOE: Right. S'about time for a little more rolling thunder for my money.

BENDERS: What about the guy at the top of the stairs?

ROSCOE: Hammerman? Last I heard he was in operations, hit an A school with some 808, now'ees on the skids. Tell you the truth, sir, we can't move it east a the Oder/Niese anymore. I don't know, sir, looks like a heck of a job to me. Maybe a massive rewrite. I don't know if we're up to it.

BENDERS: Well, I'll tell you what I'm going to do. And I don't do this lightly. It's a grave responsibility. I'm going to trans-ship the whole mess down to Attack Group Nuclear. Oh, I know it sounds a little final but at least they'll be out of our hair.

How do I look, Captain?

ROSCOE: Fine, sir.

If you want, sir, we could work out a little mix-up with the wops and/or the jugs and/or the buggars if you want. Can't say it'd get us anywhere.

BENDERS: I know, they're so erratic as allies. Though the Turk is the best goddamned mercenary you can buy. We really get our money's worth out of those little guys . . .

I wonder if there's a place for this almost Oriental utilization of mankind in Western Civ as we know it? Oh, well, not to worry, there will be a judgment on this wild bacchanalia of drunken pan-Serbianism.

We're going to be all right, aren't we, Roscoe, tell me the truth.

ROSCOE: Yes, sir, just fine. Everything is gonna be just fine.

BENDERS: What is it, Roscoe? What's the matter?

ROSCOE: Oh, nothing, sir. It's just I been squeezing them so hard lately it's like sifting sand to let it go.

BENDERS: Oh, yes, it starts to hurt as soon as it's stale. Pain, huh.

ROSCOE: Yes, sir. And my leg starts to lift.

BENDERS: Mary Jane?

ROSCOE: No, sir. Mary Ann.

BENDERS: That's a very mean combination, Roscoe. But I'll tell you, all the greats were like that and that's to your credit. Washington, von Steuben,

MacArthur, Patton. I actually knew that man's wife. She made the damndest pecan pie. I could eat that thing all night. Oh, well, you know where we go to from here.

ROSCOE: Ljubljana Gap?

BENDERS: Keep it on tap.

ROSCOE: Aye-aye, sir. One more thing, sir, this guy Lud. You don't think by any stretch of the imagination that he's on the right track, do you?

BENDERS: Well, he's not right. But then again, he's not exactly wrong. All right, Lud, pay attention. Captain, please proceed.

ROSCOE: Okay, Lud, you're just jerkin' us off and I for one ain't buyin'.

LUD: Look, Roscoe, when the interrogations start, you'll see what kind a stuff I got. I don't have to toe a line with your sort . . .

ROSCOE: An' what sort is that, Lud, you tell me what you think.

LUD: I'm not saying anything about you, Roscoe, I'm saying I got more stuff'n you could dream about on two and a half pipes.

ROSCOE: You saying I'm a hash-head, cause if you are, mister, you are a total asshole . . .

LUD: What I'm saying to you, big dick, is I think you're muff-shy . . .

ROSCOE: Why you . . . This is it. You had it, baby. Your teeth are spitballs . . .

BENDERS: Please, please, boys, you'll make me spill my drink. Roscoe, the questioning!

ROSCOE: Yes, sir. Okay. Okay. Okay, I'm gonna forget for a minute you claim you're Sam the snake and get right down to it. Okay, Lud, how low did you go? Let's have it. And remember, you're looking at a big negative.

LUD: I don't know what the hell you are talking about, Roscoe. You're trying to make something out a nothing.

ROSCOE: Don't take me off the beam with questions, Lud. Next thing you know a guy like you'd be marchin' with the Japanese. I don't mind telling you, mister, to me you are not armed forces. To me you're something else. You're nothing, that's what you are, shit dressed up like sheep.

LUD: Hell, what are you talking about, I'm a booster.

ROSCOE: Hey, you could be Joe Day for all I care. Don't talk to me, just answer questions.

LUD: I'm telling you, Roscoe, I'm a booster. My folks are ordinary folks. Doctors, brick layers, lawyers, merchants, steel workers. You got nothing on me. Rubber workers, secretaries, mechanics. You got nothing on me there.

ROSCOE: Okay, Lud, you oughta know this then, you're so red blooded Americano, what's in the books a the Bible. Tell me that, would ja?

LUD: You mean like Daughter of Babylon? Drunk on the wine of her fornication? That sort of thing?

ROSCOE: Aw, Christ, next you'll be tellin' one a those lousy jokes a yours. You go low and you know it.

LUD: Hell, no, I'm a booster. Why back in my hometown, I'm a builder. Young businessman's whatever. I'm just like them. They recognize me . . .

ROSCOE: Yeah, how'd you set it up?

LUD: Well, I done time in Chicago. Big muss a relations. Run some kind a restaurant. A regular chain gang kind a operation. The first contact was with
the bank. That's where I picked up my social collateral. You've got to be
careful you never contact the police. That's important. Everyone they do
not deal with is considered absolutely normal. One contact and it's like
"suck one cock."

BENDERS: What's that?

LUD: The old joke. You suck one cock.

BENDERS: Who sucks cock. We're all officers here, we can talk. Tell me, Lud,
you'll be offered immunity from prosecution. In the line of duty and all . . .

LUD: Nobody, sir. It's an old joke.

BENDERS: Nobody sucks cock. Oh, come off it, Lud.

ROSCOE: Let me try, sir. Maybe I can get it out of him. Okay, what's the role
of the KGB in all this?

LUD: From what I understand all they do is sit around and watch Abbott and
Costello on the tube . . .

ROSCOE: That's enough of that kind a talk. That's no more'n a rumor.

LUD: You are political, aren't you, Roscoe. I told you you wouldn't understand.
That's why we got to word process it. Otherwise it's a tower a Babylon in the
Bible.

ROSCOE: Oh, yeah, is that what those computers a yours can do? Big talk, Lud.

LUD: No, that's what I do with the computers.

BENDERS: Now don't you go getting insolent, Lud. We could be monitored from
Washington at any time and there is nothing we could do about it.

LUD: That's your problem. You got no ground. No offense intended, sir. It's just
in history it went different. I mean how we won the revolution. We worked
with armies could not be moved. Just armed settlers. You check the record
on Washington's numbers. We run this through the machines a couple a
times and we can now predict as good as the weather . . .

BENDERS: I'm impressed . . .

ROSCOE: The weather! Ha! Bullshit. That's a good one. You're lying through
teeth. We got you now. Just you tell me if it's raining outside. Huh? Ya see?
The guy's crapola. He don't know. You'd need a TV to know that.

LUD: Armies could not be moved, so King of England shipped 'em back to
Ireland. Same shitload outta Nam into the Andes . . . up on the nuclear
plateau, the new battlefield . . .

BENDERS: Silence, man!

LUD: Matter of fact, several armies still extant in the fatherland . . .

ROSCOE: Silence, mister. You are a total fool, an asshole!

BENDERS: Talk like that could sink this ship. Anyway, that sort of thing went
out with polaris class . . .

Stay with him, Chizzum, he's starting to spill. We work him right and we've got a perfectly deadly new right hand man.

ROSCOE: I read you loud and clear, Chief.

You're outta your mind, Lud. I wanna tell you so you should know. And one more thing, Lud. When the ultimate read-out comes through on the absolute truth, the real answer, which way are you going to break, for it or against it?

LUD: I got a choice?

ROSCOE: The hell you do. Where you're sitting it's shit or cut bait . . .

BENDERS: Please, Ann, when is she coming? I need it bad.

ANN: Why, General, I told you, she comes every chance she gets.

BENDERS: Ann, please!

ANN: Why, General, she's already here! Can't you see, we're all here.

GIRLS: Getting it all down for you, sir. On a tape you can take out in your pants.

BENDERS: Oh, yes, I see. I didn't notice. I hope I haven't said anything offensive. Yes. Hello, girls.

GIRLS: Hello, General Benders.

BENDERS: Oh, Ann, where's Jane. Oh, there she is. Oh, Ann, she could have me eating out of a dog bowl.

ANN: Oh, General, why would you want to do something like that?

BENDERS: That's what I keep asking myself, Ann, do you know?

ANN: No, General, I don't. That's over my head. But here's Jane, maybe she knows.

BENDERS: Jane. Jane. You know who I am, don't you. You know the wet uniform contest? I'll see that you get it. I can do that for you. I know the judge and I'm his superior officer.

JANE: Oh, General, it'd sure be a treat to win that contest and meet Mike Smith after all these years of watching his movies but wouldn't you be compromising yourself.

BENDERS: Oh, no, Jane, I'm not compromised at all, unless you consider business and sex compromising affairs.

JANE: Oh, General, you have such a way with words, such a gift for gab.

BENDERS: Oh, it's nothing, Jane.

JANE: Oh, don't say that, General. You know it's not nothing to win a contest.

BENDERS: And you will win, Jane, I promise you that. And it's for a good cause. It's important for the boys to see you girls soaked to the skin every once in a while.

JANE: The boys, yes, the boys. I can hear them crying for it!

BENDERS: And you know what, Jane, I'll let you have a crack at one of the prisoners. How would you like that, Jane?

JANE: Oh, General, you are such a sweetheart! And I'll do you proud. Believe me!

ROSCOE: I'm waiting, Lud. I'm waiting and I'm watching. Don't give us any more garbage, Lud, we need a good clean image, you hear. We know where you come from, Lud, we know where you been. Now you give, you hear. There's something in there wants out, and we're the ones what want it.

LUD: Enough. Enough. I'll give it to you, I'll give it to you as low as it goes with me.

JANE: Oooh, they've got him now.

ANN: My boy, my boy, he's going down . . .

LUD: But you're not going to understand. You see, it don't make sense in your time frame. So we have to feed it to these word processor girls and they get it stabilized and rearranged. Call it order. Call it office work. Can you understand how boring this can get, General?

BENDERS: Oh, yes! You can't beat a floppy disk.

LUD: So I have to tell these girls stories while they work on it, getting it all on tape you can take out in your pants. But while they do this you got to pay them, they don't care about any of this shit . . .

BENDERS: The point, Lud, the point. We know all this.

LUD: So I hated this guy so much I just had to fuck his old lady.

ROSCOE: Hated, kid? You're not that deep.

LUD: Oh, yeah. So what if I loved him then. I mean her. What's the difference?

BENDERS: Loved, Lud? Really. Come off it.

ROSCOE: This one, I heard this a hunnert times!

LUD: Yeah, loved. I mean, he didn't love her or anything.

ANN & JANE: Oh, sure, Lud, they were just good friends. Like your mom and dad!

LUD: And then it was easier for him because she felt this warm kind of guilt. I mean, I didn't get off that many times, maybe two dozen good ones in six months.

BENDERS: Two dozen good ones in six months. A pace like that would kill me.

LUD: So what if it broke up his home and killed him. There was a time, I mean, if he'd just touched a piece a cheese in the box or just been rimmed by a nurse he could shove it in and she'd cream and he'd float one . . .

BENDERS: Float one? Is that a technique? How abstract.

LUD: Anyway, it was later she was a widow and I had to do it to her again. She was old by that time and showing it but her pussy was still good . . . I'd slip it in her mouth cause I loved the humiliation involved in being gobbled by this old bag. But other times I'd just go right in her big drooly puss . . .

And you know who she was, Roscoe?

ROSCOE: No, who?

LUD: Your mother, that's who!

BENDERS: You're kidding, it wasn't, was it?

ROSCOE: I'll get you for this, you bastard. One way or the other, you are going to pay for this. That's it. Your flap gets razored off. You're gonna bleed your drawers off . . .

ANN: God, Lud, is that lurid. I'm eating my heart out.

JANE: Great porn, Lud, that'll stink sewers from here to Hong Kong.

ANN: God, Lud, was that lurid. I'm eating my heart out.

LUD: Are you, Ann? It's sure got shock value, don't it?

ANN: Oh, I love it, Luddy, when you talk ignorant like that. It makes me think you're going to be an animal in bed.

WENDY-GWEN: Oh, look, here comes the German priest.

ALICE: But why a German priest?

KIM: Are you kidding, they caught him red-handed. (*Houlihan and Doberman bring in German Priest in manacles.*)

BENDERS: You take it, Lud. Let's see what you can do.

ROSCOE: Careful with this one, Lud, I smell skullduggery. You know what they say.

LUD: All right. I got it. Now what's this about you're not being loyal to the Pope, huh? You know who you're talking to, don't you, padre?

GERMAN PRIEST:

Of course I know who you are. You are swine come to feed off our land, to make whores of our sisters. You are the conquering army. You are very pretty. America must be a very rich country.	Natürlich weiss ich wer Sie sind. Sie sind schweine die gekommen sind um unseres land zu zerfressen, um unsere Schwestern zu Huhren zu machen. Sie sind die Eroberungsarmee. Sie sind sehr hübsch. Amerika soll ein sehr reiches land sein.

ROSCOE: You bet it is!

BENDERS: I didn't know you spoke German, Captain.

ROSCOE: I don't. Not much, anyway. But just enough to know what a guy like this is saying. Okay, bonehead, come clean. Where are these so-called cells you guys got?

LUD: I'll handle this, Roscoe. I know my turf.

GRETCHEN: Hey, what's your name? Martin Luther?

KIM: Hey, Marty, you can nail your articles on my door any day.

ROSCOE: Okay, stay cool, okay, Kid? They got tunnels all over the place. This is a tough one and I wanna help you crack it.

LUD: I'll do it myself, Roscoe. Okay, all right. Now, you! Yeah, you in the dress. You see this piece a rubber hose? Now think a this rubber hose as the Pope's peter. And then think a how it's gonna feel on your kidneys when it starts slappin' into ya like Mike Smith's tin prick.

ROSCOE: Lud, you crazy fucker . . .

BENDERS: Lud, please . . .

LUD: Aw, hell, I didn't mean anything. I was just joshin' him cause he's clerical.

GERMAN PRIEST:

The madness of America is the madness of European history and in it you	Die Wahnsinn Amerikas ist die Wahnsinn der Europäischen

are profound in your misunderstanding. For us, America will always be a trailer camp for primitive thugs, bet on the demonstration of some justifying might.

Geschichte und in dieser haben sie ein tiefes Fehlverstandnis. Zu uns Amerika wird immer ein Zeltlagerplatz sein, ein Trailercamp für primitive Spitzbuben die nur eine Demonstration machen wollen einer art rechtvertigender Macht.

LUD: Talk, fish face, or you'll piss blood in your chalice . . . Lousy commie dupe.

GRETCHEN: Hey, who's he callin' Spitzbuben?

GERMAN PRIEST:

Look, I'll make a deal with you. I'm a practical man. I'll sell you all absolutions if you'll just get off the continent.

Kuck mal, ich werde etwas mit Ihnen abmachen. Ich bin ein praktischer Mensch. Ich werde Ihnen alle Absolutionen verkaufen wen Sie nur das Festland entraümen.

LUD: Well, don't you think you're smart-ass, talkin' donkey. Don't worry, we got a CPT speaks German.

ROSCOE: Begging your pardon, sir, we could use the old ecclesiastical stand-in routine with him . . .

BENDERS: Ah, yes, the "nobody's fool." Hmmm, not a bad idea. Put some soap on a rope and give him a Dutch rub. Only a boche could eat that garbage . . .

GERMAN PRIEST:

I am no Meister Eckhart, no anabaptist, no brother of the free spirit, no leveler, no Quaker. The universe is not a monarchy. Jesus is a voice that speaks with other voices throughout time saying, wake up man!

Ich bin kein Meister Eckhart, kein Wedertaufer, kein Bruder des freien Geistes, kein "leveler," kein Quaker. Das Weltall ist kein Konigreich. Jesus ist eine Stimme die mit anderen Stimmen durch die Zeit uns anruft und sagt: erawche Mensch!

GIRLS: Wake up, man!

BENDERS: Oh, did I doze. . . ? Did I miss something?

ROSCOE: Naw, he claims he's got relatives in Elkhart, Indiana.

GERMAN PRIEST:

I never could know how irreligious a people could be. You must be very hungry! I heard your confessions and lost my faith. It entered my system as a poison, an iridescent green gas we have never before seen . . .

LUD: Aw, go away, would ya. You're totally infiltrated. And you know why? Cause dough is infiltration, that's why. Your only choice is to go honest and get wiped out . . .

BENDERS: That's enough of this one. Bring in the next one. (*Houlihan and Doberman bring in French Schoolgirl, hands bound with rope.*)

ROSCOE: How you feel, buddy? You look good. You really softened him up.

LUD: I feel good. I feel strong.

ROSCOE: Good, baby, keep it up. You do got stuff, it's just like you said.

LUD: All right, state your name and business! You were found with a lot of books, you know, books it'd be just as smart you weren't caught reading . . .

FRENCH SCHOOLGIRL:

I wanted to study relativity but I could get no footing. I wanted to study biology but everything was dying. So I studied life and I got so depressed . . .

J'ai voulu étudier la rélativité, mais je n'ai pas pu avoir un pied-à-terre. Je voulais étudier la biologie, mais tout était éntrain de mourir. Alors, j'ai étudié la vie et ça m'a donné une grande dépression . . .

BENDERS: What's she saying?

ROSCOE: Sounds like a lot of anarchist propaganda to me.

LUD: Let's work her over.

ROSCOE: Okay, but go easy, Lud, later we wanna get pictures . . .

WENDY-GWEN: Who does your hair, sherry, Mon-sieur Kenneth de Brillo? Oh, ha ha ha.

LUD: Okay, babyface, maybe you want to be another Karen Carpenter. You know you can't eat any of this shit, you know that, don't you?

FRENCH SCHOOLGIRL:

For spiritual and intellectual purposes Europe must be one great confederation, bound to a joint action and working to a common result. This present age must be seen as one which passes . . .

L'Europe doit être une grande conféderation pour des raisons spirituelles et intellectuelles, lie pour une action d'ensemble en collaboration pour un résultat commun. On doit considerer le temps présent comme un temps qui passe.

LUD: All right, that's enough a that . . .

BENDERS: What was it, Lud?

LUD: Not much more, sir, than an invite to do a little fellow travelling. Okay, sister, maybe you want some nice little scars on that pretty face a yours . . .

BENDERS: Just a minute, Lud. And have her ears plugged. She just may speak our language.

FRENCH SCHOOLGIRL: Mais oui, mais oui, I do! I have learned it from the great stars of your moving pictures, Marilyn Monroe, Jean Seberg, Jerry Lewis . . . Look, mes amis, I can tell your fortunes. I'll give you a very good dealing from my cards, no? I'll tell you things you need to know, the affairs of the heart. I will tell you who will win the wet uniform contest! If you will leave, we can be friends. I will write to you in your country, the billêt doux.

BENDERS: Now you just attention up there, little Miss, before I motivate you out of here, because there is something I want to say to you. Should you ever be put in a position of handling manhood in the mass, and I'm sure you will . . . An operative should never announce in advance of his or her intention to proceed in any particular mode. Until you've undergone certain . . . decentralized rigors, you will remain in a real gray area. Now you just go and tell that to your masters in the Kremlin walls.

ROSCOE: That's telling her, sir. Later you oughta write your name in her dance book.

BENDERS: That's a good one, Roscoe. I'm going to use that myself sometime. It's incredible the way they use the tender members of the demi-monde to further their nefarious desires . . .

ROSCOE: Yes, sir, it's a caution.

LUD: If you don't mind, sir, I'm not going to do anything or anything, but maybe if I just scare her some she'll open up a little bit . . .

BENDERS: Oh, that's all right then . . . but don't be provoked into attack. They will bait you but never rise to the bait.

LUD: Just a minute, what's that shit I smell. . . ?

BENDERS: I don't know. Roscoe?

ROSCOE: If you're saying I smell like shit, mister . . .

LUD: What in the blazes! Donahan, Houliman, what in the sam hill do you think you're doing!

DOBERMAN: Just a little taste, sir, cause we get so bored when we're on duty.

LUD: Bored? I'll show you bored. You fuckin' hop-heads. Blowing smoke on duty. Unfucking believable. I'll give you the dirty low-down on drugs. Drugs is dangerous. You fuck with that shit, kids, you could get us all killed. And we'd never even know it. Our kids'd grow up slaves. Dead, you hear? DOD. You understand? Now shake it out your arm or you'll both be on sign in down mental hygiene.

BENDERS: You boys should listen to Colonel Lud. He knows of what he speaks.

ROSCOE: What'd you guys go an do shit like that? You off the beam?

HOULIHAN: Naw, s'not like that, sir, we just do it cause it makes us pop better.

ROSCOE: Pop, huh?

HOULIHAN: Hell, sir, you know why they call Bob minute-man, don't ja?

DOBERMAN: An you know why an elephant's "memory" is as wide as it is long? Well, that's old Gregory. Back in communications school at Bragg we called him "the trunk line."

ROSCOE: You guys are funny, no doubt about it.

HOULIHAN: But it's not just he's fast, he's a repeater. I seen him shoot off four rounds in under forty minutes an that was on a single mount.

DOBERMAN: Hell, they call Bob here the perching rocket.

HOULIHAN: Hell, one time we was locking horns on a merry widow outta Iserlohn an, well . . . (*Houlihan and Doberman dance. "Chicken Time."*)

ROSCOE: Okay. Okay. Okay, we'll let it pass at a warning. Now back to work and no more blowing shit.

LUD: You ought to talk to those kids sometime, General, they're a little hard to figure.

BENDERS: Oh, really, I've always been a little off on enlistcomm. It's a weakness. But then I've always purchased my promotions. I have a very wealthy wife. I'm like Ike that way. It's virtually the only way to really rise in the ranks. It sounds awful, doesn't it. Well, clothes make the man but it's the horse-collar makes the horse. Bring in the Dutch mother. (*Houlihan and Doberman bring in the Dutch mother.*) Who wants her? Ned, Roscoe, which one of you wants her? Suit yourselves.

ROSCOE: Let me start it up. Okay with you, Ned?

LUD: Call me Lud. You understand, Roscoe? Just cause we can work together don't mean we're close.

ROSCOE: Sure, Lud. I respect that. You can see that, can't you?

LUD: Yeah, sure. Go ahead. Wet your stick.

ROSCOE: Okay. Now, mam, if you wouldn't mind telling me, what is the exact number of fathers your different children have?

DUTCH MOTHER:

I knew it would be like this. I knew when they came my children would grow to be strangers to me. Every morning I would rise so the schools could open.	Ik wist dat het zo zou gaan. Ik wist toen ze kwamen, dat mijn kinderen vreemden voor me zouden worden. Elke morgen stond ik op, zodat de school kon beginnen.

ROSCOE: She's got kids in every network on the continent, sir. I think it must be broken.

BENDERS: Proceed, Roscoe. We are very interested.

DUTCH MOTHER:

I just can't stop crying, thinking about what's going to happen. I know it's too late. I've known that for a long time now. But I do so want them to live, even as strangers.	Als ik denk aan wat er gaat gebeuren blijf ik huilen. Ik weet dat het te laat is. Ik heb dat aldoor geweten. Maar ik wil zo graag dat ze blijven leven, zelfs als vreemden.

ROSCOE: These are nothing more, sir, than detailed plans for the manufacture of bombs and booby-traps in a clandestine drug laboratory. It's the toilet, sir.

BENDERS: Flabbergasting!! Give Jane here a shot. Come on down, Jane Babcock!

JANE: So, hi mom. It's me, you gotta remember. So how are things at home with old what's-his-panty-waste? Don't pretend you don't know me mom. It's me, the screamer! Yiha waaaaa.

I hope you're real happy now, you're rid of me. Thought that was real smart, didn't ya, never picking me up from the hospital. An don't tell me.

You never paid the bill. Yihawaaaa.

And what about the car. Did ja ever give me the car when I wanted it. When Johnny Potter called and I wanted to go out drinking. Huh, did ja? Yihaaaaaaaa.

BENDERS: That's enough, Jane, honey, I think you've made your point.

JANE: And what about the phone, did I have a princess phone of my own like the Smith kids? Did I? Whaaaaaaa.

DUTCH MOTHER:

And I know I will go on, no matter what. And I know that peace will come on an incomprehensible bridge of bodies.

En ik weet dat ik door zal gaan, hoe dan ook. Ik weet dat de vrede zal komen over een onvoorstelbare brug van lijken.

LUD: Oh, Christ, stop slobbering, will you. You remind me of my ex, always blubbering into her hankie.

ANN: Oh, no, you weren't married to one of them, were you? That's disgusting. You didn't! Not with her!

LUD: Yes, I did, Ann, but let me explain. I didn't do it any more than I had to and it wasn't all that good anyway. You see, I was young and had gone in the service to avoid a rape conviction back in the little town in the States where I grew up, a little town with no pity . . .

GIRLS: Oh, Ann, he's involved with the law . . .

LUD: Let me explain, she was the bully cock-tease of the school and she deserved what I gave her. I got the whole football team to say she'd been giving it away for free under the bleachers but they convicted me anyway. Justice is blind, I guess.

ANN: Oh, Lud, this is a dagger in my heart. When it's in me I'll always know where it's been before.

LUD: Well, I was young and alone and, well, all I can do is hope you'll forgive and understand.

ANN: Well, I do, Luddy. There, there, weren't any . . . offspring?

LUD: Oh, no, that would be criminal, wouldn't it?

ANN: Oh, yes, such a handicap for the children. Almost better they should pull the plug.

LUD: I don't know, Ann, that's something between a man and his conscience.

ANN: Oh, Luddy, you have such an enchanting manner.

LUD: Ah, Ann, you're not so bad yourself.

ANN: Oh, no, please, Lud, don't. It'll only end in tragedy. Please, not now. Later, at the party. I'll be with you there, Ned.

MARY: Sensational, honey. You hooked him good.

KIM: You have to hand it to that pigeon-toed bitch, she sure can throw a curve.

JANE: Who are you calling bird-foot. Why you're so deformed you could a been born in a can a Pepsi.

ANN: Thanks, Janey, she deserved that.

HOULIHAN: Excuse me, sir, we got something coming in top priority. It's from the next encyclical the Pope is working on. Comes outta his garbage bag. Says in his visible house it is a mistake to criminalize acts that are clearly immoral. Says it stigmatizes the sinner and turns him away from the soul. Says it leads to a morbid hoarsening of the voice of the Godhead. Thing's called "On Social Justice."

ROSCOE: If this pickle goes any farther in this direction we're gonna have him shot, and that's that.

BENDERS: Yes, let's make sure we get him briefed before he goes sticking his nose in other people's business.

WENDY-GWEN: I don't know if I can watch this much longer. I just know somebody's going to get killed.

DUTCH MOTHER:

When the mind of a great Roman theologian jumps with the common mind of a Dutch folk, we ought to be able to take the result with some security. An ontwerp now, and upward. I know that even in their homeland these men are babu . . .

Als de geest van een groot Rooms theoloog samensmelt met het boerenverstand van een gewone Hollander zouden we het resultaat moeten kunnen vertrouwen. Een ontwerp nu, en erop los. Ik weet dat deze kerels zelfs in hun eigen land van God los zijn.

BENDERS: Isn't it incredible what people will say when they finally look death in the face and turn to the gods of sleep. But I think some of those reports on damage in the collateral zone are highly inflammatory. Oh, well, to a bigger and better lockup, I always say, with many more of the amenities of gender. And I rest so secure in this knowledge. Isn't that wonderful?

ROSCOE: Yes, sir.

BENDERS: Well, let's finish up real quick. What about the Italian politico?

LUD: Russo? Aw, he hung himself in his cell or something.

BENDERS: Too bad! And kind of good looking in that reddish way of the northerners. But no Valentino.

ROSCOE: No, sir, no Valentino.

BENDERS: And the certain English lady?

LUD: Last I heard, sir, she was overboard without so much as a sanitary napkin, if you'll pardon the expression, sir.

BENDERS: Oh, God, Lud, you're getting as bad as Chizzum. And Chizzum, you navy men are just too much. Ah, now we're all good friends. Let's get to the club. Oh, I love the club. It's a place where I feel I can be me, away from the everyday cares of being alive. (*All sing "Goodbye Old Paint."*)

SCENE 7

(*The Officers Club. The Dutch people, in costume, stand at the bar. Bernice, the Bartender, comes and goes serving drinks. All enter dancing. "Jungle Beat."*)

BENDERS: Well, yes, but they took it with them to the grave. There's no point in thinking about them. Believe you me, it'll only get you dead. But I'll tell you, these young people are a real worry to me.

ROSCOE: Sit down, Lud. Take a load off.

LUD: I ain't got a load on, Roscoe. Maybe you noticed. I dumped it.

BENDERS: I'm hungry. Let's order. Look at this mess in here. Bernice, bring me the spaceship happy meal and a double. She's such a wonderful girl, always smiling, always so happy.

ROSCOE: Relax, kid, you're gonna like it here at the club. We aim to have a good time. Have a few drinks. You'll get the picture.

LUD: Bitch me all you want, Roscoe. In the end it's brain over brawn.

ROSCOE: Yeah, z'at what you think, Ludski. Well, it seems there's some question like that in this issue a the gun bible, ah, some question as to whether a gun is a, ah, body or a brain. Real interesting kinda material. You know, Lud, you know what it is?

LUD: Lemme see that thing.

ROSCOE: Set em up, Bernice.

BENDERS: I'm supposed to be at some Shape reception. But I'll be damned if I'll be their bemedalled gigolo. Not for anything. Don't you think I'm right, Jane?

JANE: Begging your pardon, sir?

BENDERS: Well, I'm supposed to go to a party and then I'm supposed to dance with those battle axes. Then we all throw our dog tags into a chaffing dish. It's disgusting, what you end up doing. It's not really my cup of tea, you know.

JANE: I know, sir, I can see it's not your cup of tea.

BENDERS: It's just my wife, she bores me so. And the thought of that enormous clam with all those sticky fluids . . .

JANE: Oh, General, you just don't stop the high speed imaging, do you . . .

BENDERS: What's that, Jane? I'll buy you jewelry, you know that, don't you? I have always been a man who could talk to women.

WENDY-GWEN: I never want to go to outer space. I just hate outer space, cause there's always those stupid funny creatures around me.

ALICE: I know what you mean, and it's so cold and dark.

ROSCOE: Where do you pick up these diseased tramps, Ann?

BENDERS: Oh, Jane, I'd eat a couple of your smelly little love apples if you'd let me.

JANE: Oh, General, you are so poetic!

BENDERS: I mean it, Jane, I would and I don't know why. Do you? Bernice, another round.

ROSCOE: Benders' a weird dude. Kept a butter cow sweet enough to ride. And did, from what I hear. Gotta wife the name a Shan. Sh'was pathetic. Made him eat ash samitch. Some kinda tycoon, though. Bought him everything he's got. But then this is a peace time picture. Two weeks a combat an he'd be pushin' a broom. Huh, bullshit. There's a shadow service means to fight it out to the end when these dicks go yellow. No war in sight unless we say so. When you're sitting on megatonnage like us . . . Guy's a real big-wig lightweight.

BENDERS: Oh, no, Jane, I am trying. I'm compromising as fast as I can. I'm just worried the whole thing is going to go off in your hands like a ripe banana.

ANN: Ooooh, Houlihan, you're a real man . . .

MARY: And you, Doberman, you're big too . . .

ROSCOE: What's goin' on back there?

LUD: I don't know. Some tom dickin' harry scene. Looks like doomsday to me.

ROSCOE: Like in Operation Mincemeat, right?

LUD: Never heard of it.

ROSCOE: But you heard of mince pie, right?

LUD: What's she really? She ain't no colonel.

ROSCOE: Naw, no way. She's a junior leuie, maybe even an ensign. Benders got her an operational promotion so she can work the club.

LUD: Christ, what a crude device. I've never seen such a crude device.

ROSCOE: Forget her, Lud. What'd she promise she'd do, scrub your nuts with her hair brush?

LUD: You wouldn't believe the things I got to do to make a living.

ROSCOE: Hell, we're all married men. We can talk. Is it our fault we're in the service. Somebody's got to do it. What am I, a recreation vehicle?

ANN: Excuse me, Rosc, I've got to go talk to the girls. Give me some money for the powder room, would you?

ROSCOE: Oh, sure, honey, here.

ANN: Oh, thanks. See you in a minute. I've got to fix my face. Oh, hi Luddy. Do you mind if you don't smoke. The yukkie smell and those ugly stains.

GIRLS: Ugly stains, she don't like ugly stains.

ROSCOE: Easy, Lud, that there, that is the answer to a fighting boy's prayer. She sucks more cock'n a Dutch housewife. Ha, ha, ha. She do not deny it, she do not deny it. Bernice, another round. I mean what I mean to say is there ain't a lot to talk about these days. I mean, what do we do all day but listen to the radio?

MARY: Maybe you, Roscoe, but I got other things going on in my life but that cheap negativity of yours. You know what I'd be making on the outside?

ROSCOE: Don't kid me, you'd be doing time.

MARY: The shit, I'm a builder. I got a list of things in my life.

ROSCOE: Yeah, name one.

MARY: Here's one you never heard of Roscoe. Love. Yes, love, Roscoe. You think about it.

ROSCOE: I will. You know, Mary, I like you.

BENDERS: Let me tell you, Bernice, you could have had me anytime you wanted before I got married. But now, now my desires are so various. Indeed, I can barely define them. Oh, Bernice, won't you let me lick it, just once?

BERNICE: Get outta here, ya bum. You guys are always crying about it.

BENDERS: Well, I'm not crying. And I haven't compromised myself. Unless you think of sex and business as compromising affairs.

GRETCHEN: Come on in, Lud, it's a jerk off cult. You wanna join.

KIM: Come on over, honey, I'll give it to you on a plate.

ROSCOE: You know, I just may have to leave the service. They always say the best soldiers are on the outside. Go work for the boss, get it in jewelers' bars . . .

Wasa matter, Lud, walls startin' to move?

LUD: You're startin' to sound like that wine salesman, what's his name, Franco Bollo . . .

ROSCOE: It's negative, Lud, negative. It'll never sell. Hell, I'm so sold out you could wring shit outta my tax return. How 'bout you, Lud.

LUD: Well, I'm not too bad off. I been sellin' a few defense secrets for about three years now. Just to make ends meet.

ROSCOE: No shit, you get good money for that?

LUD: You bet, top dollar.

ROSCOE: Well, no harm. Don't do no harm. Who you sell em to?

LUD: Well, of course his name isn't really his. Z'a little guy with a toupee and a moustache. Meet him in museums and opera houses, places like that.

ROSCOE: You don't worry about getting busted?

LUD: Hell no. It's a business like any other. I got a real sweetheart deal. It's double blind. They'll never know who I am. I pay my taxes, support the schools, go to church. Like I said, I'm a booster. I'm a builder. You should see the little survivalist place I got up in the mountains. Got stuff all dried up. And it's an arsenal, believe me. Anyone tries to come close to me or mine, kabloom!

ROSCOE: You know Hank Knam?

LUD: The promoter?

ROSCOE: Yeah, the guy from Santa Barbara. He does that.

LUD: I'll have to look him up.

ROSCOE: There's a whole gang of them up in New Hampshire that do that. Make a good living. Ever hear of Bobby Chipuka? Bernie Jogisches? Colonel Bykov?

LUD: Naw, never heard of him.

ROSCOE: Hey, Lud, what's wrong. Hey, when you're off duty, relax.

LUD: I feel bad about the way I busted those two guys for blowing smoke.

ROSCOE: Them? Forget it. What do they know? Screw it, drink. Bernice, another round. It all comes down to drink, sooner or later. Down the hatch.

LUD: What's it all about, Roscoe.

ROSCOE: Be like me. I just like to lie around and watch Benders get laid a couple a times, watch him pop some snot.

LUD: Hell, I'm so polluted you could wring shit outta my tax return.

ROSCOE: Ah, forget it. Hey, you're as pure as a vegetarian in Vermont. Send me some of that schwartzwasser'n soda, will ya, Bernice,. It's negative, Lud, negative. It'll never sell.

LUD: It'll sell, I tell you. It'll sell. It's positive.

ROSCOE: Naw, s'negative.

LUD: You gotta see it an you're just callin' it by some other name. The opposite. You are like some one-way mirror, Chizzum.

ROSCOE: You guessed it, two face. Negative is negative to me. Like I say, I'm a scientist.

LUD: Double negative, I get it.

ROSCOE: You wouldn't get your mail, kid, if your mother didn't give it to you with a letter opener. Aw, don't take it so hard, Lud, I give you a hard time. Maybe you are armed forces, after all.

LUD: You think so, Roscoe?

ROSCOE: No, I don't, Lud. Look, does "without baggage" mean anything to you?

LUD: No, nothing.

ROSCOE: You'll figure it out, don't worry. Learn to live, kid. Look at what's available. The stuff you can get for a dollar and a quarter is incredible. I never seen such scuzz, these chicks.

LUD: Watch it, Roscoe, you're talking about the woman I love. I don't care what she does.

ROSCOE: Oh, aren't you a regular King Farouk! Look, once you go for it, get a taste for that slime, you never go back. You take that brunette over there takin' it from Benders. Just one thrust at that thing on your face ud leave you seeing gray sparks for half an hour, your tongue ud be sprung and you'd need a neck brace for six weeks. If you know what I'm talking about. Come on, get realistic. You can get in real trouble out here.

LUD: You talking about me? What are you talking about. I've got to make a move here somewhere . . .

ROSCOE: There was this guy so crazy for this slit I shot him. Shot him dead. (Roscoe pulls a pistol.)

LUD: Put it away, Roscoe, you're all liquored up.

ROSCOE: You bet, baby, you bet. An this is the way I'm gonna stay. I could stop a tank with this thing. I'm tellin' you, I had to do it. I'm warning you. It was disgusting. He like made us vulnerable. Not to speak a being a security risk. Another round, Bernice. On to Dubrovnik. I'm gonna drink Stolny outta Joe Stalin's skull.

BERNICE: Okay, boys, but this better be the last. I got to close up.

LUD: D'jou say slant?

ROSCOE: What'd you say, Willamowitz?

LUD: Name's Lud.

ROSCOE: Oh, yeah, what'jou say Lud?

LUD: D'jou say slant?

ROSCOE: How would I know what I said. I ain't got time for that. What'd I say? I'm so wasted on this shit I can't sit straight. You boys may have to strap me down before it's over. You know what I mean?

Hell, here I am bawling like Sepp Dietrich at Horst Wessel's funeral. Ah, the sands a Iwo Jima.

MARY: Don't mess with him, Roscoe, I hear he's in policy.

ROSCOE: Ah, don't worry about me, Mare, I can take care a myself.

ANN: Oh, no, Luck, Lucky, don't. You animal. Can't you see, it's tragic and it's doomed. I'll always be an American kinda girl.

LUD: Don't try to deceive me, Ann, I know you're not a real colonel.

ANN: Oh, no, Lud, who told you.

LUD: Never mind, Ann, I'm in intelligence and I got ways of finding out.

ANN: Oh, Lud, be careful. They really are crazy, you know that, don't you?

LUD: Yeah, that's kind a the way I had it figured.

ANN: Do you have any idea about what it's about?

LUD: I ain't got a clue.

ANN: Well, that's okay, Lud, cause a lot of guys just make it on native drive, instinct and good looks.

LUD: They do. You think I'm good lookin, Ann?

ANN: Sure you are, honey. Now you just sit down some more. I got to go talk to the girls. Girls, girls, come here.

ROSCOE: General Benders, sir, almost time for your address.

BENDERS: 4756 Loganrita Drive, Encino, California.

ROSCOE: No, sir, your address to the men.

BENDERS: Roscoe, call me Rod.

ROSCOE: Okay, Rod. Better get ready, sir.

BENDERS: Who are those people at the bar, Roscoe?

ROSCOE: Those are the Dutch people, sir. Rod.

GIRLS: What is it, Ann? Whazit?

ANN: Look, girls, I've got something to tell you and I don't know how you'll take it.

GIRLS: We'll take it lying down, thanks, Ann.

JANE: Hey, you know what they say, declining bucket follows the sun. What is this shit, a tennis match. Don't fuck with me, Ann. What's going on?

ANN: Jane, honey, you know I don't like it when you talk like that.

JANE: There's only one kind a language you do understand, Ann, and you know it as good as any four-legged animal.

ANN: Jane, I'll conveniently forget you said that. We'll take it up in your chambers. It's not so good to talk in front of the girls.

Girls, I've got something to tell you that some of you may find hard to take. Some of you may ralph so keep your distance. Girls, there is no wet uniform contest.

GIRLS: Aw, what'd'ya mean. There's always something like that at something like this.

ANN: Not only that, but this whole thing is a dumby. It's all make believe. We're not doing anything here, honest. It's just like playing house. The real action is five hundred miles farther north.

JANE: Ann, you big shit, you told me this was going to be the real thing.

ANN: Don't be silly, Janey, honey, you just heard that one on the radio. You can't get any action in a club like this. The real action is out in the street. Out where you hustle your stuff and find out what you're really worth.

BENDERS: I've won so much in different drawing rooms. So much in so many refrigerators.

ROSCOE: It's about time for your address, General.

BENDERS: Call me Rod.

ROSCOE: Begging your pardon, sir, you could be Joe Day for all I know.

BENDERS: Joe Day? Never head of him. Roscoe, who are those people standing at the bar?

ROSCOE: Those are Dutch people, sir.

BENDERS: Ah, the Dutch, such a warm and wonderful people. And such great allies. What do they want, Roscoe, why are they looking at me like that?

ROSCOE: They have an entertainment in mind for you, sir, a little skit of theirs, like a cabaret.

BENDERS: Ah, like when I was in Bali and the natives danced. Oh, those naked torsos . . . (*Exit Benders and Jane. Dutch entertainment. Benders on p.a.*) My god, Jane, what are they saying. I can't understand a word.

JANE: (*On p.a.*) Oh, look, General, the girls are translating. (*Girls translate into hand-jive.*)

BENDERS: (*On p.a.*) Make them stop, Roscoe, please. I'm so unhappy. Won't they stop.

ROSCOE: Benders is so wasted all the dude can do's a slow drool.

JANE: (*On p.a.*) Is this the tape, General?

BENDERS: (*On p.a.*) Mike me, I'm mumbling. Men. Men. This is your commanding officer. Can you hear me? Am I on the air?

GIRLS: What's he doing, Jane?

JANE: (*On p.a.*) Oh, nothing. Playing gorf under my skirt.

GIRLS: Oh, Fort Lobo!

CRYSTAL: I can't believe there's no wet uniform contest.

KIM: Yeah, well, we'll see about that. There's water and we all got uniforms!

GIRLS: Yeah.

GRETCHEN: And I wanted to wash my hair!

WENDY-GWEN: And I thought tonight was going to be my night. I'm ready to do it!

ANN: I'm sorry, hon, we don't throw coming out parties.

MARY: Ann, this is brilliant. I'm puttin you in for real colonel.

GIRLS: Yeah for Ann!!

KIM: Well, I'm still mad at you, Ann.

ANN: Oh, don't be silly, Kim. It's an endless shuffle, the big brown bus. These are all minor characters, except Lud. But then he's going to die. I just know it.

KIM: Well, I guess you're all right in my book, Ann.

ANN: But that is such a short, boring book, Kimmy.

WENDY-GWEN: I still can't believe it, Ann! You're telling us there is no wet uniform contest. You mean Mike Smith is not making a movie.

ANN: No, Gwen, nothing. And I'm happy to see you're not taking it hard.

WENDY-GWEN: Oh, it's nothing, Ann, old Gwendy is an old pro.

ANN: Oh, don't put yourself down, hon, you're too old for that.

ALICE: Well, is there any way we can make a little more money.

ANN: No, forget about that, girls. It's all nine to five where I stand. Be satisfied with petty pilfering. It's the American way.

WENDY-GWEN: Is it really, Ann?

ANN: Oh shut up, you ugly old bitch. There is no American way. There's a constitution and it's strict interpretation. I'm not talking idealist bull-caca, I'm talking . . .

KIM: Well, what about Mike Smith?

ANN: There is no Mike Smith, Kim, that's just a name I made up to keep you girls going. You could be a detective if you want, sweetheart, but you'd have to stand up more than you'd want to with those round heels of yours.

CRYSTAL: I think you're right, Ann, let's not peel any more moss off that tree.

KIM: Are you saying my bra straps are green, cause if you are, soldier, you are going to pay in more than pixie dust . . .

CRYSTAL: Now just calm down, Kimmy, honey. Don't go getting us all heated up.

KIM: Well, you'll never fool us again, sister. Getting us worked up for nothing.

ANN: Oh, yes I will. I can do it any time I want. And if you don't believe me, think again.

ALICE: No Mike Smith, I can't believe it. I heard he was Mr. Pogo.

ANN: Oh, no, Bill Jones is Mr. Pogo. You girls listen to anything you hear. I'm one of the only female colonels around to encourage a little independent action.

BENDERS: (On p.a.) No, dogface, there is nothing worse than feeling or even being a little militarily patriotic. A strong force is still needed. And in order to feel strong and capable requires good and reliable people in positions of leadership. Every man and woman in uniform today is needed. The defense of our freedom is first and foremost. No one can make you choose a career of dedicated service. It's your choice. But without you staying in the military, that choice could be lost to future generations. One hundred years ago our president, George Washington, told the nation, your roof tiles will blow off while you fight the Huns, it happened to me in Trenton, it could happen to you. But we can't be strong without a dedicated force of willing people. People willing to sacrifice personal needs and desires in order to maintain our cherished freedoms. This all sounds like flag waving? I don't know a better flag to wave, do you?

BERNICE: This is your check, soldier?

DOBERMAN: Yes, sir, you see . . .

BERNICE: And it is stamped insufficient funds? Isn't it, soldier?

DOBERMAN: Yes, sir, let me explain, sir. My account's back home in Idaho. My wife writes all the checks there, I write the checks here. It's all sort of confusing, sir, mam.

BENDERS: (On p.a.) You bet it is, Charlie, real confusing. You better set up your account at your duty station banking facility. And keep your records straight, Charlie. Bad checks are bad news. Keep em good.

ANN: Oh, how am I going to motivate those people?

BENDERS: (On p.a.) I don't think there's a single one of us who hasn't thrilled to see her carried in a parade. There are many things about displaying her you may not know. You can display her after dark, even twenty-four hours a day if properly illuminated. She should always have the marching right or prior place except during church services at sea. There's a lot of fascinating reading about her. Check it out at your base library.

SOUTH KOREAN JUDGE: (On p.a.) Gne no ba dee gbog eeh dadm man kid kid kip.

JANE: (Translating on p.a.) You have been found guilty of stealing an automobile.

HOULIHAN: Your honor, I was a little tipsy. I just borrowed the car. I knew the owner.

SOUTH KOREAN JUDGE: (On p.a.) Gne no ba dee gbog eeh dad man kid kip wa.

JANE: (Translating on p.a.) Order, I won't have any more outbursts. You are sentenced to three years in a South Korean prison. This proceeding is adjourned.

LUD: Why a South Korean prison?

ROSCOE: Don't even talk to me about Korea. They got a big lock up there.

BENDERS: (On p.a.) Hassles? Service members who are accused of crimes overseas may be in for the hassle of their lives. Learn your rights as a citizen, but remember you are a guest in a host country. If you're charged with violating a foreign law, the government will help in every way possible. Officials will help you get a fair trial, a defense council and an interpreter. But sometimes because of local laws and practices, it may be too little, too late. Learn the laws. It's your responsibility to adjust to foreign laws, customs and practices. Make your tour a positive experience. Sometimes we forget about the blue skies, snow capped peaks and rolling fields of grain. Sometimes we get confused and do things we know we shouldn't. It's important you understand the simple truth that being a serviceman does not provide you with immunity to the laws of the host country. You can end up in a foreign prison. If you do, we will not forget you to the extent permitted by local law. You will be provided with the same items and services you would receive if confined by your own forces. The blue skies, snow capped peaks, the rolling fields of grain are still there. Take care of yourself. Know and respect the laws of the host country. How do you navy men say, a fair wind and following seas. Goodbye, son.

JANE: (*On p.a.*) Is this the tape, General?

LUD: We're promoting independent action and we're the only people in the world who do . . .

BENDERS: (*On p.a.*) Yes, Jane, take it. Take it. Take it all. (*Roscoe pulls pistol and shoots Lud in the head. Girls scream.*)

ROSCOE: You're a bad seed, baby.

LUD: I can't believe it. Ned Lud is dying. I can't believe it. Look at him. He's dying. I never thought this would happen.

ROSCOE: Face it. That's the way it is.

GIRLS: Oh, Roscoe! That's perfectly lurid.

ROSCOE: Ah, shit! I did it again.

BENDERS: (*On p.a.*) Roscoe, you've been a very bad boy! You'd better go and sit in my office.

ROSCOE: Aw, he stepped over a line. He was all confused. It's a decision you've got to make in this business. I didn't like the direction he was going in. Anyway, he was a new dealer, the snail darter type. A Fritz, a renegade, a momma's boy. (*Girls giggle.*)

BENDERS: (*On p.a.*) Now let's not get into personality! Well, Roscoe, this is going to be hard to cover. Oh, dear. It may take my entire personal fortune to keep this thing off page one.

ROSCOE: Ah, come on, give me a break, will ya. I always played ball with you guys. What am I, a french fry? So I killed a guy! Big deal. I'm innocent until proven guilty. And you try and prove it! I'll hang you up in appeals until doomsday! He was a bully. So I 86'd him. Ain't I got rights?

BENDERS: (*On p.a.*) Well, I don't know. I'd be going out on a limb. Girls, what do you think? Should we give the captain the benefit of the doubt?

ROSCOE: You'll never regret it!

BENDERS: (*On p.a.*) What do you say, girls? How about it? And don't worry about a thing, we'd make it worth your while. Would you give us a boost?

GIRLS: Ah, hell. We don't know. (*Girls all light cigarettes. Inhale. Exhale.*)

ROSCOE: Look, Ned Lud is dead, there's nothing any of us can do about that. We're all going to miss him. Ann, you'll miss him more than most.

LUD: I can't imagine a normal guy holding a grudge just because another guy's stopped being a sucker.

ANN: Yes, I'll miss him. He was a worried soldier. He was drowned in the army. He talked to me like I was his mother. His mind was being deadened. He never read the Bible. It's a kind of dark picture. He had a leadership complex. He was so homesick and young. And though he didn't look young he knew Europo'd gone west. He knew there was something wrong with this, all this. What can I say?

LUD: People are gonna wonder who I was, what kind of guy was Ned Lud? After the autopsy's in, after you discount the lone assassin theory . . .

ROSCOE: You see, they're already startin' to talk, next thing they'll be sayin he died by his own hand, say he took his own life. But that is all just unfounded rumor, grist from the mill. Pretty soon there'll be so much controversy nobody'll ever get to the bottom of it. I'm just trying to find out the truth, each in his own way, it's the meaning of democracy! Come on, gimme a break, it's insulting to the dignity of the dead. (*Houlihan and Doberman cover Lud with sheet.*)

GIRLS: (*On the edge of the sheet.*) Ah, hell. The hell with it. Let's throw one and get him off our ass. Sure, we'll buy. But you're not gonna like the price. (*Girls giggle.*)

BENDERS: (*On p.a.*) Well, all right then. I need men like like you, Captain Chizzum, men of initiative who can take control of a situation. All in all, it's just a spot of bother over the death of a would-be reformer. Let's not trouble ourselves overly. No profit in it, really.

ROSCOE: No, sir, we've got to keep the bottom line in mind.

BENDERS: (*On p.a.*) So we'll do it then! We'll get the girls to go along and sell them a line a mile long. We'll say he was dangerous. We'll put it into code. Hell, when it's over they'll think the guy was Joe Day himself. Why, if he were alive, he'd think it. He would! I just know he would. I know boys like that, so many boys like that!

GIRLS 1: Oh look, he's trying to write something!

GIRLS 2: Oh, gee, I didn't know he could write! (*Lud scrawls these letters on the wall: Howdy Ose.*)

GIRLS 1: Howdy Ose! What's that supposed to mean?

GIRLS 2: Gee, he's not much of a writer.

LUD: . . . But just consider the rug by itself. She gave me a rug. I have it. I have the damn thing. The girls saw it. I have it in my house.

GIRLS 1: What rug? We didn't see no rug. A vicuna coat, maybe . . .

GIRLS 2: Poor kid, he's raving. This must be the end.

LUD: Now what would you do assuming you were unjustly accused, and the man said, "Why, you got a rug from us," and you had a rug but you did not get it from us? What do you do with the rug? You bring it in and say to the rug man, "Is this the damn rug?" No! Who do I show it to. I show it to the girls and they're cutting it up like I'm Jimmy the Greek. No! The thing to do when you are unjustly accused is to come in and prove that that is not the rug. The Navy can't go out and subpeona rugs belonging to the defendant . . . Bring it in here! Let us look at it. Let the expert look at it. "That is one of the four rugs I sold!" Bang. Guilty. Bang. That's for Sweeney. That's actually for Sweeney. Don't do it that way. That proves I'm guilty. I didn't do it. They're putting the Murphy on me. I was framed.

BENDERS: Time to take that long walk, son. It's time to go. (*Overture to "Git Along Little Doggies."*)

ROSCOE: So, it's okay. Went off like clockwork.

ANN: Yeah, but who likes clocks.

ROSCOE: Ann, what's with the girls? They look like they got a beef.

ANN: Well, I had to cut them out of the operation and cancelled the wet uniform contest in the process.

ROSCOE: I don't know. They look rebellious.

ANN: Put that away, Roscoe. Hasn't there been enough killing for one day?

ROSCOE: Okay, Ann, if you say so. What about Benders.

ANN: Just let him run off at the mouth.

ROSCOE: Ann, any chance of our getting together later for a little romance?

ANN: I'm sorry, Rosc, I've got an awful headache. (*Anchor chains fall offstage.*)

ROSCOE: What the fuck port is this? We ain't supposed to be here. Who are those guys with the torches? What is go the fucking on? (*All sing "Git Along Little Doggies." All dance a Shaker dance.*)

CRYSTAL: Well, hell, I'm gonna cruise the fo'c's'le an see if I can get a date with a couple a the Gatlin boys.

JANE: Aw, honey, they wouldn't date you. Stop kidding yourself.

WENDY-GWEN: Ooooh, one of the glasses in my glasses broke.

GRETCHEN: Ooooh, poopsie, you're skin is so dry. S'like onion skin. You know, you'd really do better with one of those heavy oils.

KIM: Like motor oil maybe. By the way, love the gel back and the fluffy fringe. D'jou do that with horse piss?

GRETCHEN: Oh, dear, you're complexion's so gloomy. Do you like milk.

WENDY-GWEN: Whack-o stuff, huh, sis?

ALICE: You mean milk for my face.

CRYSTAL: Ooooh, there's a trout in my drawers! Who put that there?

GRETCHEN: Oh, no, I'm talking about a different sort of milk.

KIM: Let's go down the hashstroy an see what Uncle Nick cooked up.

JANE: (*On p.a.*) So, that's my job, to jerk you off?

BENDERS: (*On p.a.*) Girls, by the way, you're all under arrest.

GIRLS: Aw, what for?

BENDERS: (*On p.a.*) For trying to rig the wet uniform contest. I mean it. This is serious. Sergeant! A cordon! The guard house. We can't have frauds like you running around on the loose. (*Girls scream and run. Lud rises up under a sheet. Lud, Roscoe and Ann chase each other around. Benders, on p.a.*) Men, men, this is your commanding officer. Obey the laws of your host country until I can get you out of here. Somehow . . . Can you hear me? Am I on the air? Testing, one, two, three, four . . . (*"Elephant Walk" or "Prairie Dog Pass."*)

END

Sunday in the Park with George

James Lapine and Stephen Sondheim

Sunday in the Park with George was first performed at the Booth Theatre in New York City on May 2, 1984 with the following cast:

ACT I

George	*Mandy Patinkin*
Dot	*Bernadette Peters*
Old Lady	*Barbara Bryne*
Nurse	*Judith Moore*
Franz	*Joseph Kolinski*
Boy	*Sherri Lynn Leidy*
Young Man	*Nancy Opel*
Man	*T. J. Meyers*
Jules	*John Cunningham*
Yvonne	*Pamela Burrell*
Boatman	*William Parry*
Celeste 1	*Melanie Vaughan*
Celeste 2	*Betsy Joslyn*
Louise	*Sherri Lynn Leidy*
Frieda	*Nancy Opel*

Louis	*T. J. Meyers*
Soldier	*Jeff Keller*
Man	*David Bryant*
Little Girl	*Sarah Reynolds*
Woman	*Sue Anne Gershenson*
Mr.	*Ray Gill*
Mrs.	*Judith Moore*

ACT II

George	*Mandy Patinkin*
Marie	*Bernadette Peters*
Dennis	*Joseph Kolinski*
Bob Greenberg	*John Cunningham*
Naomi Eisen	*Pamela Burrell*
Harriet Pawling	*Judith Moore*
Billy Webster	*T. J. Meyers*
Photographer	*Sue Anne Gershenson*
Museum Assistant	*David Bryant*
Charles Redmond	*William Parry*
Alex	*Jeff Keller*
Betty	*Nancy Opel*
Lee Randolph	*Ray Gill*
Blair Daniels	*Barbara Bryne*
Waitress	*Betsy Joslyn*
Elaine	*Melanie Vaughan*

Director: James Lapine
Music and Lyrics: Stephen Sondheim
Scenery: Tony Straiges
Costumes: Patricia Zipprodt & Ann Hould-Ward
Lighting: Richard Nelson

CHARACTERS

ACT I

George, an artist
Dot, his mistress
an Old Lady
her Nurse
Jules, another artist
Yvonne, his wife
a Boatman
Celeste no. 1, a shop girl
Celeste no. 2, another shop girl
Louise, a little girl
Franz, a coachman
Frieda, a cook
a Soldier
Mr. & Mrs., a foreign couple
Louis, a baker
Hornplayer
Woman with baby carriage
Man with bicycle

ACT II

George, an artist
Marie, his grandmother
Bob Greenberg, the museum director
Dennis, a technician
Naomi Eisen, a composer
Harriet Pawling, a patron of the arts
Billy Webster, her friend
a Waitress
Charles Redmond, a visiting curator
Betty, an artist
Alex, an artist
a Museum Assistant
Blair Daniels, an art critic
Lee Randolph, the museum's publicist
a Photographer
Elaine, George's former wife

MUSICAL NUMBERS

ACT I

Sunday in the Park With George	Dot
No Life	Jules, Yvonne
Color and Light	Dot, George
Gossip	Celeste no. 1, Celeste no. 2, Boatman, Nurse, Old Lady, Jules, Yvonne
The Day Off	George, Nurse, Franz, Frieda, Soldier, Celeste no. 1, Celeste no. 2, Yvonne, Louise, Jules, Louis
Everybody Loves Louis	Dot
Finishing the Hat	George
We Do Not Belong Together	Dot, George
Beautiful	Old Lady, George
Sunday	Company

ACT II

It's Hot Up Here	Company
Chromolume no. 7	George, Marie
Putting It Together	George, Company
Children and Art	Marie
Lesson no. 8	George
Move On	George, Dot
Sunday	Company

ACT ONE

(*A white stage. White floor, slightly raked and extended in perspective. Four white portals define the space. The proscenium arch continues across the bottom as well, creating a complete frame around the stage. George enters downstage. He is an artist. Tall, dark beard, wearing a soft felt hat with a very narrow brim crushed down at the neck, and a short jacket. He looks rather intense. He is seated downstage on the apron at an easel with a large drawing pad and a box of chalk. He stares momentarily at the pad before turning to the audience.*)

GEORGE: White. A blank page or canvas. The challenge: bring order to the whole. (*Arpeggiated chord. A tree flies in stage right.*) Through design. (*Four arpeggiated chords. The white portals fly out and the white ground cloth comes off, revealing a grassy-green expanse and portals depicting our park scene.*) Composition. (*Two arpeggiated chords. Two trees descend.*) Balance. (*Two arpeggiated chords. A tree tracks on from stage left.*) Light. (*Arpeggiated chord. The lighting bumps, giving the impression of an early morning sunrise on the island of La Grande Jatte—harsh shadows and streaming golden light through the trees.*) And harmony. (*The Music coalesces into a theme:* Sunday, *as a cut-out of a couple rises at the back of the stage. George goes to the wings and escorts Dot towards the audience. She wears a traditional 19th century outfit: full length dress with bustle, etc. When he gets her downstage left, he turns her profile, then returns downstage to his easel. He begins to draw. She turns to him. Music continues under. Annoyed.*) No. Now I want you to look out at the water.

DOT: I feel foolish.

GEORGE: Why?

DOT: (*Indicating bustle.*) I hate this thing.

GEORGE: Then why wear it?

DOT: Why wear it? Everyone is wearing them!

GEORGE: (*Begins sketching.*) Everyone . . .

DOT: You know they are. (*She begins to move.*)

GEORGE: Stand still, please.

DOT: (*Sigh.*) I read they're even wearing them in America.

GEORGE: They are fighting Indians in America—and you cannot read.

DOT: I can read . . . a little. (*Pause.*) Why did we have to get up so early?

GEORGE: The light.

DOT: Oh. (*George lets out a moan.*) What's the matter?

GEORGE: (*Erasing feverishly.*) I hate this tree. (*A tree rises back into the fly space. Music stops.*)

DOT: (*Hurt.*) I thought you were drawing me.

GEORGE: (*Muttering.*) I am. I am. Just stand still. (*Dot is oblivious to the moved tree. Through the course of the scene the landscape can continue to change. At this point a sailboat begins to slide into view.*)

DOT: I wish we could go sailing. I wouldn't go this early in the day, though.

GEORGE: Could you drop your head, please. (*She obliges.*) Dot. If you wish to be a good model you must learn to concentrate. Hold the pose. Look out at the water. (*She obliges.*) Thank you. (*Towards the far upstage corner, an Old Lady comes into view.*)

OLD LADY: Where is that tree? (*Pause.*) NURSE! NURSE!

DOT: (*Startled.*) My God! (*Sees Old Lady.*) She is everywhere. (*Nurse enters. She wears an enormous headdress.*)

OLD LADY: NURSE!

NURSE: What is it, Madame?

OLD LADY: The tree. The tree. Where is our tree?

NURSE: What tree?

OLD LADY: The tree we always sit near. Someone has moved it.

NURSE: No one has moved it, Madame. It is right over there. (*Nurse attempts to help the Old Lady along.*)

OLD LADY: Do not push me!

NURSE: I am not pushing. I am helping.

OLD LADY: You are pushing and I do not need any help.

NURSE: (*She crosses the stage and sits.*) Yes, Madame.

OLD LADY: And this is not our tree! (*She continues her shuffle.*)

NURSE: Yes, Madame.

DOT: I do not envy the nurse.

GEORGE: (*Under his breath.*) She can read . . .

DOT: They were talking about you at La Coupole.

GEORGE: Oh.

DOT: Saying strange things . . .

GEORGE: They have so little to speak of, they must speak of me?

DOT: Were you at the zoo, George? (*No response.*) Drawing the monkey cage?

GEORGE: Not the monkey cage.

DOT: They said they saw you.

GEORGE: The monkeys, Dot. Not the cage.

DOT: (*Giggling.*) It is true? Why draw monkeys?

OLD LADY: (*Finally reaches the tree.*) What is that, Nurse?

NURSE: What, Madame?

OLD LADY: (*Points offstage.*) That! Off in the distance.

NURSE: They are making way for the exposition.

OLD LADY: What exposition?

NURSE: The International Exposition. They are going to build a tower.

OLD LADY: Another exposition . . .

NURSE: They say it is going to be the tallest structure in the world.

OLD LADY: More foreigners. I am sick of foreigners.

GEORGE: More boats. (*An arpeggiated chord. A tugboat appears.*) More trees. (*Two Chords. More trees track on.*)

DOT: George. (*Chord.*) Why do you always get to sit in the shade while I have to stand in the sun? (*Chord. No response.*) George? (*Still no response.*) Hello, George? (*Chord.*) There is someone in this dress! (*Twitches slightly, mutters to herself.*)

A TRICKLE OF SWEAT.
  (*Twitch.*)
THE BACK OF THE HEAD.
  (*Twitch.*)
HE ALWAYS DOES THIS.
  (*Twitch.*)
NOW THE FOOT IS DEAD
SUNDAY IN THE PARK WITH GEORGE.
ONE MORE SU—
  (*Twitch.*)
THE COLLAR IS DAMP.
BEGINNING TO PINCH
  (*Slow twitch.*)
THE BUSTLE'S SLIPPING—
  (*Hiss and twitch, partly pleasure.*)
I WON'T BUDGE ONE INCH.
  (*Undulating with some pleasure, mingled with tiny twitches of vexation.*)
WHO WAS AT THE ZOO, GEORGE?
WHO WAS AT THE ZOO?
THE MONKEYS AND WHO, GEORGE?
THE MONKEYS AND WHO?

GEORGE: Don't move, please.

DOT: (*Still.*)
ARTISTS ARE BIZARRE, FIXED. COLD.
THAT'S YOU, GEORGE, YOU'RE BIZARRE. FIXED. COLD
I LIKE THAT IN A MAN. FIXED. COLD.
GOD, IT'S HOT OUT HERE.

WELL, THERE ARE WORSE THINGS

THAN STARING AT THE WATER ON A SUNDAY.
THERE ARE WORSE THINGS
THAN STARING AT THE WATER
AS YOU'RE POSING FOR A PICTURE
BEING PAINTED BY YOUR LOVER
IN THE MIDDLE OF THE SUMMER
ON AN ISLAND IN THE RIVER ON A SUNDAY.

(*George rearranges her a bit, as if she were an object, then resumes sketching.*)
Dot hisses, twitching again.)

THE PETTICOAT'S WET—
WHICH ADDS TO THE WEIGHT.
THE SUN IS BLINDING.

(*Closing her eyes.*)

ALL RIGHT, CONCENTRATE

GEORGE: Eyes open, please.

DOT: (*Starting to twitch and undulate out of her dress.*)

SUNDAY IN THE PARK WITH GEORGE.

GEORGE: Look out at the water. Not at me.

DOT:

SUNDAY IN THE PARK WITH GEORGE.

(*Dot has now left the dress completely. It remains upright; George continues sketching it as if she were still inside. During the following, Dot moves around the stage, continuing to undulate, taking representative poses as punctuation to the music, which is heavily rhythmic.*)

CONCENTRATE. CONCENTRATE.
WELL, IF YOU WANT BREAD
AND RESPECT
AND ATTENTION—
NOT TO SAY CONNECTION—
MODELING'S NO PROFESSION.

(*Poses.*)

IF YOU WANT, INSTEAD,
WHEN YOU'RE DEAD,
SOME MORE PUBLIC
AND MORE PERMANENT
EXPRESSION—

(*Pose.*)

OF AFFECTION—

(*Pose.*)

YOU WANT A PAINTER—

(*Brief, sharp poses throughout the following.*)

POET
SCULPTOR, PREFERABLY:

GRANITE, MARBLE, BRONZE.
DURABLE.
SOMETHING NICE WITH SWANS
THAT'S DURABLE
FOREVER.
ALL IT HAS TO BE IS GOOD.
   (*Looking over George's shoulder at his work, then at George.*)
AND GEORGE, YOU'RE GOOD.
YOU'RE REALLY GOOD.

GEORGE'S STROKE IS TENDER,
GEORGE'S TOUCH IS PURE.
   (*Sits or stands nearby and watches him intently.*)
YOUR EYES, GEORGE.
I LOVE YOUR EYES, GEORGE.
I LOVE YOUR BEARD, GEORGE.
I LOVE YOUR SIZE, GEORGE.
BUT MOST, GEORGE,
OF ALL,
BUT MOST OF ALL,
I LOVE YOUR PAINTING . . .

I THINK I'M FAINTING . . .
   (*Steps back into dress, resumes pose, gives a twitch and a wince, then sings
   sotto voce again.*)

THE TIP OF A STAY.
   (*Wince.*)
RIGHT UNDER THE TIT.
NO, DON'T GIVE IN, JUST –
   (*Shifts.*)
LIFT THE ARM A BIT . . .
GEORGE: Don't lift the arm, please.
DOT:
   SUNDAY IN THE PARK WITH GEORGE.
GEORGE: The bustle high, please.
DOT:
   NOT EVEN A NOD.
   AS IF I WERE TREES.
   THE GROUND COULD OPEN,
   HE WOULD STILL SAY "PLEASE."

NEVER KNOW WITH YOU, GEORGE,

WHO COULD KNOW WITH YOU?
THE OTHERS I KNEW, GEORGE.
BEFORE WE GET THROUGH,
I'LL GET TO YOU, TOO.

GOD, I AM SO HOT!

WELL, THERE ARE WORSE THINGS
THAN STARING AT THE WATER ON A SUNDAY.
THERE ARE WORSE THINGS
THAN STARING AT THE WATER
AS YOU'RE POSING FOR A PICTURE
AFTER SLEEPING ON THE FERRY
TO COME OVER TO AN ISLAND
IN THE MIDDLE OF A RIVER
HALF AN HOUR FROM THE CITY
ON A SUNDAY.
ON A SUNDAY IN THE PARK WITH—

GEORGE: (*The music stopping.*) Don't move the mouth. (*Dot holds absolutely still for a very long beat.*)

DOT: (*Music resuming, as she pours all her extremely mixed emotions into one word.*) —GEORGE.
(*After the applause.*) I am getting tired. The sun is too strong today.

GEORGE: Almost finished.

DOT: I'd rather be in the studio, George.

GEORGE: I know.

OLD LADY: (*Looking across the water.*) They are out early today.

NURSE: It is Sunday, Madame.

OLD LADY: That is what I mean, Nurse. Young boys swimming so early on a Sunday?

NURSE: Well, it is very warm.

OLD LADY: Hand me my parasol.

NURSE: I am, Madame. (*Nurse stands up and opens the parasol for the Old Lady. Franz enters. Stares at the Two Women for a moment, then moves downstage. He sees George, and affects a pose as he sits.*)

DOT: Oh, no.

GEORGE: What?

DOT: Look. Look who is over there.

GEORGE: So?

DOT: When he is around, you know who is likely to follow?

GEORGE: You have moved your arm.

DOT: I think they are spying on you, George. I really do.

GEORGE: Are you going to hold you head still? (*The Nurse has wandered over in the vicinity of Franz.*)

NURSE: You are here awfully early today.

FRANZ: So are you.

NURSE: And working on a Sunday.

FRANZ: Ya . . .

NURSE: It is a beautiful day.

FRANZ: It is too hot.

NURSE: Do you think?

OLD LADY: Where is my fan!

NURSE: I have to go back.

OLD LADY: My fan, Nurse!

NURSE: You did not bring it today, Madame.

OLD LADY: Of course I brought it!

FRANZ: Perhaps we will see each other later.

NURSE: Perhaps . . .

OLD LADY: There it is. Over there. (*Old Lady picks up the fan.*)

NURSE: That is my fan—

OLD LADY: Well I can use it. Can I not? It was just lying there . . . What is all that commotion?

FRANZ: *Jungen! Nicht so laut! Ruhe, bitte!* (*Music. Laughter from off right. A wagon tracks on showing likeness of* Une Baignade Asnières.)

BOY: Yoo-hoo! Dumb and fat!

YOUNG MAN: Hey! Who are you staring at?

PERVERT: Look at the lady with the rear! (*The Young Man gives a loud Bronx cheer.*)

BOY: Yoo-hoo—kinky beard!

PERVERT: Kinky beard.

YOUNG MAN, BOY: Kinky beard! (*George gestures—All freeze. A frame comes in around them. Jules and Yvonne stroll on.*)

JULES: Ahh . . .

YVONNE: Ooh . . .

JULES: Mmm . . .

YVONNE: Oh, dear.

JULES: Oh, my.

YVONNE: Oh, my dear.

JULES:
  IT HAS NO PRESENCE.

YVONNE:
  NO PASSION.

JULES:
  NO LIFE.
    (*They laugh*)
  IT'S NEITHER PASTORAL

NOR LYRICAL.

YVONNE: (*Giggling.*)

YOU DON'T SUPPOSE THAT IT'S SATIRICAL?

(*They laugh heartily.*)

JULES:

JUST DENSITY

WITHOUT INTENSITY —

YVONNE:

NO LIFE.

Boys with their clothes off —

JULES: (*Mocking.*) *I* must paint a factory next!

YVONNE:

IT'S SO MECHANICAL.

JULES:

METHODICAL.

YVONNE:

IT MIGHT BE IN SOME DREARY

SOCIALISTIC PERI-

ODICAL.

JULES: (*Approvingly.*) Good.

YVONNE:

SO DRAB, SO COLD.

JULES:

AND SO CONTROLLED.

BOTH:

NO LIFE.

JULES: His touch is too deliberate, somehow.

YVONNE: The dog. (*They shriek with laughter.*)

JULES:

THESE THINGS GET HUNG —

YVONNE: Hmm.

JULES:

AND THEN THEY'RE GONE.

YVONNE: Ahhh.

OF COURSE HE'S YOUNG —

(*Jules shoots her a look.*)

YVONNE: (*Hastily.*)

BUT GETTING ON.

JULES: Hanh.

ALL MIND, NO HEART.

NO LIFE IN HIS ART.

YVONNE:

NO LIFE IN HIS *LIFE* —

(*Jules nods in approval.*)
BOTH:
  NO—
    (*They giggle and chortle.*)
BOTH:
  LIFE.
    (*Arpeggio. The Boy in the picture gives a loud Bronx cheer. Jules and Yvonne turn and slowly stroll around; the sky and the trees return.*)
NURSE: (*Seeing Jules.*) There is that famous painter—what is his name . . .
OLD LADY: What *is* his name?
NURSE: I can never remember their names. (*Jules tips his hat towards the Ladies. The Couple continues towards George.*)
JULES: George! Out very early today. (*George nods as he continues sketching. Dot drops her head even further.*)
GEORGE: Hello, Jules.
YVONNE: A lovely day . . .
JULES: I couldn't be out sketching today—it is too sunny!
GEORGE: Have you seen the painting yet?
JULES: Yes. I was just going to say! Boys bathing—what a curious subject. (*Catches himself.*) We must speak.
YVONNE: (*Sincere.*) I loved the dog.
JULES: I *am* pleased there was an independent exhibition.
GEORGE: Yes . . .
JULES: We *must* speak. Really. (*Beat.*)
YVONNE: Enjoy the weather.
JULES: Good day. (*As they exit, Yvonne stops Jules and points to Dot.*)
YVONNE: That dress! (*They laugh and exit.*)
DOT: I hate them.
GEORGE: Jules is a fine painter.
DOT: I do not care. I hate them. (*Jules and Yvonne return.*)
JULES: Franz!
YVONNE: We are waiting! (*They exit.*)
FRANZ: Ya, Madame, Monsieur. At your service. (*Franz, who has been eyeing the Nurse, quickly gets up and dashes offstage after Jules and Yvonne. George closes his pad. Dot remains frozen.*)
GEORGE: Thank you.
DOT: (*Moving.*) I began to do it.
GEORGE: What?
DOT: Concentrate. Like you said.
GEORGE: (*Patronizing.*) You did very well.
DOT: Did I really?
GEORGE: (*Gathering his belongings.*) Yes. I'll meet you back at the studio.
DOT: (*Annoyed.*) You are not coming?

GEORGE: Not now. (*Angry, Dot begins to exit.*) We'll go to the Follies tonight. (*She stops, looks at him, then walks off. George walks to the Nurse and Old Lady.*) Bonjour.

NURSE: *Bonjour, Monsieur.*

GEORGE: Lovely morning, ladies.

NURSE: Yes.

GEORGE: I have my pad and crayons today.

NURSE: Oh, that would—

OLD LADY: Not today!

GEORGE: (*Disappointed.*) Why not today?

OLD LADY: Too warm.

GEORGE: It *is* warm, but it will not take long. You can go—

OLD LADY: (*Continues to look out across the water.*) Some other day, monsieur. (*Beat.*)

GEORGE: It's George, Mother.

OLD LADY: (*As if it is to be a secret.*) Sssh . . .

GEORGE: Yes. I guess we will all be back. (*He exits as Lights fade to black. Upstage, George on a scaffold, behind a large canvas, which is a scrim. He is painting. Downstage, Dot [in a likeness of "La Poudreuse"] is at her vanity, powdering her face. Steady, unhurried, persistent rhythmic figure underneath.*)

DOT: (*As she powders rhythmically.*) George taught me all about concentration. "The art of being still," he said. (*Checks herself, then resumes powdering.*) I guess I did not learn it soon enough. (*Dips puff in powder.*) George likes to be alone. (*Resumes powdering.*) Sometimes he will work all night long painting. We fought about that. I need sleep. I love to dream. George doesn't need as much sleep as everyone else. (*Dips puff, starts powdering neck.*) And he never tells me his dreams. George has many secrets. (*Lights down on Dot, up on George. A number of brushes in his hand, He is covering a section of the canvas—the face of the woman in the foreground—with tiny specks of paint, in the same rhythm as Dot's powdering.*)

GEORGE: (*Pauses, checks.*) Order. (*Dabs with another color, pauses, checks, dabs with another color, pauses, checks, dabs palette.*) Design. (*Dabs with another brush.*) Composition. Tone. Form. Symmetry. Balance. (*Sings.*)
MORE RED.
(*Dabs with more intensity.*)
AND A LITTLE MORE RED.
(*Switches brushes.*)
BLUE BLUE BLUE BLUE
BLUE BLUE BLUE BLUE
EVEN EVEN . . .
(*Switches quickly.*)
GOOD . . .
(*Humming.*)

BUMBUM BUM BUMBUMBUM
BUMBUM BUM ...
  (*Paints silently for a moment.*)
MORE RED ...
  (Switches brushes again.)
MORE BLUE ...
  (*Again.*)
MORE BEER ...
  (*Takes a swig from a nearby bottle, always eyeing the canvas, puts the bottle down.*)
MORE LIGHT!
  (*He dabs assiduously, delicately attacking the area he is painting.*)
COLOR AND LIGHT.
THERE'S ONLY COLOR AND LIGHT.
YELLOW AND WHITE.
JUST BLUE AND YELLOW AND WHITE.
  (*Addressing the woman he is painting.*)
LOOK AT THE AIR, MISS—
  (*Dabs at the space in front of her.*)
SEE WHAT I MEAN?
NO, LOOK OVER THERE, MISS—
  (*Dabs at her eye, pauses, checks it.*)
THAT'S DONE WITH GREEN ...
  (*Swirling a brush in the orange cup.*)
CONJOINED WITH ORANGE ...
  (*Lights down on George, up on Dot, now powdering her breasts and armpits. Rhythmic figure persists underneath.*)
DOT: Nothing seems to fit me right. (*Giggles.*) The less I wear, the more comfortable I feel. (*Sings, checking herself.*)
MORE ROUGE
  (*Puts puff down, gets rouge, starts applying it in small rhythmic circles, speaks.*)
George is very special. Maybe I'm just not special enough for him.
  (*Puts rouge down, picks up eyebrow tweezers, sings.*)
IF MY LEGS WERE LONGER.
  (*Plucks at her eyebrow.*)
IF MY BUST WAS SMALLER.
  (*Plucks.*)
IF MY HANDS WERE GRACEFUL.
  (*Plucks.*)
IF MY WAIST WAS THINNER.
  (*Checks herself.*)
IF MY HIPS WERE FLATTER.
  (*Plucks.*)

IF MY VOICE WAS WARM.
  (*Plucks.*)
IF I COULD CONCENTRATE—
  (*Abruptly, her feet start to can-can under the table.*)
I'D BE IN THE FOLLIES.
I'D BE IN A CABARET.
GENTLEMEN IN TALL SILK HATS
AND LINEN SPATS
WOULD WAIT WITH FLOWERS.
I COULD MAKE THEM WAIT FOR HOURS.
WITH FANCY FLATS
WHO'D DRINK MY HEALTH,
AND I WOULD BE AS
HARD AS NAILS . . .
  (*Looks at her nails, reaches for the buffer.*)
IF I WAS A FOLLY GIRL.
AH, I WOULDN'T LIKE IT MUCH.
MARRIED MEN AND STUPID BOYS
AND TOO MUCH SMOKE AND ALL THAT NOISE
AND ALL THAT COLOR AND LIGHT . . . . . .
  (*Lights up on George, talking to the woman in the painting. rhythmic figure continues underneath.*)

GEORGE: Aren't you proper today, Miss? Your parasol so properly cocked, your bustle so perfectly upright. No doubt your chin rests at just the proper angle from your chest. (*Addressing the figure of the man next to her.*) And you, sir. Your hat so black. So black to you, perhaps. So red to me. (*The rhythmic figure drops out momentarily.*)

DOT: (*Spraying herself rhythmically with perfume.*)
  NONE OF THE OTHERS WORKED AT NIGHT . . .

GEORGE: So composed for a Sunday.

DOT:
  HOW DO YOU WORK WITHOUT THE RIGHT
    (*Spray.*)
  BRIGHT
    (*Spray.*)
  WHITE
    (*Spray.*)
  LIGHT?
    (*Spray.*)
  HOW DO YOU FATHOM GEORGE?
    (*Rhythmic figure returns underneath.*)

GEORGE: (*Muttering, trance-like, as he paints.*)
  RED RED RED RED

RED RED ORANGE
RED RED ORANGE
ORANGE PICK UP BLUE
PICK UP RED
PICK UP ORANGE
FROM THE BLUE-GREEN BLUE-GREEN
BLUE-GREEN CIRCLE
ON THE VIOLET DIAGONAL
DI-AG-AG-AG-AG-AG-O-NAL-NAL
YELLOW COMMA YELLOW COMMA
  (*Humming, massaging his numb wrist.*)
NUMNUM NUM NUMNUMNUM
NUMNUM NUM . . .
  (*Sniffs, smelling Dot's perfume.*)
BLUE BLUE BLUE BLUE
BLUE STILL SITTING
RED THAT PERFUME
BLUE ALL NIGHT
BLUE-GREEN THE WINDOW SHUT
DUT DUT DUT
DOT DOT SITTING
DOT DOT WAITING
DOT DOT GETTING FAT FAT FAT
MORE YELLOW
DOT DOT WAITING TO GO
OUT OUT OUT BUT
NO NO NO GEORGE
FINISH THE HAT FINISH THE HAT
HAVE TO FINISH THE HAT FIRST
HAT HAT HAT HAT
HOT HOT HOT IT'S HOT IN HERE . . .
  (*Whistles a bit, then joyfully.*)
SUNDAY!

  COLOR AND LIGHT!
DOT: (*Pinning up her hair.*) But how George looks. He could look forever.
GEORGE:
  THERE'S ONLY COLOR AND LIGHT.
DOT: As if he sees you and he doesn't all at once.
GEORGE:
  PURPLE AND WHITE . . .
DOT: What is he thinking when he looks like that?

GEORGE:

   . . . AND RED AND PURPLE AND WHITE.

DOT: What does he see? Sometimes, not even blinking.

GEORGE: (*To the young girls in the painting.*)

   LOOK AT THIS GLADE, GIRLS,

   YOUR COOL BLUE SPOT.

DOT: His eyes. So dark and shiny.

GEORGE:

   NO, STAY IN THE SHADE, GIRLS,

   IT'S GETTING HOT . . .

DOT: Some think cold and black.

GEORGE:

   IT'S GETTING ORANGE . . .

DOT: (*Sings.*)

   BUT IT'S WARM INSIDE HIS EYES . . .

GEORGE: (*Dabbing more intensely.*)

   HOTTER . . .

DOT:

   AND IT'S SOFT INSIDE HIS EYES . . .

   (*George steps around the canvas to get paint or clean a brush. He glances at Dot. Their eyes meet for a second, then Dot turns back to her mirror.*)

DOT:

   AND HE BURNS YOU WITH HIS EYES . . .

GEORGE: Look at her looking.

DOT:

   AND YOU'RE STUDIED LIKE THE LIGHT.

GEORGE: Forever with that mirror. What does she see? The round face, the tiny pout, the soft mouth, the creamy skin . . .

DOT:

   AND YOU LOOK INSIDE THE EYES.

GEORGE: The pink lips, the red cheeks . . .

DOT:

   AND YOU CATCH HIM HERE AND THERE.

GEORGE: The wide eyes. Studying the round face, the tiny pout . . .

DOT:

   BUT HE'S NEVER REALLY THERE.

GEORGE: Seeing all the parts and none of the whole.

DOT:

   SO YOU WANT HIM EVEN MORE.

GEORGE: (*Sings.*)

   BY THE WAY SHE CATCHES THE LIGHT . . .

DOT:

   AND YOU DROWN INSIDE HIS EYES . . .

GEORGE:
  AND THE COLOR OF HER HAIR . . .
DOT:
  I COULD LOOK AT HIM
  FOREVER . . .
GEORGE: (*Continued.*)
  I COULD LOOK AT HER
  FOREVER . . .
    (*A long beat. Music holds under, gradually fading.*)
GEORGE: (*Continued. Matter-of-fact.*) It's going well . . .
DOT: Should I wear my red dress or blue?
GEORGE: Red. (*Beat.*)
DOT: Aren't you going to clean up?
GEORGE: Why?
DOT: The Follies, George! (*Beat.*)
GEORGE: I have to finish the hat. (*He returns to his work. Dot slams down her brush and stares at the back of the canvas. She exits. Lights fade downstage as the rhythmic figure resumes.*)
GEORGE: (*As he paints.*) Damn. The Follies. Will she yell or stay silent? Go without me or sulk in the corner? Will she be in the bed when the hat and the grass and the parasol have finally found their way? (*Sings.*)
  TOO GREEN . . .
  Do I care?
  TOO BLUE . . .
  Yes . . .
  TOO SOFT. . .
  What should I do?
    (*Thinks for a moment.*)
  Well . . .
  Red. (*Continues painting as music and lights fade. Afternoon. Another Sunday on the island. Downstage right George sketches the Boatman; a cut-out of a black dog stands close by; Nurse and Old Lady sit near their tree. Celeste 1 and Celeste 2 sit on a bench stage left.*)
BOATMAN: The water looks different on Sunday.
GEORGE: It is the same water you boat on all week.
BOATMAN: (*Contentious.*) It looks different from the park.
GEORGE: You prefer watching the boats to the people promenading?
BOATMAN: (*Laughing.*) People all dressed up in their Sunday best pretending? Sunday is just another day. (*Dot and Louis enter arm in arm. They look out at the water.*)
BOATMAN: I wear what I always wear—then I don't have to worry.
GEORGE: Worry?
BOATMAN: They leave me alone dressed like this. No one comes near. (*Celeste 1*

and Celeste 2 enter. Gossip music under.)

CELESTE 1: Look who's over there.

CELESTE 2: Dot. Who is she with?

CELESTE 1: Looks like Louis the baker.

CELESTE 2: Well, how did Dot get to be with Louis?

CELESTE 1: She knows how to make dough rise!

NURSE: (*Noticing Dot.*) There is that woman.

OLD LADY: Who is she with?

NURSE: (*Squinting.*) Looks like the baker.

OLD LADY: Moving up I suppose.

NURSE: The artist is more handsome.

OLD LADY: You cannot eat paintings, my dear—not when there's bread in the oven. (*Jules and Yvonne appear. They stand to one side and strike a pose. Music continues under, slow and stately.*)

JULES: They say he is working on an enormous canvas.

YVONNE: I heard somewhere he's painting little specks.

JULES: You heard it from me! A large canvas of specks. Really . . .

YVONNE: Look at him. Drawing a slovenly boatman.

JULES: I think he is trying to play with light.

YVONNE: What next?

JULES: A monkey cage, they say. (*They laugh.*)

BOATMAN: Sunday hypocrites. That's what they are. Muttering and murmuring about this one and that one. I'll take my old dog for company any day. A dog knows his place. Respects your privacy. Makes no demands. Right, Spot?

SPOT (GEORGE): Ruff.

CELESTE 1:
THEY SAY THAT GEORGE HAS ANOTHER WOMAN.

CELESTE 2:
I'M NOT SURPRISED.

CELESTE 1:
THEY SAY THAT GEORGE ONLY LIVES WITH TRAMPS.

CELESTE 2:
I'M NOT SURPRISED.

CELESTE 1:
THEY SAY HE PROWLS THROUGH THE STREETS
IN HIS TOP HAT AFTER MIDNIGHT—

CELESTE 2:
NO!

CELESTE 1:
—AND STANDS THERE STARING UP AT THE LAMPS.

CELESTE 2:
I'M NOT SURPRISED.

BOTH:
ARTISTS ARE SO CRAZY . . .
OLD LADY:
THOSE GIRLS ARE NOISY.
NURSE: Yes, Madame.
OLD LADY: (*Referrring to Jules.*)
THAT MAN IS FAMOUS.
NURSE: Yes, Madame.
OLD LADY: (*Referring to Boatman.*)
THAT MAN IS FILTHY.
NURSE: Your son seems to find him interesting.
OLD LADY:
THAT MAN'S DELUDED.
(*Nurse thinks, nods.*)
CELESTES:
ARTISTS ARE SO CRAZY.
OLD LADY, NURSE:
ARTISTS ARE SO PECULIAR.
YVONNE: Monkeys!
BOATMAN:
OVERPRIVILEGED WOMEN
COMPLAINING,
SILLY LITTLE SIMPERING
SHOPGIRLS,
CONDESCENDING ARTISTS
"OBSERVING,"
"PERCEIVING" . . .
WELL, SCREW THEM!
ALL:
ARTISTS ARE SO—
CELESTE 2:
—CRAZY.
CELESTE 1:
—SECRETIVE.
BOATMAN:
—HIGH AND MIGHTY.
NURSE:
—INTERESTING.
OLD LADY:
—UNFEELING.
BOATMAN: What do you do with these drawings, anyway?
DOT: (*To Louis.*) That's George. (*All heads turn, first to Dot then to George.*)
JULES: There's a move on to include his work in the next group show.

YVONNE: Never!

JULES: I agree. (*Pause.*) I agree. (*They exit.*)

CELESTE 1: He draws anyone.

CELESTE 2: Old boatman!

CELESTE 1: Peculiar man.

CELESTE 2: Like his father, I said.

CELESTE 1: I said so first. (*Dot enters and goes to a park bench left. She has a lesson book in hand. Very slowly, she reads aloud.*)

DOT: Lesson number eight. Pro-nouns. (*Proudly, she repeats the word.*) Pronouns. (*She reads.*) What is a pronoun? A pronoun is the word used in the place of a noun. Do you recall what a noun is? (*Looks up.*) Certainly, I recall. (*She pauses, then quickly flips back in the book to the earlier lesson on nouns. She nods her head knowingly, then flips back to the present lesson. She reads.*) Example: Charles has a book. Marie wants Charles's book. (*To herself.*) Not Marie again . . . (*Reads.*) Marie wants *his* book. Fill in the blanks. Charles ran with Marie's ball. Charles ran with . . . (*She writes as she spells aloud.*) h-e-r ball. (*To herself.*) Get the ball back, Marie. (*Louise enters upstage.*)

OLD LADY: Children should not go unattended.

NURSE: She is very young to be alone.

OLD LADY: I do not like what I see today, Nurse.

NURSE: (*Confused.*) What do you see?

OLD LADY: Lack of discipline.

NURSE: Oh.

OLD LADY: Not the right direction at all.

BOATMAN: Fools rowing. Call that recreation!

GEORGE: Almost finished. (*Louise has come up to pet the dog. Boatman turns on her in a fury.*)

BOATMAN: Get away from that dog! (*All eyes turn to the Boatman. Louise screams and goes running offstage crying. All the other parties engage in animated whispering.*)

GEORGE: That was hardly necessary.

BOATMAN: How do you know what's necessary? Who are you, with your fancy pad and crayons. You call that work? You smug goddam holier-than-thou shitty little men in your fancy clothes—born with pens and pencils, not pricks. You don't know! (*Boatman storms off. George, stunned, begins to draw the dog.*)

CELESTE 1: Well, what are you going to do—now that you have no one to draw?

CELESTE 2: Sshh. Don't talk to him.

GEORGE: I am drawing his dog.

CELESTE 2: His dog!

CELESTE 1: Honestly . . .

GEORGE: I have already sketched you ladies.

CELESTE 1: What!

CELESTE 2: You have?

CELESTE 1: I do not believe you.

CELESTE 2: When? (*During the above, the Old Lady and Nurse have exited.*)

GEORGE: A few Sundays ago.

CELESTE 1: But we never sat for you.

GEORGE: I studied you from afar.

CELESTE 2: No!

CELESTE 1: Where were you?

CELESTE 2: I want to see.

GEORGE: Someday you shall.

CELESTE 1: When?

GEORGE: Good day. (*George exits. Gossip music begins.*)

CELESTE 1: He did not so much as ask. (*They exit. George has crossed to Dot.*)

GEORGE: Good afternoon.

DOT: Hello.

GEORGE: Lesson number eight?

DOT: Yes. Pronouns. My writing is improving. I even keep notes in the back.

GEORGE: Good for you.

DOT: How is your painting coming along?

GEORGE: Slowly.

DOT: Are you getting more work done now that you have fewer distractions in the studio?

GEORGE: (*Beat.*) It has been quiet there. (*Louis bounds onstage with a pastry tin.*)

LOUIS: I made your favorite— (*He stops when he sees George.*)

GEORGE: Good day. (*George goes cross stage, then moves downstage to Spot and sits. Dot watches him, then turns to Louis.*)

LOUIS: (*Opens the tin.*) Creampuffs! (*The bench on which they are sitting tracks off-stage as Dot continues to look at George. George, who has been staring at his sketch of Spot, looks over and sees they have left. Vamp. He begins to lose himself in his work. Lights change, leaving the dog [Spot] alone onstage. George is sketching the dog. Music under, stops. George stands back a moment, then resumes briefly. He stops again.*)

GEORGE:
IF THE HEAD WAS SMALLER . . .
IF THE TAIL WERE LONGER . . .
IF HE FACED THE WATER . . .
IF THE PAWS WERE HIDDEN . . .
IF THE NECK WAS DARKER . . .
IF THE BACK WAS CURVED . . .
MORE LIKE THE PARASOL . . .

BUMBUM BUM BUMBUMBUM

BUMBUM BUM . . .

MORE SHADE . . .
MORE TAIL . . .

MORE GRASS! . . .
WOULD YOU LIKE SOME MORE GRASS?
MMMM . . .

SPOT (GEORGE): *(Barks.)*
  RUFF! RUFF!
THANKS, THE WEEK HAS BEEN
  (Barks.)
ROUGH!
WHEN YOU'RE STUCK FOR LIFE ON A GARBAGE SCOW–
  (Sniffs around.)
ONLY FORTY FEET LONG FROM STERN TO PROW,
AND A CRACKPOT IN THE BOW–WOW, ROUGH!
  (Sniffs.)
THE PLANKS ARE ROUGH
AND THE WIND IS ROUGH
AND THE MASTER'S DRUNK AND MEAN AND–
  (Sniffs.)
GRRRRUFF! GRUFF!
WITH THE FISH AND SCUM
AND PLANKS AND BALLAST . . .
  (Sniffs.)
THE NOSE GETS NUMB
AND THE PAWS GET CALLOUSED.
AND WITH SPLINTERS IN YOUR ASS,
YOU LOOK FORWARD TO THE GRASS
ON SUNDAY.
THE DAY OFF.
  (Barks.)
OFF! OFF!
OFF!

The grass needs to be thicker. Perhaps a few weeds. With some ants, if you would. I love fresh ants.

ROAMING AROUND ON SUNDAY,
POKING AMONG THE ROOTS AND ROCKS,
NOSE TO THE GROUND ON SUNDAY,
STUDYING ALL THE SHOES AND SOCKS
EVERYTHING'S WORTH IT SUNDAY,
THE DAY OFF.

(*Sniffs.*)
BITS OF PASTRY . . .
    (*Sniffs.*)
PIECE OF CHICKEN
    (*Sniffs.*)
THERE'S A THISTLE . . .
    (*Sniffs.*)
THAT'S A SHALLOT . . .
    (*Sniffs.*)
THAT'S A DRIPPING
FROM THE LOONY WITH THE PALETTE . . .
    (*Fifi, the pug dog, appears.*)

FIFI (GEORGE):
YAP! YAP!
    (*Pants.*)
YAP!
OUT FOR THE DAY ON SUNDAY,
OFF OF MY LADY'S LAP AT LAST.
YAPPING AWAY ON SUNDAY
HELPS YOU FORGET THE WEEK JUST PAST—
    (*Yelps.*)
YEP!
EVERYTHING'S WORTH IT SUNDAY,
THE DAY OFF.
YEP!
STUCK ALL WEEK ON A LADY'S LAP.
NOTHING TO DO BUT YAWN AND NAP.
CAN YOU BLAME ME IF I YAP?

SPOT:
NOPE.

FIFI: There's just so much attention a dog can take.
BEING ALONE ON SUNDAY,
ROLLING AROUND IN MUD AND DIRT.

SPOT:
BEGGING A BONE ON SUNDAY,
SETTLING FOR A SPOILED DESSERT.

FIFI:
EVERYTHING'S WORTH IT.

SPOT:
SUNDAY.

FIFI:
THE DAY OFF.

SPOT: (*Sniffs.*)

SOMETHING FUZZY . . .

FIFI: (*Sniffs.*)

SOMETHING FURRY . . .

SPOT: (*Sniffs.*)

SOMETHING PINK
THAT SOMEONE TORE OFF IN A HURRY . . .

FIFI:

WHAT'S THE MUDDLE
IN THE MIDDLE?

SPOT:

THAT'S THE PUDDLE
WHERE THE POODLE DID THE PIDDLE.

> (*Hornplay rises from the stage. Two horn calls. Vamp. Enter Franz, Frieda, Celeste 1 and 2, Nurse and possibly the Boatman.*)

GEORGE:

TAKING THE DAY ON SUNDAY,
NOW THAT THE DREARY WEEK IS DEAD.
GETTING AWAY ON SUNDAY
BRIGHTENS THE DREARY WEEK AHEAD.
EVERYONE'S ON DISPLAY ON SUNDAY—

ALL:

THE DAY OFF!

> (*George flips open a page of his sketchbook and starts to sketch the Nurse as she clucks at the ducks.*)

GEORGE:

BONNET FLAPPING,
BUSTLE SLIDING,
LIKE A ROCKING HORSE THAT NOBODY'S BEEN RIDING.
THERE'S A DAISY—
AND SOME CLOVER—
AND THAT INTERESTING FELLOW LOOKING OVER . . .

OLD LADY: (*Offstage.*) Nurse!

NURSE & GEORGE:

ONE DAY IS MUCH LIKE ANY OTHER
LISTENING TO HER SNAP AND DRONE.

NURSE:

STILL, SUNDAY WITH SOMEONE'S DOTTY MOTHER
IS BETTER THAN SUNDAY WITH YOUR OWN

MOTHERS MAY DRONE, MOTHERS MAY WHINE—
TENDING TO HIS, THOUGH, IS PERFECTLY FINE.
IT PAYS FOR THE NURSE THAT IS TENDING TO MINE
ON SUNDAY—

MY DAY OFF.

(*The Celestes enter with fishing poles. "Celeste" Music.*)

CELESTE 2: This is just ridiculous.
CELESTE 1: Why shouldn't we fish.
CELESTE 2: No one will notice us anyway.
CELESTE 1: Look.
CELESTE 2: Where?
CELESTE 1: Soldiers.
CELESTE 2: Alone.
CELESTE 1: What did I tell you?
CELESTE 2: They'll never talk to us if we fish. Why don't we—
CELESTE 1: It's a beautiful day for fishing. (*She smiles in the direction of the Soldiers.*)
SOLDIER: (*Looking to his companion.*) What do you think? (*Companion nods.*) I like the one in the light hat. (*Horn call. Louis enters, notices Frieda and Franz, and dashes over to them.*)
LOUISE: Frieda, Frieda—
FRANZ: Oh, no.
FRIEDA: Not now, Louise.
LOUISE: I want to play.
FRANZ: Go away, Louise. We are not working today.
LOUISE: Let's go throw stones at the ducks.
FRIEDA: Louise! Do not throw stones at the ducks!
LOUISE: Why not?
FRANZ: You know why not, and you know this is our day off, so go find your mother and throw some stones at her, why don't you.
FRIEDA: Franz!
LOUISE: I'm telling.
FRANZ: Good. Go!
FRIEDA: Franzel—relax.
FRANZ: Ya . . . Relax. (*George flips a page and starts to sketch Franz and Frieda.*)
GEORGE, FRIEDA:
  SECOND BOTTLE . . .
GEORGE, FRANZ: (*As Franz looks at the Nurse.*)
  AH, SHE LOOKS FOR ME . . .
FRIEDA:
  HE IS BURSTING TO GO . . .
FRANZ:
  NEAR THE FOUNTAIN . . .
FRIEDA:
  I COULD LET HIM . . .

FRANZ:
> HOW TO MANAGE IT—?

FRIEDA:
> NO.

You know, Franz—I believe that artist is drawing us.

FRANZ: Who?

FRIEDA: Monsieur's friend.

FRANZ: (*Sees George. They pose.*) Monsieur would never think to draw us! We are only people he looks down upon. (*Pause.*) I should have been an artist. I was never intended for work.

FRIEDA: Artists work, Franz. I believe they work very hard.

FRANZ:
> WORK! . . .
> WE WORK.
> WE SERVE THEIR FOOD,
> WE CARVE THEIR MEAT,
> WE TEND TO THEIR HOUSE,
> WE POLISH THEIR
> SILVERWARE.

FRIEDA:
> THE FOOD WE SERVE
> WE ALSO EAT.

FRANZ:
> FOR THEM WE RUSH,
> WASH AND BRUSH,
> WIPE AND WAX—

FRIEDA:
> FRANZ, RELAX.

FRANZ:
> WHILE HE "CREATES"
> WE SCRAPE THEIR PLATES
> AND DUST THEIR KNICKNACKS,
> HUNDREDS TO A SHELF.
> WORK IS WHAT I DO FOR OTHERS,
> LIEBCHEN,
> ART IS WHAT YOU DO FOR YOURSELF.

JULES: Working on Sunday again? You should give yourself a day off.

GEORGE: Why?

JULES: You must need time to replenish—or does your well never run dry? (*Laughs; notices that George is drawing Frieda and Franz.*) Drawing my servants? Certainly, George, you could find more colorful subjects.

GEORGE: Who should I be sketching?

JULES: How about that pretty friend of yours? Now why did I see *her* arm-in-arm with the baker today? (*George looks up.*) *She* is a pretty subject.

GEORGE: Yes . . .

JULES: Your life needs spice, George. Go to some parties. That is where you'll meet prospective buyers. Have some fun. The work is bound to reflect—

GEORGE: You don't like my work, do you?

JULES: I did once.

GEORGE: You find it too tight.

JULES: People are talking about your work. You have your admirers, but you—

GEORGE: I'm using a different brushstroke.

JULES: (*Getting angry.*) Always changing! Why keep changing?

GEORGE: Because I do not paint for your approval. (*Beat.*)

JULES: And I suppose that is why I like you. (*Begins to walk away.*) Good to see you, George. (*Jules crosses as if to exit.*)

GEORGE: (*Calling after him.*) Jules. I would like you to come to the studio sometime. See the new work . . .

JULES: For my approval?

GEORGE: No, for your opinion.

JULES: Very well. (*George flips a page over and starts sketching the Boatman.*)

GEORGE, BOATMAN:
YOU AND ME, PAL
WE'RE THE LOONIES.
DID YOU KNOW THAT?
BET YOU DIDN'T KNOW THAT.

BOATMAN:
'CAUSE WE TELL THEM THE TRUTH!
WHO YOU DRAWING?
WHO THE HELL YOU THINK YOU'RE DRAWING?
ME?
YOU DON'T KNOW ME!
GO ON DRAWING.
SINCE YOU'RE DRAWING ONLY WHAT YOU WANT TO SEE.
ANYWAY!
   (*Points to his patch.*)
ONE EYE, NO ILLUSION—
THAT YOU GET WITH TWO:
   (*Points to George's eye.*)
ONE FOR WHAT IS TRUE.
   (*Points to the other.*)
DRAW YOUR WRONG CONCLUSION,
ALL YOU ARTISTS DO.
I SEE WHAT IS TRUE . . .
   (*Music continues under.*)

BOATMAN: Sitting here, looking everyone up and down. Studying every move

like *you* see something different, like your eyes know more—
YOU AND ME, PAL,
WE'RE SOCIETY'S FAULT.

ALL:
TAKING THE DAY ON SUNDAY
AFTER ANOTHER WEEK IS DEAD.

OLD LADY:
NURSE!

ALL:
GETTING AWAY ON SUNDAY
BRIGHTENS THE DREARY WEEK AHEAD.

OLD LADY:
NURSE!

ALL:
LEAVING THE CITY PRESSURE
BEHIND YOU,
OFF WHERE THE AIR IS FRESHER,
WHERE GREEN, BLUE,
BLIND YOU—

DOT: (*Looking offstage in the direction of George's exit.*)
HELLO, GEORGE . . .
WHERE DID YOU GO, GEORGE?
I KNOW YOU'RE NEAR, GEORGE.
I CAUGHT YOUR EYES, GEORGE.
I WANT YOUR EAR, GEORGE.
I'VE A SURPRISE, GEORGE . . .

EVERYBODY LOVES LOUIS,
LOUIS' SIMPLE AND KIND.
EVERYBODY LOVES LOUIS,
LOUIS' LOVABLE.

FRANZ:
LOUIS!

DOT:
SEEMS WE NEVER KNOW, DO WE,
WHO WE'RE GOING TO FIND?
  (*Tenderly.*)
LOUIS THE BAKER IS NOT WHAT I HAD IN MIND.
BUT . . .

LOUIS' REALLY AN ARTIST:
LOUIS' CAKES ARE AN ART.
LOUIS ISN'T THE SMARTEST—

LOUIS' POPULAR.
EVERYBODY LOVES LOUIS:
LOUIS BAKES FROM THE HEART . . .

THE BREAD, GEORGE.
I MEAN THE BREAD, GEORGE.
AND THEN IN BED, GEORGE . . .
I MEAN HE KNEADS ME—
I MEAN LIKE DOUGH, GEORGE . . .
HELLO, GEORGE . . .

LOUIS' ALWAYS SO PLEASANT,
LOUIS' ALWAYS SO FAIR.
LOUIS MAKES YOU FEEL PRESENT,
LOUIS' GENEROUS.
THAT'S THE THING ABOUT LOUIS:
LOUIS IS ALWAYS "THERE."
LOUIS' THOUGHTS ARE NOT HARD TO FOLLOW,
LOUIS' ART IS NOT HARD TO SWALLOW.

NOT THAT LOUIS' PERFECTION—
THAT'S WHAT MAKES HIM IDEAL.
HARDLY ANYTHING WORTH OBJECTION:
LOUIS DRINKS A BIT,
LOUIS BLINKS A BIT.
LOUIS MAKES A CONNECTION,
THAT'S THE THING THAT YOU FEEL . . .

WE LOSE THINGS.
AND THEN WE CHOSE THINGS.
AND THERE ARE LOUIS'S
AND THERE ARE GEORGE'S—
WELL, LOUIS'S
AND GEORGE.
BUT GEORGE HAS GEORGE,
AND I NEED—
SOMEONE—
LOUIS—
    (*Louis gives her a pastry and exits.*)
EVERYBODY LOVES LOUIS,
HIM AS WELL AS HIS CAKES.
EVERYBODY LOVES LOUIS,
ME INCLUDED, GEORGE.

NOT AFRAID TO BE GOOEY,
LOUIS SELLS WHAT HE MAKES.
EVERYBODY GETS ALONG WITH HIM.
THAT'S THE TROUBLE, NOTHING'S WRONG WITH HIM.

LOUIS HAS TO BAKE HIS WAY,
GEORGE CAN ONLY BAKE HIS . . .
  (*Licks a pastry.*)
LOUIS IT IS.
  (*Enter a foreign couple, Mr. and Mrs., followed by George who sketches them.*
  Mr. and Mrs. are eating French pastries and studying the people in the park.)
MR.: Paris looks nothing like the paintings.
MRS.: I know.
MR.: (*Looking about.*) I don't see any passion, do you?
MRS.: None.
MR.: The French are so placid.
MRS.: I don't think they have much style, either.
MR.: What's all the carryin' on back home? Delicious pastries, though.
MRS.: Mmmm, excellent.
MR.: Looking at those boats over there makes me think of our return voyage.
MRS.: I long to be back home.
MR.: You do?
MRS.: How soon could we leave?
MR.: You're that anxious to leave? But Peaches, we just arrived . . .
MRS.: I know.
MR.: (*Gives it a moment's thought.*) I don't like it here either! We'll go right
  back to the hotel and I'll book passage for the end of the week. We'll go to
  the galleries this afternoon and then we'll be on our way home!
MRS.: Oh, I am so relieved. (*As they exit.*) I'll miss these pastries, though.
MR.: We'll take a baker with us, too.
MRS.: Oh, wonderful. (*They exit.*)
CELESTE 1: You really should try using that pole.
CELESTE 2: It will not make any difference.
CELESTE 1: (*Yelping as if she had caught a fish.*) Oh! Oh!
CELESTE 2: What is wrong?
CELESTE 1: Just sit. there. (*Celeste 1 carries on some more [*"something huge!"*]*
  looking in the direction of the Two Soldiers. Soldiers converse for a moment, then
  come over.)
SOLDIER: May we be of some service, Madame?
CELESTE 1: Mademoiselle.
CELESTE 2: She has a fish.
CELESTE 1: He knows.
SOLDIER: Allow me. (*Soldier takes the pole from her and pulls in the line and hook.*

There is nothing on the end.)

CELESTE 1: Oh. It tugged so . . .

SOLDIER: There's no sign of a fish here.

CELESTE 1: Oh me. My name is Celeste. This is my friend.

CELESTE 2: Celeste. (*Soldier fools with fishing pole.*)

CELESTE 1: Do you have a name?

SOLDIER: I beg your pardon. Napoleon. Some people feel I should change it.

CELESTE 2: And your friend?

SOLDIER: Yes. He is my friend. (*Music.*)

CELESTE 1: (*Giggling, to Soldier.*) He's very quiet.

SOLDIER: Yes. Actually he is. He lost his hearing during combat exercises.

CELESTE 1: Oh. What a shame.

SOLDIER: He can't speak, either.

CELESTE 2: Oh. How dreadful.

SOLDIER: We have become very close, though.

CELESTE 1: (*Nervous.*) So I see.

SOLDIER AND GEORGE: (*Sudden and loud.*)

> MADEMOISELLES,
> I AND MY FRIEND,
> WE ARE BUT SOLDIERS!
> (*Rumble from his companion: Soldier raises hand to quiet him.*)

SOLDIER:

> PASSING THE TIME
> IN BETWEEN WARS
> FOR WEEKS AT AN END.

CELESTE 1:

> (*Aside.*) BOTH OF THEM ARE PERFECT.

CELESTE 2:

> YOU CAN HAVE THE OTHER.

CELESTE 1:

> I DON'T WANT THE OTHER.

CELESTE 2:

> I DON'T WANT THE OTHER EITHER.

SOLDIER:

> AND AFTER A WEEK
> SPENT MOSTLY INDOORS
> WITH NOTHING BUT SOLDIERS,
> LADIES, I AND MY FRIEND
> TRUST WE WILL NOT OFFEND –
> WHICH WE'D NEVER INTEND –
> BY SUGGESTING WE SPEND

BOTH CELESTES: (*Excited.*)

> OH, SPEND –

SOLDIER:

   –THIS MAGNIFICENT SUNDAY–

BOTH CELESTES: (*A bit deflated.*)

   OH, SUNDAY–

SOLDIER:

   –WITH YOU AND YOUR FRIEND.

     (*Soldier offers his arm. Both Celestes rush to take it; Celeste 1 gets there first. Celeste 2 tries to get in between the Soldiers, can't, and rather than join the companion, takes the arm of Celeste 1. They all start to promenade.*)

CELESTE 2: (*To Celeste 1.*)

   THE ONE ON THE RIGHT'S AN AWFUL BORE . . .

CELESTE 1:

   HE'S BEEN IN A WAR.

SOLDIER: (*To Companion.*)

   WE MAY GET A MEAL AND WE MIGHT GET MORE . . .

ALL: (*To themselves, as they exit.*)

   IT'S CERTAINLY FINE FOR SUNDAY . . .

   IT'S CERTAINLY FINE FOR SUNDAY . . .

     (*From offstage.*)

   IT'S CERTAINLY FINE FOR SUNDAY . . .

     (*George is alone. He moves downstage, near Fifi the pug who rises, and sits.*)

GEORGE: (*Leafing back through his sketches.*)

   MADEMOISELLES . . .

     (*Flips a page.*)

   YOU AND ME, PAL . . .

   SECOND BOTTLE . . .

   AH, SHE LOOKS FOR ME . . .

     (*Flips.*)

   BONNET FLAPPING . . .

     (*Flips.*)

   YAPPING . . .

     (*Flips.*)

   RUFF! . . .

   CHICKEN . . .

   PASTRY . . .

     (*Licks lip.*)

   YES, SHE LOOKS FOR ME–GOOD.

   LET HER LOOK FOR ME TO TELL ME WHY SHE LEFT ME–

   AS I ALWAYS KNEW SHE WOULD.

   I HAD THOUGHT SHE UNDERSTOOD.

   THEY HAVE NEVER UNDERSTOOD,

   AND NO REASON THAT THEY SHOULD.

BUT IF ANYBODY COULD . . .

FINISHING THE HAT,
HOW YOU HAVE TO FINISH THE HAT,
HOW YOU WATCH THE REST OF THE WORLD
FROM A WINDOW
WHILE YOU FINISH THE HAT.

MAPPING OUT A SKY,
WHAT YOU FEEL LIKE, PLANNING A SKY,
WHAT YOU FEEL WHEN VOICES THAT COME
THROUGH THE WINDOW
GO
UNTIL THEY DISTANCE AND DIE,
UNTIL THERE'S NOTHING BUT SKY.

AND HOW YOU'RE ALWAYS TURNING BACK TOO LATE
FROM THE GRASS OR THE STICK
OR THE DOG OR THE LIGHT,
HOW THE KIND OF WOMAN WILLING TO WAIT'S
NOT THE KIND THAT YOU WANT TO FIND WAITING
TO RETURN YOU TO THE NIGHT,
DIZZY FROM THE HEIGHT,
COMING FROM THE HAT,

STUDYING THE HAT,
ENTERING THE WORLD OF THE HAT,
REACHING THROUGH THE WORLD OF THE HAT
LIKE A WINDOW,
BACK TO THIS ONE FROM THAT.

STUDYING A FACE,
STEPPING BACK TO LOOK AT A FACE
LEAVES A LITTLE SPACE IN THE WAY LIKE A WINDOW,
BUT TO SEE—
IT'S THE ONLY WAY TO SEE.

AND WHEN THE WOMAN THAT YOU WANTED GOES,
YOU CAN SAY TO YOURSELF "WELL, I GIVE WHAT I GIVE."
BUT THE WOMAN WHO WON'T WAIT FOR YOU KNOWS
THAT, HOWEVER YOU LIVE,
THERE'S A PART OF YOU ALWAYS STANDING BY,
MAPPING OUT THE SKY,

FINISHING A HAT . . .
(*Showing sketch to Fifi.*)
LOOK, I MADE A HAT . . .
WHERE THERE NEVER WAS A HAT . . .
(*After the song, Mr. and Mrs. enter stage right. They are lost. The Boatman crosses near them and they stop him in his path.*)
MR.: Excusez, Masseur. We are lost.
BOATMAN: What do you want?
MRS.: Let me try, Daddy. We are alien here. Unable to find passage off island.
BOATMAN: Why don't you just walk into the water until your lungs fill up and you die. (*Boatman crosses away from them, laughing.*)
MRS.: I detest these people.
MR.: (*Spotting Louis, who has entered in search of Dot.*) Isn't that the baker?
MRS.: Why, yes it is! (*They cross to Louis. George brings on the Hornplayer cutout. Old Lady enters.*)
OLD LADY: Where is that tree? Nurse? NURSE! (*Horn call. Dot enters, and suddenly she and George are still, staring at one another. Everyone onstage turns slowly to them. People begin to sing fragments of songs. Dot and George move closer to one another, circling each other like gun duelers. The rest of the cast close in around them until Dot and George stop, opposite each other. Silence. Dot takes her bustle and defiantly turns it around, creating a pregnant stance. There is an audible gasp from the onlookers. Lights fade to black. Music. Lights slowly come up on George in his studio painting. We see Dot enter and cross into the studio. George continues painting as she watches. He stops for a moment when he sees her, then continues working.*)
DOT: You are almost finished.
GEORGE: If I do not change my mind again. And you?
DOT: Two more months.
GEORGE: (*Chuckles.*) You can not change your mind.
DOT: Nor do I want to. (*Beat.*) Is it going to be exhibited?
GEORGE: I am not sure. Jules is coming over to look at it. Any minute, in fact.
DOT: Oh. I hope you don't mind my coming.
GEORGE: What is it that you want, Dot?
DOT: George. I would like my painting.
GEORGE: Your painting?
DOT: The one of me powdering.
GEORGE: I did not know that it was yours.
DOT: You said once that I could have it.
GEORGE: In my sleep?
DOT: I want something to remember you by.
GEORGE: You don't have enough now?
DOT: I want the painting, too. (*George stops painting.*)
GEORGE: I understand you and Louis are getting married.

DOT: Yes.

GEORGE: He must love you very much to take you in that condition.

DOT: He does.

GEORGE: I didn't think you would go through with it. I did not think that was what you really wanted.

DOT: I don't think I can have what I really want. Louis is what I think I need.

GEORGE: Yes. Louis will take you to the Follies! Correct?

DOT: George, I didn't come here to argue. (*Jules and Yvonne enter.*)

JULES: George?

GEORGE: Back here, Jules.

DOT: I will go.

GEORGE: Don't leave! It will only be a minute—

JULES: (*Enters.*) There you are. I brought Yvonne along.

YVONNE: May I take a peek?

DOT: I will wait in the other room.

YVONNE: (*Sees Dot.*) I hope we are not interrupting you. (*George nods. She and Jules step back and study the painting. George looks at Dot as she exits to the other room.*)

JULES: It is so large. How can you get any perspective? And this light . . . (*George pulls a lantern close to the canvas.*)

GEORGE: Stand here.

YVONNE: Extraordinary! Excuse me. (*Yvonne exits into the other room. Dot is sitting at her table, which is now cleared of her belongings. Yvonne and Dot look at each other for a moment.*) Talk of painting bores me. It is hard to escape it when you are with an artist. (*Beat.*) I do not know how you can walk up all those steps in your condition. I remember when I had Louise. I could never be on my feet for long periods of time. Certainly could never navigate steps.

DOT: Did someone carry you around?

YVONNE: Why are you so cool to me?

DOT: Maybe I don't like you.

YVONNE: What ever have I done to make you feel that way?

DOT: "What ever have I done . . .?" Maybe it is the way you speak. What are you really doing here?

YVONNE: You know why we are here. So Jules can look at George's work.

DOT: I do not understand why George invites you. He knows you do not like his painting.

YVONNE: That is not entirely true. Jules has great respect for George. And he has encouraged him since they were in school.

DOT: That is not what I hear. Jules is jealous of George now.

YVONNE: (*Beat.*) Well . . . jealousy is a form of flattery, is it not? I have been jealous of you on occasion. (*Dot looks surprised.*) When I have seen George drawing you in the park. Jules has rarely sketched me.

DOT: You are his wife.

YVONNE: Too flat. Too angular.

DOT: Modeling is hard work. You wouldn't like it anyway.

YVONNE: It is worth it, don't you think?

DOT: Sometimes . . .

YVONNE: Has your life changed much now that you are with the baker?

DOT: I suppose. He enjoys caring for me.

YVONNE: You are very lucky. Oh, I suppose Jules cares—but there are times when he just does not know Louise and I are there. George always seems so oblivious to everyone. (*Lowers her voice.*) Jules says that is what is wrong with his painting. Too obsessive. You have to have a life! Don't you agree? (*Dot nods.*)

JULES: George . . . I do not know what to say. What *is* this?

GEORGE: What is the dominant color? The flower on the hat?

JULES: Is this a school exam, George?

GEORGE: What is that color?

JULES: (*Bored.*) Violet. (*George takes him by the hand and moves him closer to the canvas.*)

GEORGE: See? Red and blue. Your eye made the violet.

JULES: So?

GEORGE: So, your eye is perceiving both red and blue *and* violet. Only eleven colors—no black—divided, not mixed on the palette, mixed by the eye. Can't you see the shimmering? (*Jules approaches the canvas.*)

JULES: George . . .

GEORGE: Science, Jules. Fixed laws for color, like music.

JULES: You are a painter, not a scientist! You cannot even see these faces!

GEORGE: I am not painting faces! I am—

JULES: George! I have touted your work in the past, and now you are embarrassing me! People are talking—

GEORGE: Why should I paint like you or anybody else? I am trying to get through to something new. Something that is my own.

JULES: And I am trying to understand.

GEORGE: And I want you to understand. Look at the canvas, Jules. Really look at it.

JULES: George! Let us get to the point. You have invited me here because you want me to try to get this included in the next group show.

GEORGE: (*Beat—embarrassed.*) It will be finished soon. I want it to be seen. (*Yvonne, who has been at the studio door, leans into the room.*)

YVONNE: Jules, I am sorry to interrupt, but we really must be going. You know we have an engagement.

JULES: Yes.

YVONNE: Thank you, George.

JULES: Yes. Thank you.

GEORGE: Yes. Thank you for coming.

JULES: I will give the matter some thought. (*They exit. George stands motionless for a moment staring at the canvas, then he immediately dives into his work.*)

GEORGE: He does not like you. He does not understand or appreciate you. He can only see you as everyone else does. Afraid to take you apart and put you back together again for himself. But we will not let anyone deter us, will we? (*Hums.*)

BUMBUM BUM BUMBUMBUM BUMBUM—

DOT: (*Calling to him.*) George! (*George, embarrassed, crosses around. He begins to speak. Dot tries to interrupt him.*)

GEORGE: Excuse me—speaking with Jules about the painting—well, I just picked up my brushes—I do not believe he even looked at the painting though—(*Pause.*)

DOT: You asked me to stay, George, and then you forget that I am even here. George!

DOT: I have something to tell you.

GEORGE: Yes. Now, about "your" painting—

DOT: I may be going away. (*Beat.*) To America.

GEORGE: Alone.

DOT: Of course not! With Louis. He has work.

GEORGE: When?

DOT: After the baby arrives.

GEORGE: You will not like it there.

DOT: How do you know?

GEORGE: (*Getting angry.*) I have read about America. Why are you telling me this? First, you ask for a painting that is *not* yours—then you tell me this. (*Beginning to return to the studio.*) I have work to do. (*Chord; music continues under.*)

DOT: Yes, George, run to your work. Hide behind your painting. I have come to tell you I am leaving because I thought you might *care* to know—foolish of me, because you care about nothing—

GEORGE: I care about many things—

DOT: Things—not people.

GEORGE: People, too. I cannot divide my feelings up as neatly as you and, I am not hiding behind my canvas—I am living in it.

DOT: (*Sings.*)

WHAT YOU CARE FOR IS YOURSELF.

GEORGE: I care about this painting. *You* will be in this painting.

DOT: (*Sings.*)

I AM SOMETHING YOU CAN USE.

GEORGE: (*Sings.*)

I HAD THOUGHT YOU UNDERSTOOD.

DOT:

IT'S BECAUSE I UNDERSTAND THAT I LEFT—

THAT I AM LEAVING.

GEORGE:

THEN THERE'S NOTHING I CAN SAY,
IS THERE?

DOT:

YES, GEORGE, THERE IS:

YOU COULD TELL ME NOT TO GO.
SAY IT TO ME,
TELL ME NOT TO GO.
TELL ME THAT YOU'RE HURT,
TELL ME YOU'RE RELIEVED,
TELL ME THAT YOU'RE BORED—
ANYTHING, BUT DON'T ASSUME I KNOW.
TELL ME WHAT YOU FEEL!

GEORGE:

WHAT I FEEL?
YOU KNOW EXACTLY HOW I FEEL.
WHY DO YOU INSIST
YOU MUST HEAR THE WORDS,
WHEN YOU KNOW I CANNOT GIVE YOU WORDS?
NOT THE ONES YOU NEED.

THERE'S NOTHING TO SAY.
I CANNOT BE WHAT YOU WANT.

DOT:

WHAT DO *YOU* WANT, GEORGE?

GEORGE:

I NEEDED YOU AND YOU LEFT.

DOT:

THERE WAS NO ROOM FOR ME—

GEORGE: (*Overriding her.*)

YOU WILL NOT ACCEPT WHO I AM.
I AM WHAT I DO!
WHICH YOU KNEW,
WHICH YOU ALWAYS KNEW,
WHICH I THOUGHT YOU WERE A PART OF—!

DOT:

NO,
YOU ARE COMPLETE, GEORGE,
YOU ARE YOUR OWN.
WE DO NOT BELONG TOGETHER.
YOU ARE COMPLETE, GEORGE,

YOU ALL ALONE.
I AM UNFINISHED,
I AM DIMINISHED
WITH OR WITHOUT YOU.

WE DO NOT BELONG TOGETHER,
AND WE SHOULD HAVE BELONGED TOGETHER
WHAT MADE IT SO RIGHT TOGETHER
IS WHAT MADE IT ALL WRONG.

NO ONE IS YOU, GEORGE,
THERE WE AGREE,
BUT OTHERS WILL DO, GEORGE.
NO ONE IS YOU AND
NO ONE CAN BE,
BUT NO ONE IS ME, GEORGE,
NO ONE IS ME.
WE DO NOT BELONG TOGETHER.
AND WE'LL NEVER BELONG—!

YOU HAVE A MISSION,
A MISSION TO SEE.
NOW I I HAVE ONE TOO, GEORGE.
AND WE SHOULD HAVE BELONGED TOGETHER.

I HAVE TO MOVE ON.

(*They stand looking at each other for a moment as the music becomes quieter. Dot leaves. George is left standing alone onstage. The lights fade, leaving him lit in special. The set changes back to the park scene around him. When the change is complete, he moves downstage right with the Old Lady, and begins to draw her. They are alone onstage, except for the cut-out of the Soldier, which stands towards the rear of the stage. There is a change of tone in both George and the Old Lady. She has assumed a kind of loving attitude, soft and dream-like. George is rather sullen in her presence.*)

OLD LADY: (*Staring across the water.*) I remember when you were a little boy. You would rise up early on a Sunday morning and go for a swim . . .
GEORGE: I do not know how to swim.
OLD LADY: The boys would come by the house to get you . . .
GEORGE: I have always been petrified of the water.
OLD LADY: And your father would walk you all to the banks of the Seine . . .
GEORGE: Father was never faithful to us.
OLD LADY: And he would give you boys careful instruction, telling you just

how far to swim out . . .

GEORGE: And he certainly never instructed . . .

OLD LADY: And now, look across there—in the distance—all those beautiful trees cut down for a foolish tower.

GEORGE: (*Music under.*) I do not think there were ever trees there.

OLD LADY: How I loved the view from here . . .
CHANGING.

GEORGE: I am quite certain that was an open field . . .

OLD LADY:
IT KEEPS CHANGING.

GEORGE: I used to play there as a child.

OLD LADY:
I SEE TOWERS
WHERE THERE WERE TREES.

GOING,
ALL THE STILLNESS,
THE SOLITUDE,
GEORGIE.

SUNDAYS,
DISAPPEARING
ALL THE TIME,
WHEN THINGS WERE BEAUTIFUL . . .

GEORGE:
ALL THINGS ARE BEAUTIFUL,
MOTHER,
ALL TREES, ALL TOWERS,
BEAUTIFUL.
THAT TOWER—
BEAUTIFUL, MOTHER,
SEE?
(*Gestures.*)
A PERFECT TREE.

PRETTY ISN'T BEAUTIFUL, MOTHER,
PRETTY IS WHAT CHANGES.
WHAT THE EYE ARRANGES
IS WHAT IS BEAUTIFUL.

OLD LADY:
FADING . .

GEORGE:
I'M CHANGING.
YOU'RE CHANGING.
OLD LADY:
IT KEEPS FADING . . .
GEORGE:
I'LL DRAW US BEFORE WE FADE,
MOTHER.
OLD LADY:
IT KEEPS MELTING
BEFORE OUR EYES.
GEORGE:
YOU WATCH
WHILE I REVISE THE WORLD.
OLD LADY:
CHANGING,
AS WE SIT HERE—
QUICK, DRAW IT ALL,
GEORGIE . . .
GEORGE:
MOTHER . . .
BOTH:
SUNDAYS—
OLD LADY:
DISAPPEARING,
AS WE LOOK—
GEORGE: Look! . . . Look! . . .
OLD LADY: (Not listening, fondly.)
YOU MAKE IT BEAUTIFUL.
(Music continues.)
Oh, Georgie, how I long for the old view. (Music out. The Soldier [sans partner] and Celeste 2 enter arm-in-arm and promenade.)
SOLDIER: (Noticing his companion.) I am glad to be free of him.
CELESTE 2: Friends can be confining.
SOLDIER: He never understood my moods.
CELESTE 2: She only thought of herself.(Mr. and Mrs. enter. He is carrying a big steamer trunk. She is carrying a number of famous paintings, framed, under her arm. They are followed by Dot, who is carrying her baby bundled in white, and Louis.)
SOLDIER: It felt as if I had this burden at my side.
MR.: This damned island again! I do not understand why we are not going' straight to our boat.

CELESTE 2: She never really cared about me.

MRS.: They wanted to come here first.

SOLDIER: We had very different tastes.

MR.: That much I figured out–but why? Didn't you ask them?

CELESTE 2: She had no taste.

MRS.: I don't know.

SOLDIER: She did seem rather pushy.

CELESTE 2: Very! And he was so odd.

SOLDIER: (Annoyed.) He is not odd.

(Mr. and Mrs. are stopped by the Soldier's line "He is not odd.")

CELESTE 2: No. No. I didn't really mean odd . . . (*Louis has skipped onstage. Boatman enters, and seeing her, rushes towards her.*)

BOATMAN: (*Mutters as he chases after Louise.*) . . . you better hope I don't get my hands on you, you little toad. (*Louise puts her hand over her eye and stiffens her leg in imitation of the Boatman, who chases her offstage.*) Now stop that!

MR.: Are we ever going to get home?! (*Dot has crossed downstage to George.*)

GEORGE: (*Not looking up.*) You are blocking my light.

DOT: Marie and I came to watch. (*Pause.*)

GEORGE: (*Mutters.*) Marie . . . (*Pause.*) You know I do not like anyone staring over my shoulder.

DOT: Yes, I know. (*She moves to another position.*) George, we are about to leave for America. I have come to ask for the painting of me powdering again. I would like to take it with me.

GEORGE: (*He stops for a moment.*) Oh? I have repainted it. (*He draws.*)

DOT: Dot?

GEORGE: Another model.

DOT: You knew I wanted it.

GEORGE: Perhaps if you had remained still –

DOT: Perhaps if you would look up from your pad! What is wrong with you, George? Can you not even look at your own child?

GEORGE: She is not my child. Louis is her father.

DOT: Louis is not her father.

GEORGE: Louis is her father now. Louis will be a loving and attentive father. I cannot because I cannot look up from my pad.(*She stands speechless for a moment, then begins to walk away.*)

GEORGE: Dot. I am sorry. (*George drawing Old Lady.*)

OLD LADY: I worry about you, George.

GEORGE: Could you turn slightly toward me, please. (*She does so.*)

OLD LADY: No future in dreaming.

GEORGE: Drop the head a little, please. (*She does so. Mr., Mrs., Dot and Louis exit. Celeste 1 enters and goes to the Soldier cut out.*)

OLD LADY: I worry about you and that woman, too.

GEORGE: I have another woman in my life now.

OLD LADY: They are all the same woman.

GEORGE: (*Chuckles.*) Variations on a theme.

OLD LADY: Ah, you always drifted as a child.

GEORGE: (*Muttering.*) Shadows are too heavy.

OLD LADY: You were always in some other place—seeing something no one else could see.

GEORGE: Softer light. (*Lights dim slowly.*)

OLD LADY: We tried to get through to you, George. Really we did. (*George stops drawing. He looks at her. Looks at the page.*)

GEORGE: (*Laments.*) Connect, George. (*Trails off.*) Connect . . . (*Frieda and Jules enter again. They seem to be hiding.*)

FRIEDA: Are you certain you wish to do this?

JULES: (*Uncertain.*) Of course. We just have to find a quiet spot. I've wanted to do it outside for a long time.

FRIEDA: Franz would kill you—

JULES: (*Panics.*) Is he in the park?

FRIEDA: I am not certain.

JULES: Oh. Well. Perhaps some other day would be better.

FRIEDA: Some other day? Always some other day. Perhaps you do not really wish to—

JULES: (*Subservient.*) I do. I do! I love tall grass.

FRIEDA: Ya. Tall grass. You wouldn't toy with my affections, would you?

JULES: No. No. Of course not.

FRIEDA: I see a quiet spot over there.

JULES: (*Pointing where she did, nervous.*) Over there. There are people in that grove—(*Frieda places his hand on her breast. They are interrupted by Celeste 2 and the Soldier. Frieda and Jules exit.*) Bonjour.

SOLDIER: Do you suppose there is a violation being perpetrated by that man?

CELESTE 2: What?

SOLDIER: There is something in the air today . . .

CELESTE 1: (*With the Soldier's companion.*) Being alone is nothing new for me.

SOLDIER: (*Noticing Celeste 1.*) Look who is watching us.

CELESTE 1: Sundays are such a bore. I'd almost rather be in the shop. Do you like your work? I hate mine!

CELESTE 2: I do not care if she never speaks to me again.

SOLDIER: She won't. (*Franz and the Nurse enter as if to rendezvous.*)

YVONNE: FRANZ! (*Nurse exits. Yvonne goes to Franz.*) Franz, have you seen Louise?

FRANZ: Nein, Madame.

YVONNE: I thought Frieda was going to care for her today.

FRANZ: But it's Sunday.

YVONNE: What of it?

FRANZ: Our day off.

YVONNE: Oh. But I have just lost my little girl! (*Franz shrugs his shoulders and begins looking for Louise.*)

SOLDIER: Let's go say hello to Celeste.

CELESTE 2: (*Indignant.*) I do not wish to speak with her!

SOLDIER: Come. It will be fun! (*Soldier takes Celeste 2 towards Celeste 1. Louise comes running in breathless. She immediately goes to Yvonne's side.*)

YVONNE: Louise! Where have you been, young lady?!

LOUISE: With Frieda.

YVONNE: There, you see.

FRANZ: Frieda?

LOUISE: And with Father.

YVONNE: Your father is in the studio.

LOUISE: No he's not. He's with Frieda. I saw them.

FRANZ: Where?

LOUISE: Over there. Tonguing. (*Franz exits. Music under, agitated.*)

OLD LADY: Manners. Grace. Respect.

YVONNE: (*Beginning to spank Louise.*)
How dare you, young lady!

LOUISE: It's true. It's true!

(*Soldier and Celeste 2 get to Celeste 1.*)

(*Jules enters, somewhat sheepishly.*)

CELESTE 1: What do you want?

SOLDIER: We've come for a visit.

YVONNE: Where the hell have you been? What are you doing here?

CELESTE 1: I don't want to say hello to her. Cheap Christmas wrapping.

JULES: Darling, I came out here looking for Louise.

CELESTE 2: Cheap! Look who is talking. You have the worst reputation of anyone in Paris.

LOUISE: (*Crying.*) You came to tongue.

CELESTE 1: At least I have a reputation. You could not draw a fly to flypaper!

(*Boatman enters and begins chasing Louise around the stage. All hell breaks loose and the arguments erupt into total chaos.*)

YVONNE: How dare you, Jules! (*She goes to him and begins striking him.*)

SOLDIER: Ladies, you mustn't fight.

CELESTE 2: I seem to be doing just fine.

JULES: Nothing. I swear.

YVONNE: Nothing. Look. (*Franz drags in Frieda.*) Have you been with my husband?

FRIEDA: Madame, he gave me no choice.

FRANZ: What do you mean he gave you no choice?

JULES: (*Letting go of Louise, who drifts off to the side.*) That is not so. Your wife lured me.

FRIEDA: Lured you! You all but forced me—

JULES: You are both fired!

FRANZ: FIRED! You think we would continue to work in your house?

YVONNE: Jules, you cannot change the subject. What were you doing?

CELESTE 1: Hah. With a diseased soldier!

SOLDIER: Wait just one minute.

CELESTE 1: Disgusting sores everywhere.

CELESTE 2: Don't say that about him.

SOLDIER: Yes, don't say that—

CELESTE 1: I'll say whatever I like. You are both ungrateful, cheap, ugly, diseased, disgusting garbage . . .

SOLDIER: Listen here, Lady, if in fact there is anything ladylike about you. You should be glad to take what you can get, any way you can get it and I—

CELESTE 2: You think you know everything. You are not so special, and far from as pretty as you think, and everyone that comes into the shop knows exactly what you are and what—

(*Everyone has slowly fought their way to the middle of the stage, creating one big fight. George and the Old Lady have been watching the chaos. Arpeggiated chord, as at the beginning of the play. Everybody suddenly freezes in place.*)

OLD LADY: Remember, George. (*She turns back to the water.*)

(*Another chord. George turns to the group.*)

GEORGE: (*Mutters.*) Order.

(*Another chord. Everyone turns simultaneously to George. As chords continue, George looks at each of the people one by one and we see his ultimate power over his subjects. He nods to them, and each ends up in one of the posed positions that they held at some point earlier in the act.*)

GEORGE: Design.

(*Chord. George nods to Frieda and Franz and they cross downstage right onto the apron. Chord. George nods to Mr. and Mrs. and they cross upstage.*)

GEORGE: Tension.

(*Chord. George nods to Celeste 1 and 2 and they cross downstage. Another chord. Jules and Yvonne cross upstage.*)

GEORGE: Balance.

(*Chord. Old Lady crosses right as Dot crosses center. Another chord. Soldier crosses upstage right. Chord. George gestures to the Boatman, who crosses downstage right.*)

The Music becomes calm, stately, triumphant.)

GEORGE: Harmony.

(*George turns front. The Promenade begins. Throughout the song, George is moving about, setting trees, cut-outs and figures—making a perfect picture.*)

ALL:
SUNDAY,
BY THE BLUE
PURPLE YELLOW RED WATER
ON THE GREEN
PURPLE YELLOW RED GRASS,
LET US PASS
THROUGH OUR PERFECT PARK,
PAUSING ON A SUNDAY
BY THE COOL
BLUE TRIANGULAR WATER
ON THE SOFT
GREEN ELLIPTICAL GRASS
AS WE PASS
THROUGH ARRANGEMENTS OF SHADOWS
TOWARDS THE VERTICALS OF TREES
FOREVER . . .
   (*The horn sounds.*)
BY THE BLUE
PURPLE YELLOW RED WATER
ON THE GREEN
ORANGE VIOLET MASS
OF THE GRASS
IN OUR PERFECT PARK,
MADE OF FLECKS OF LIGHT
AND DARK,

AND PARASOLS:
PEOPLE STROLLING THROUGH THE TREES
OF A SMALL SUBURBAN PARK
ON AN ISLAND IN THE RIVER
ON AN ORDINARY SUNDAY . . .
    (The horn sounds. Chimes. They all reach their positions.)
SUNDAY . . .
    (The horn again. Everyone turns, into their final poses, as George freezes them. He comes out to the apron.)
SUNDAY . . .

(The horn. They all suddenly shut their mouths. The picture is complete. At the last moment, George rushes back into the frame and removes Louise's eyeglasses. As he dashes back on to the apron, the completed canvas flies in. Final chord. Very slow fade, or long freeze and sudden blackout.)

ACT TWO

(Lights slowly fade up, and we see everyone frozen in the tableau. There is a very long pause before we begin. The audience should feel the tension as they wait for something to happen. Finally, music begins.)

DOT:
> IT'S HOT UP HERE.

YVONNE:
> IT'S HOT AND MONOTONOUS.

LOUISE:
> I WANT MY GLASSES.

FRANZ:
> THIS IS NOT MY GOOD PROFILE.

NURSE: Nobody can even *see* my profile.

CELESTE 1:
> I HATE THIS DRESS.

CELESTE 2:
> THE SOLDIERS HAVE FORGOTTEN US.

FRIEDA:
> THE BOATMAN SCHWITZES.

JULES: I'm completely out of proportion.

SOLDIER:
> THESE HELMETS WEIGH A LOT ON US.

OLD LADY:
> THIS TREE IS BLOCKING MY VIEW.

LOUISE:
> I CAN'T SEE ANYTHING.

BOATMAN:
> WHY ARE THEY COMPLAINING?
> IT COULD HAVE BEEN RAINING.

DOT:
> I HATE THESE PEOPLE.

ALL:
> IT'S HOT UP HERE
> A LOT UP HERE.
> IT'S HOT UP HERE
> FOREVER.

> A LOT OF FUN
> IT'S NOT UP HERE.
> IT'S HOT UP HERE,
> NO MATTER WHAT.

> THERE'S NOT A BREATH
> OF AIR UP HERE,
> AND THEY'RE UP HERE
> FOREVER.

> IT'S NOT MY FAULT
> I GOT UP HERE.
> I'LL ROT UP HERE,
> I AM SO HOT UP HERE.

YVONNE: Darling, don't clutch Mother's hand quite so tightly. Thank you.
CELESTE 1:
> IT'S HOT UP HERE.

FRIEDA:
> AT LEAST YOU HAVE A PARASOL.

SOLDIER, NURSE, YVONNE, LOUISE:
> WELL, LOOK WHO'S TALKING,
> SITTING IN THE SHADE.

JULES: (To Dot.) I trust my cigar is not bothering you—unfortunately, it never goes out. (She pays him no attention.) You have excellent concentration.
SOLDIER: (To companion.)
> IT'S GOOD TO BE TOGETHER AGAIN.

CELESTE 2: (To Celeste 1)
> SEE, I TOLD YOU THEY WERE ODD.

CELESTE 1:
> DON'T SLOUCH.

LOUISE:
> HE TOOK MY GLASSES!

YVONNE:
> YOU'VE BEEN EATING SOMETHING STICKY.

NURSE:
> I PUT ON ROUGE TODAY, TOO . . .

FRIEDA: (To Boatman.)
> DON'T YOU EVER TAKE A BATH?

OLD LADY:
  NURSE! HAND ME MY FAN.
NURSE:
  I CAN'T.
FRANZ:
  AT LEAST THE BRAT IS WITH HER MOTHER.
LOUISE:
  I HEARD THAT!
JULES: (*To Dot.*)
  DO YOU LIKE TALL GRASS?
FRIEDA:
  HAH!
YVONNE:
  JULES!
BOATMAN:
  BUNCH OF ANIMALS . . .
DOT:
  I HATE THESE PEOPLE.
ALL:
  IT'S HOT UP HERE
  AND STRANGE UP HERE,
  NO CHANGE UP HERE FOREVER.

  HOW STILL IT IS,
  HOW ODD IT IS,
  AND GOD, IT IS
  SO HOT!
SOLDIER: I like the one in the light hat.
DOT:
  HELLO, GEORGE.
  I DO NOT WISH TO BE REMEMBERED
  LIKE THIS, GEORGE,
  WITH THEM, GEORGE.
  MY HEM, GEORGE:
  THREE INCHES OFF THE GROUND
  AND THEN THIS MONKEY
  AND THESE PEOPLE, GEORGE—

  THEY'LL ARGUE TILL THEY FADE
  AND WHISPER THINGS AND GRUNT.
  BUT THANK YOU FOR THE SHADE,
  AND PUTTING ME IN FRONT.
  YES, THANK YOU, GEORGE, FOR THAT . . .

AND FOR THE HAT . . .

CELESTE 1:
   IT'S HOT UP HERE.

YVONNE:
   IT'S HOT AND IT'S MONOTONOUS.

LOUISE:
   I WANT MY GLASSES!

FRANZ:
   THIS IS NOT MY GOOD PROFILE.

(*Simultaneously:*)

CELESTE 1:
   I HATE THIS DRESS.

CELESTE 2:
   THE SOLDIERS HAVE FORGOTTEN US.

CELESTE 1:
   DON'T SLOUCH!

BOATMAN:
   ANIMALS . . .

JULES:
   ARE YOU SURE YOU DON'T LIKE TALL GRASS?

NURSE:
   I PUT ON ROUGE TODAY, TOO . . .

FRIEDA:
   DON'T YOU EVER TAKE A BATH?

SOLDIER:
   IT'S GOOD TO BE TOGETHER AGAIN.

OLD LADY:
   NURSE, HAND ME MY FAN.

DOT:
   IT'S HOT UP HERE.

YVONNE:
   IT'S HOT AND IT'S MONOTONOUS.

LOUISE:
   HE TOOK MY GLASSES, I WANT MY GLASSES!

FRANZ:
   THIS IS NOT MY GOOD PROFILE.

ALL:
   AND FURTHERMORE,

FINDING YOU'RE
                    FADING
IS VERY DEGRADING
AND GOD, I AM SO HOT!

ALL:
WELL, THERE ARE WORSE THINGS THAN SWEATING
BY A RIVER ON A SUNDAY.
THERE ARE WORSE THINGS THAN SWEATING BY A RIVER

BOATMAN:
WHEN YOU'RE SWEATING IN A PICTURE
THAT WAS PAINTED BY A GENIUS

FRANZ:
AND YOU KNOW THAT YOU'RE IMMORTAL

FRIEDA:
AND YOU'LL ALWAYS BE REMEMBERED

NURSE:
EVEN IF THEY NEVER SEE YOU

OLD LADY:
AND YOU'RE LISTENING TO DRIVEL

SOLDIER:
AND YOU'RE PART OF YOUR COMPANION

LOUISE:
AND YOUR GLASSES HAVE BEEN STOLEN

YVONNE:
AND YOU'RE BORED BEYOND ENDURANCE

LOUIS:
AND THE BABY HAS NO DIAPERS

CELESTE 1: (*To Celeste 2.*)
YOU'RE SLOUCHING

CELESTE 2:
I AM NOT!

JULES:
AND YOU ARE OUT OF ALL PROPORTION

DOT:
AND I HATE THESE PEOPLE!

ALL:
YOU NEVER GET
A BREEZE UP HERE,
AND SHE'S (HE'S) UP HERE
FOREVER.

YOU CANNOT RUN
AMOK UP HERE,

YOU'RE STUCK UP HERE
IN THIS GAVOTTE.

PERSPECTIVES DON'T
MAKE SENSE UP HERE.
IT'S TENSE UP HERE
FOREVER.

THE OUTWARD SHOW
OF BLISS UP HERE
IS DISAPPEAR-
ING DOT BY DOT.
    (*Long pause. Vamp continues endlessly.*)
AND IT'S HOT!

(*They puff at their faces. In the following section, the characters break from their pose when they speak, and they exit when they finish. Accompanying their exit, a piece of scenery will fly out, so that by the time the Boatman exits at the end of the sequence, the set will be returned to its original white configuration.*)

CELESTE 2: Thirty-one . . .
CELESTE 1: It is hard to believe.
CELESTE 2: Yes.
CELESTE 1: It seems like only yesterday we were posing for him.
CELESTE 2: We never posed for him!
CELESTE 1: Certainly we did! We are in a painting, aren't we?
CELESTE 2: It's not as if he asked us to sit!
CELESTE 1: If you had sat up straight, he might have.
CELESTE 2: Oh, you do not know what you are talking about.
CELESTE 1: How dare you speak to me in that tone! You have picked up some
    terrible manners, young lady.
CELESTE 2: I have learned all my manners from you, and you—
SOLDIER: Will you just keep QUIET! (*Celestes exit.*) I hardly knew the man.
    I would spend my Sundays here, and I would see him sketching, so I was sur-
    prised when he stopped showing up. Of course, I did not notice right away.
    But one day, I realized, something was different—like a flash of light, right
    through me, the way that man would stare at you when he sketched—I
    knew, he was no longer. (*Soldier exits. Louise breaks away from her Mother and
    dashes downstage.*)
LOUISE: I am going to be a painter when I grow up! (*Louise runs off.*)
BOATMAN: If you live.
FRIEDA: Honestly!
BOATMAN: Keep your mouth shut!

FRIEDA: It is my mouth and I shall do as I please!

FRANZ: Quiet! George was a gentleman.

FRIEDA: Soft spoken.

FRANZ: And he was a far superior artist to *Monsieur.*

FRIEDA: George had beautiful eyes.

FRANZ: Ya, he—beautiful eyes?

FRIEDA: Ya . . . well . . . eyes that captured beauty.

FRANZ: (*Suspicious.*) Ya . . . he chose his subjects well. (*They exit.*)

DOT: I was in Charleston when I heard. At first, I was surprised by the news. Almost relieved, in fact. Perhaps I knew this is how it would end—perhaps we both knew. (*Dot exits.*)

OLD LADY: A parent wants to die first. But George was always off and running, and I was never able to keep up with him.

NURSE: No one knew he was ill until the very last days. I offered to care for him, but he would let no one near. Not even her. (*Old Lady and Nurse exit.*)

JULES: (*Too sincere.*) George had great promise as a painter. It really is a shame his career was ended so abruptly. He had an unusual flair for color and light, and his work was not as mechanical as some have suggested. I liked George. He was dedicated to his work—seldom did anything but work—and I am proud to have counted him among my friends.

YVONNE: George stopped me once in the park—it was the only time I had ever spoken to him outside the company of Jules. He stared at my jacket for an instant, then muttered something about beautiful colors and just walked on. I rather fancied George. (*Jules looks at her.*) Well, most of the women did! (*Jules and Yvonne exit.*)

BOATMAN: They all wanted him and hated him at the same time. They wanted to be painted—splashed on some fancy salon wall. But they hated him, too. Hated him because he only spoke when he absolutely had to. Most of all they hated him because they knew he would always be around. (*Boatman exits. The stage is bare.*)

(*Lights change. Electronic music. It is 1984. We are in the auditorium of the museum where the painting now hangs. Enter George. He wheels in his grandmother, Marie [played by Dot], who is ninety-eight and confined to a wheelchair. Dennis, George's technical assistant, rolls on a control console. An immense white machine rolls on. Our contemporary George is an inventor-sculptor, and this is his lates invention, the Chromolume no. 7. The machine is postmodern in design and is dominated by a four-foot in diameter sphere at the top. It glows a range of cool colored light. Marie sits on one side of the machine, and George is at the console on the other side. Behind them is a full-stage projection screen.*)

GEORGE: Ladies and gentlemen, in 1983 I was commissioned by this museum to do a piece commemorating Georges Seurat's painting "A Sunday Afternoon on the Island of La Grand Jatte." My latest Chromolume stands before you now, the seventh in a continuing series. Because I have a special association to this painting, the museum director, Robert Greenberg, suggested I assemble a short presentation to precede the activation of my latest invention. I have brought my grandmother along to give me a hand.

(What follows is a coordinated performance of music, text [read from index cards by George and Marie], film projections and light emissions from the machine. The first section is accompanied by film projections.)

GEORGE: My grandmother, Marie.

MARIE: I was born in Paris, France, ninety-eight years ago. My grandson, George.

GEORGE: I was born in Lodi, New Jersey, thirty-two years ago.

MARIE: My mother was married to Louis, a baker. They left France when I was an infant to travel to Charleston, South Carolina.

GEORGE: George Seurat.

MARIE: Born: December 2, 1859.

GEORGE: It was through his mother that the future artist was introduced to the lower-class Parisian parks. Seurat received a classical training at the Beaux Arts.

MARIE: Like his father, he was not an easy man to know.

GEORGE: He lived in an age when science was gaining influence over romantic principles.

MARIE: He worked very hard.

GEORGE: His first painting, at the age of twenty-four, "Bathing At Asnières," was rejected by the Salon, but was shown by the Group of Independent Artists.

MARIE: They hung it over a refreshment stand. Wasn't that awful?

GEORGE: On Ascension Day 1884, he began work on his second painting, "A Sunday Afternoon on the Island of La Grand Jatte." He was to work two years on this painting.

MARIE: He always knew where he was going before he picked up a paint brush.

GEORGE: He denied conventional perspective and conventional space.

MARIE: He was unconventional in his lifestyle as well. *(Off-the-cuff.)* So was I! I was a flora-dora girl for a short time—when I left Charleston and before I was married to my first husband—

GEORGE: Marie. Marie! *(She looks over to him.)* The film is running.

MARIE: Excuse me. *(She reads.)* They hung it over the refreshment stand.

GEORGE: Marie! *(He reads.)* Having studied scientific findings on color, he developed a new style of painting. He found by painting tiny particles, color next to color, that at a certain distance the eye would fuse the specks optically, giving them greater intensity than any mixed pigments.

MARIE: He wanted to paint with colored lights.

GEORGE: Beams of colored light, he hoped.

MARIE: It was shown at the eighth and last Impressionist Exhibition.

GEORGE: Monet, Renoir and Sisley withdrew their submissions because of his painting.

MARIE: They placed it in a small room off to the side of the main hall, too dark for the painting to truly be seen.

GEORGE: The painting was ridiculed by most. But there were also a handful of believers in his work.

MARIE: He went on to paint six more major paintings before his sudden death at the age of thirty-one. He never sold a painting in his lifetime.

GEORGE: On this occasion, I present my latest Chromolume —

MARIE: — Number seven —

GEORGE: — which pays homage to "La Grand Jatte" and to my grandmother, Marie. The score for this presentation has been composed by Naomi Eisen. (*Naomi enters, bows, and exits.*)

MARIE: (*She reads a stage direction by mistake.*) George begins to activate the Chromolume machine as . . .

GEORGE: No. Don't read that part, Grandmother.

MARIE: Oh . . . don't read this . . .

(*Music begins to increase in volume and intensity. Strobe lights begin emitting from the machine along with side shafts of brilliant light. Colors begin to fill the stage and audience, creating a pointillist look. Just as the sphere begins to illuminate, producing various images from the painting, there is a sudden EXPLOSION of sparks and smoke. The lighting system flickers on and off until everything dies, including music. There is a moment of chaos in the darkness.*)

GEORGE: Robert Greenberg?

GREENBERG: (*From the back of the house.*) Just a minute, George! (*Some light returns to the stage. The stage is filled with smoke.*) It's the regulator, George.

(*Lights come up on George who is looking inside the machine. He steps downstage toward the audience.*)

GEORGE: I'm sorry, ladies and gentlemen. For precise synchronization of all the visual elements, I've installed a new state-of-the-art Japanese micro-computer which controls the voltage regulator. I think that the surge from the musical equipment has created an electrical short. (*Beat.*) Unfortunately, no electricity, no art. Give us a moment and we'll be able to bypass the regulator and be back in business. (*After "no electricity, no art" Greenberg has entered and stands to the side of the apron. Dennis enters. George, who has been working on the machine, grabs him and pulls him over.)*

GREENBERG: I am very sorry, ladies and gentlemen. We seem to be having a little electrical difficulty. (*Naomi has entered and rushed to the machine, Dennis and George.*)

NAOMI: There's no juice!

GREENBERG: You must realize this is the first time we have had a collaboration like this at the museum and it has offered some extraordinary challenges to us here. (*George, Naomi and Dennis exit arguing loudly. George returns to the machine.*) Now, I hope to see all of you at the reception which will follow the presentation. It's right down the hall in the main gallery, where the painting hangs. And, after dinner, we have a very special treat for you. As I am sure you have noticed, in order to raise additional funds we have chosen to sell the air rights to the museum—and some of the twenty-seven flights of condominiums that stand above us now will be open for your inspection. You may want to even become one of our permanent neighbors!

GEORGE: We're definitely ready, Bob.

GREENBERG: Well . . . proceed. Proceed!

GEORGE: (*Into his headset.*) Dennis! Lights. (*Lights dim and the presentation continues. Music gathers momentum. The Chromolum begins several seconds before the speaking resumes.*)

MARIE: When I was young, Mother loved telling me tales of her life in France, and of her work as an artist's model.

GEORGE: She showed her this great painting and pointed to this woman and said that it was she.

MARIE: And she pointed to a couple in the back—they were holding an infant child—and she said that was me!

GEORGE: Shortly before my great-grandmother's death, she spoke of her association with the artist of this painting. She told Marie that he was her real father.

MARIE: I was shocked.

GEORGE: My parents never believed this story. After all, there was no proof. I do not—

MARIE: (*Produces the red book, unbeknownst to George.*) My mother gave me this small red book.

GEORGE: Marie!

GEORGE: Oh, George, I wanted to bring the book and show it. (*To audience.*) In the back are notes about his great-grandfather, the artist.

GEORGE: Actually, this book is really just a grammar book in the handwriting of a child, and though there *are* notes in the back which mention Georges—they could be referring to anyone.

MARIE: But they do not.

GEORGE: I do not know whether there is any validity to this story.

MARIE: Of course there is validity! (*To the audience.*) He has to have everything spelled out for him!

GEORGE: The facts are sketchy. The tales are many. I would like to invite you into my "Sunday: Island of Light." It will be on exhibition here in the upstairs gallery until August first.

(*Music crescendos, as lasar beams burst through the audience, passing all about. When they complete their course, the sphere begins to turn, sending out a blinding burst of light. The painting flies in. We are at the museum where the painting is hanging and in front of which the reception is beginning. Harriet and Billy enter, closely followed by Redmond, Greenberg, Alex, Betty, and Naomi. Cocktail music under.*)

BILLY: Well, I can't say that *I* understand what that machine has to do with this painting.

HARRIET: Darling, it's a theme and variation.

BILLY: Oh. Theme and variation.

GREENBERG: (*To Redmond.*) Times change too quickly.

REDMOND: Lord knows.

GREENBERG: That's the challenge of our work. You never know what movement is going to hit next. Which artist to embrace.

(*Rhumba Vamp.*)

NAOMI: I thought it went very well, except for that electrical foulup. What did you guys think?

ALEX: Terrible.

BETTY: Terrific. (*Short embarrassed pause.*)

HARRIET:
I MEAN, I DON'T UNDERSTAND COMPLETELY –

BILLY:
I'M NOT SURPRISED.

HARRIET:
BUT HE COMBINES ALL THESE DIFFERENT TRENDS.

BILLY:
I'M NOT SURPRISED.

HARRIET:
YOU CAN'T DIVIDE ART TODAY
INTO CATEGORIES NEATLY –

BILLY:
OH.

HARRIET:
WHAT MATTERS IS THE MEANS, NOT THE ENDS.

BILLY:
I'M NOT SURPRISED.

BOTH:
> THAT IS THE STATE OF THE ART, MY DEAR,
> THAT IS THE STATE OF THE ART.

GREENBERG:
> IT'S NOT ENOUGH KNOWING GOOD FROM ROTTEN—

REDMOND:
> YOU'RE TELLING ME—

GREENBERG:
> IT'S ONLY NEW, THOUGH, FOR NOW—

REDMOND:
> NOUVEAU.

GREENBERG:
> BUT YESTERDAY'S FORGOTTEN.

REDMOND: (*Nods.*)
> AND TOMORROW IS ALREADY PASSÉ.

GREENBERG:
> THERE'S NO SURPRISE.

BOTH:
> THAT IS THE STATE OF THE ART, MY FRIEND,
> THAT IS THE STATE OF THE ART.

BETTY:
> HE'S AN ORIGINAL.

ALEX: Was.

NAOMI:
> I LIKE THE IMAGES.

ALEX: Some.

BETTY:
> COME ON.
> YOU HAD YOUR MOMENT,
> NOW IT'S GEORGE'S TURN—

ALEX:
> IT'S GEORGE'S TURN?
> I WASN'T TALKING TURNS,
> I'M TALKING ART.

BETTY: (*To Alex.*)
> YOU'RE TALKING CRAP.

ALEX: (*To Naomi.*)
> BUT IS IT REALLY NEW?

NAOMI:
> WELL, NO . . .

ALEX: (*To Betty.*)
> HIS OWN COLLABORATOR—!

BETTY: (*To Naomi.*)
> IT'S MORE THAN NOVELTY.

NAOMI:
> WELL, YES . . .

BETTY: (*To Alex.*)
> IT'S JUST IMPERSONAL, BUT—

ALEX:
> IT'S ALL PROMOTION, BUT THEN—

ALEX, BETTY: (*To Naomi.*)
> THAT IS THE STATE OF THE ART,
> ISN'T IT?

NAOMI:
> WELL . . .

BILLY: (*To Harriet.*)
> ART ISN'T EASY—

HARRIET: (*Nodding.*)
> EVEN WHEN YOU'VE AMASSED IT—

BETTY:
> FIGHTING FOR PRIZES—

GREENBERG:
> NO ONE CAN BE AN ORACLE.

REDMOND: (*Nodding.*)
> ART ISN'T EASY.

ALEX:
> SUDDENLY YOU'RE—
> > (*Snaps fingers.*)
> PAST IT.

NAOMI:
> ALL COMPROMISES—

HARRIET: (*To Billy.*)
> AND THEN WHEN IT'S ALLEGORICAL—!

REDMOND, GREENBERG:
> ART ISN'T EASY—

ALL:
> ANY WAY YOU LOOK AT IT.

(*Chord. Fanfare. George makes a grand entrance with Marie, who is in a wheelchair, and Elaine. Applause from guests. George and Marie move towards the painting. Lights come down on George, who sings.*)

GEORGE:
> ALL RIGHT, GEORGE.
> AS LONG AS IT'S YOUR NIGHT, GEORGE . . .
> YOU KNOW WHAT'S IN THE ROOM GEORGE:
> ANOTHER CHROMOLUME, GEORGE.

IT'S TIME TO GET TO WORK . . .

MARIE: George, look. All these lovely people in front of our painting. (*Greenberg comes up to George.*)

GREENBERG: George, I want you to meet one of our board members. (*Greenberg steers him over to Billy and Harriet.*) This is Harriet Pawling.

HARRIET: What a pleasure. And this is my friend, Billy Webster.

BILLY: How do you do.

GREENBERG: Well, I'll just leave you three to chat. (*Greenberg exits.*)

BILLY: Harriet was so impressed by your presentation.

HARRIET: This is the third piece of yours I've seen. They are getting so large!

BILLY: What heading does your work fall under?

GEORGE: Most people think of it as sculpture.

BILLY: Sculpture . . .

GEORGE: Actually, I think of myself as an inventor as well as a sculptor.

BILLY: It's so unconventional for sculpture.

(*Lights down on George.*)

GEORGE:
SAY "CHEESE," GEORGE
PUT THEM AT THEIR EASE, GEORGE.
YOU'RE UP ON THE TRAPEZE, GEORGE.
MACHINES DON'T GROW ON TREES, GEORGE.
START PUTTING IT TOGETHER . . .

(*Lights up.*)

HARRIET: I bet your great-grandfather would be very proud! (*They are joined by Marie and Elaine who have been nearby and overheard the conversation.*)

MARIE: Yes. He would have loved this evening.

BILLY: How do you know?

MARIE: I just know. I'm like that.

HARRIET: Hi. I'm Harriet Pawling.

BILLY: Billy Webster.

MARIE: How do you do. This is Elaine—George's former wife.

ELAINE: Hello.

MARIE: Elaine is such a darling, I will always think of her as my granddaughter. I am so happy that these children have remained close. Isn't that nice?

BILLY: Yes. Harriet has just gone through a rather messy divorce—

HARRIET: Bill! (*Awkward pause.*) What a fascinating family you have!

MARIE: Many people say that. George and I are going back to France next month to visit the island where the painting was made, and George is going to bring the Lomochrome.

(*Music.*)

GEORGE: Chromolume.

(*Music.*)

GEORGE: I've been invited by the government to do a presentation of the machine on the island.

MARIE: George has never been to France.

GEORGE: (*To us.*)
ART ISN'T EASY—
(*He raises a cutout of himself in front of Billy and Harriet.*)
EVEN WHEN YOU'RE HOT.

BILLY: (*Ignoring Marie's question, to Cutout.*) Are these inventions of yours one of a kind?

GEORGE:
ADVANCING ART IS EASY—
(*To Billy, but front.*)
Yes.
FINANCING IT IS NOT.

MARIE: They take a year to make.

GEORGE: (*To us.*)
A VISION'S JUST A VISION
IF IT'S ONLY IN YOUR HEAD.

MARIE: The minute he finishes one, he starts raising money for the next.

GEORGE:
IF NO ONE GETS TO SEE IT,
IT'S AS GOOD AS DEAD.

MARIE: Work. Work. Work.

GEORGE:
IT HAS TO COME TO LIGHT!

(*Music continues under. George speaks as if to Billy and Harriet, but away from them, and front.*)

GEORGE: I put the names of my contributors on the side of each machine.

ELAINE: Some very impressive people!

HARRIET: Well, we must speak further. My family has a foundation and we are always looking for new projects.

GEORGE: (*To us.*)
BIT BY BIT,
PUTTING IT TOGETHER . . .

MARIE: Family—it's all you really have.

GEORGE:

PIECE BY PIECE—
ONLY WAY TO MAKE A WORK OF ART.
EVERY MOMENT MAKES A CONTRIBUTION,
EVERY LITTLE DETAIL PLAYS A PART.
HAVING JUST THE VISION'S NO SOLUTION,
EVERYTHING DEPENDS ON EXECUTION:
PUTTING IT TOGETHER—
THAT'S WHAT COUNTS.

HARRIET: Actually, the Board of the foundation is meeting next week . . .

GEORGE:

OUNCE BY OUNCE
PUTTING IT TOGETHER . . .

HARRIET: You'll come to lunch.

GEORGE:

SMALL AMOUNTS,
ADDING UP TO MAKE A WORK OF ART.
FIRST OF ALL, YOU NEED A GOOD FOUNDATION,
OTHERWISE IT'S RISKY FROM THE START.
TAKES A LITTLE COCKTAIL CONVERSATION,
BUT WITHOUT THE PROPER PREPARATION,
HAVING JUST THE VISION'S NO SOLUTION,
EVERYTHING DEPENDS ON EXECUTION.

THE ART OF MAKING ART
IS PUTTING IT TOGETHER
BIT BY BIT . . .

(*Charles Redmond corners George; the Cutout remains, as Billy and Harriet talk to it. Marie falls asleep; Elaine rocks her gently. Vamp continues under.*)

REDMOND: We have been hearing about you for some time. We haven't met. Charles Redmond. County Museum of Texas.

GEORGE: Nice to meet you.

REDMOND: Your work is just tremendous.

GEORGE: Thank you.

(*Chord.*)

REDMOND: I don't mean to bring business up during a social occasion, but I wanted you to know we're in the process of giving out some very sizable commissions—

(*Vamp.*)

GREENBERG: You're not going to steal him away, are you?

(*George raises a cut-out of himself as before, and leaves his drink in its hand, then steps forward.*)

GEORGE:
    LINK BY LINK,
    MAKING THE CONNECTIONS . . .
    DRINK BY DRINK,
    FIXING AND PERFECTING THE DESIGN.
    ADDING JUST A DAB OF POLITICIAN
    (ALWAYS KNOWING WHERE TO DRAW THE LINE).
    LINING UP THE FUNDS BUT IN ADDITION
    LINING UP A PROMINENT COMMISSION,
    OTHERWISE YOUR PERFECT COMPOSITION
    ISN'T GOING TO GET MUCH EXHIBITION.

    ART ISN'T EASY.
    EVERY MINOR DETAIL
    IS A MAJOR DECISION,
    HAVE TO KEEP THINGS IN SCALE,
    HAVE TO HOLD TO YOUR VISION—
        (*Pauses for a split second.*)
    EVERY TIME I START TO FEEL DEFENSIVE,
    I REMEMBER LASERS ARE EXPENSIVE.
    WHAT'S A LITTLE COCKTAIL CONVERSATION
    IF IT'S GOING TO GET YOU YOUR FOUNDATION,
    LEADING TO A PROMINENT COMMISSION
    AND AN EXHIBITION IN ADDITION?

(*Promenade.*)

ALL: (*Except Marie, who is asleep.*)
    ART ISN'T EASY—
ALEX, BETTY:
    TRYING TO MAKE CONNECTIONS—
ALL:
    WHO UNDERSTANDS IT—?
HARRIET, BILLY:
    DIFFICULT TO EVALUATE—
ALL:
    ART ISN'T EASY—

GREENBERG, REDMOND:
  TRYING TO FORM COLLECTIONS—
ALL:
  ALWAYS IN TRANSIT—
NAOMI: (*To whoever will listen.*)
  AND THEN WHEN YOU HAVE TO COLLABORATE—
ALL:
  ART ISN'T EASY,
  ANY WAY YOU LOOK AT IT . . .

(*Chord. Cocktail piano. During the above, Blair Daniels, an art critic, has entered. George is approached by Lee Randolph with Marie.*)

MARIE: George, you have to meet Mr. Randolph!
RANDOLPH: Hello! Lee Randolph. I handle the public relations for the museum.
GEORGE: How do you do. (*Naomi joins them.*)
NAOMI: There you are, George! Hi, Marie. (*To Randolph.*) Naomi Eisen.
RANDOLPH: Delighted. You kids made quite a stir tonight.
NAOMI: You see, George—that electrical screw up didn't hurt our reception.
RANDOLPH: There's a lot of opportunity for some nice press here.

(*George gestures; a third cut-out of himself slides in from the wings and stops in front of Naomi and Randolph. George steps forward and sings.*)

GEORGE:
  DOT BY DOT,
  BUILDING UP THE IMAGE.
    (*Flash. Photograph starts taking pictures of the cut-out.*)
  SHOT BY SHOT,
  KEEPING AT A DISTANCE DOESN'T PAY.
  STILL, IF YOU REMEMBER YOUR OBJECTIVE,
  NOT TO GIVE ALL YOUR PRIVACY AWAY—
    (*Flash. Beat; he glances at the first cut-out*)
  A LITTLE BIT OF HYPE CAN BE EFFECTIVE,
  LONG AS YOU CAN KEEP IT IN PERSPECTIVE.
  AFTER ALL, WITHOUT SOME RECOGNITION
  NO ONE'S GOING TO GIVE YOU A COMMISSION,
  WHICH WILL CAUSE A CRACK IN THE FOUNDATION.
  YOU'LL HAVE WASTED ALL THAT CONVERSATION.

(*Music stops suddenly as Dennis, George's technician and assistant, comes over, disheveled and apologetic. Dennis is something of a nerd.*)

DENNIS: I am really sorry, George. (*Cocktail music.*) I spoke with Naomi in great detail about how much electricity her synthesizer was going to use—I computed the exact voltage—

GEORGE: Dennis! It's okay.

DENNIS: The laser was beautiful, George.

GEORGE: It was, wasn't it? Now go get yourself a drink, Dennis. Mingle.

DENNIS: George. I have one more thing I wanted to talk to you about. I was going to wait—no, I'll wait—

GEORGE: What?

DENNIS: I'm quitting.

(*Music stops suddenly.*)

GEORGE: Quitting?

DENNIS: I am going back to NASA. There is just too much pressure in this line of work.

GEORGE: Dennis, don't make any rash decisions. Just take it easy, sleep on it, and we'll talk about it tomorrow.

DENNIS: Okay, George.

GEORGE: (*To us. Vamp under.*)
    ART ISN'T EASY . . .

(*Alex and Betty approach.*)

BETTY: Hey, it's the brains.

GEORGE:
    EVEN IF YOU'RE SMART . . .

ALEX: Little technical screw-up tonight, Dennis? (*Dennis exits.*)

GEORGE:
    YOU THINK IT'S ALL TOGETHER . . .
    AND SOMETHING FALLS APART . . .

(*Vamp continues under.*)

BETTY: I love the new machine, George.

GEORGE: Thanks. That means a lot to me.

ALEX: We saw you talking to Redmond from Texas.

GEORGE: Yeah.

BETTY: Did you get one of the commissions?

GEORGE: We talked about it. You guys?

ALEX: Her. My stuff is a little too inaccessible.

GEORGE: I love your work, Alex. I'll put in a good word for you.

ALEX: (*Defensive.*) He knows my work!

GEORGE: (*Uncomfortable.*) It's all politics, Alex. Maybe if you just lightened up

once in a while.
BETTY: (*Mollifying.*) Texas would be fun!

(*George beckons and a fourth cut-out slides in and heads toward Betty and Alex.*)

GEORGE: (*Front.*)
   ART ISN'T EASY.
      (*Gesturing towards Alex.*)
   OVERNIGHT YOU'RE A TREND
   YOU'RE THE RIGHT COMBINATION –
      (*Behind him cut-out 1 begins sinking slowly into the floor.*)
   THEN THE TREND'S AT AN END,
   YOU'RE SUDDENLY LAST YEAR'S SENSATION . . .
      (*Notices the cut-out, goes to raise it during the following.*)
   SO YOU SHOULD SUPPORT THE COMPETITION,
   TRY TO SET ASIDE YOUR OWN AMBITION,
   EVEN WHILE YOU JOCKEY FOR POSITION –
      (*Cut-out 4 has slid in too far, and Betty and Alex have turned away; George, un-*
      flustered, pushes or gestures it back into place, and Betty and Alex start talking
      to it.)
   IF YOU FEEL A SENSE OF COALITION,
   THEN YOU NEVER REALLY STAND ALONE.
   IF YOU WANT YOUR WORK TO REACH FRUITION,
   WHAT YOU NEED'S A LINK WITH YOUR TRADITION,
   AND OF COURSE A PROMINENT COMMISSION –
      (*Cut-out 1 starts to sink again; George hastens to fix it.*)
   PLUS A LITTLE FORMAL RECOGNITION,
   SO THAT YOU CAN GO ON EXHIBI –
      (*Getting flustered.*)
   SO THAT YOUR WORK CAN GO ON EXHIBITION –

(*Loud promenade, very brief, during which cut-out 1 starts to go again, but stops just*
as George reaches it. As he does so, Blair Daniels comes up to him. Chord.)

DANIELS: There's the man of the hour.
GEORGE: Blair. Hello. (*Chord.*) I read your piece on neo-expressionism –

(*Chord.*)

DANIELS: Just what the world needs – another piece on neo-expressionism.
GEORGE: Well, I enjoyed it.

(*Chords continue under, irregularly.*)

DANIELS: Good for you! Now, I had no idea you might be related to nine-teenth century France.

GEORGE: It's a cloudy ancestral line at best.

DANIELS: I'm dying to meet your grandmother. It was fun seeing the two of you onstage with your invention. It added a certain humanity to the proceedings.

GEORGE: Humanity?

DANIELS: George. Chromolume 7?

GEORGE:

BE NICE, GEORGE . . .

(*Gestures for a cut-out; it doesn't arise.*)

DANIELS: I was hoping it would be a series of three—four at the most.

GEORGE:

YOU HAVE TO PAY A PRICE, GEORGE . . .

(*Gestures again; nothing.*)

DANIELS: We have been there before, you know.

GEORGE: You never suffer from a shortage of opinions, do you, Blair?

DANIELS: You never minded my opinions when they were in your favor!

DANIELS: I have touted your work from the beginning, you know that. You were really on to something with these light machines— once. Now they're just becoming more and more about less and less.

GEORGE:

THEY LIKE TO GIVE ADVICE, GEORGE—

(*Gestures offstage; nothing.*)

DON'T THINK ABOUT IT TWICE, GEORGE . . .

(*Gestures again; nothing.*)

GEORGE: I disagree.

(*Vamp. Blair Daniels turns briefly away from him, rummaging through her purse for a cigarette. George takes advantage of this to rush offstage and bring on cut-out 5, which he sets up in front of her during the following.*)

DANIELS: Don't get me wrong. You're a talented guy. If you weren't, I wouldn't waste our time with my opinions. I think you are capable of far more. Not that you couldn't succeed by doing Chromolume after Chromolume—but there are new discoveries to be made, George. (*She holds up her cigarette and waits for a light from the cut-out.*)

GEORGE:

BE NEW, GEORGE.
THEY TELL YOU TILL THEY'RE BLUE, GEORGE:
YOU'RE NEW OR ELSE YOU'RE THROUGH, GEORGE,
AND EVEN IF IT'S TRUE, GEORGE—

YOU DO WHAT YOU CAN DO . . .
(*Wandering among cut-outs, checking them.*)
BIT BY BIT,
PUTTING IT TOGETHER.
PIECE BY PIECE,
WORKING OUT THE VISION NIGHT AND DAY.
ALL IT TAKES IS TIME AND PERSEVERANCE,
WITH A LITTLE LUCK ALONG THE WAY,
PUTTING IN A PERSONAL APPEARANCE,
GATHERING SUPPORTERS AND ADHERENTS . . .

(*Vamp stops. Blair, getting impatient for her light, leaves the cut-out to join another group. George notices. Beat.*)

HARRIET:
. . . BUT HE COMBINES ALL THESE DIFFERENT TRENDS . . .

(*Beat. The cut-out with Harriet and Billy falters.*)

GEORGE: (*Moving to it smoothly as Vamp resumes.*)
MAPPING OUT THE RIGHT CONFIGURATION –
(*Adjusting it.*)
STARTING WITH A SUITABLE FOUNDATION –
BETTY:
. . . HE'S AN ORIGINAL . . .
ALEX:
. . . WAS . . .

(*During the following, all the cut-outs falter sporadically, causing George to move more and more rapidly among them. Simultaneously with George:*)

GEORGE:
LINING UP A PROMINENT COMMISSION –
AND AN EXHIBITION IN ADDITION –
HERE A LITTLE DAB OF POLITICIAN –
THERE A LITTLE TOUCH OF PUBLICATION –
TILL YOU HAVE A BALANCED COMPOSITION –
EVERYTHING DEPENDS ON PREPARATION –
EVEN IF YOU DO HAVE THE SUSPICION
THAT IT'S TAKING ALL YOUR CONCENTRATION:

BETTY:
I LIKE THOSE IMAGES.
ALEX:
SOME.
BETTY:
THEY'RE JUST HIS PERSONAL RESPONSE.
ALEX:
TO WHAT?
BETTY:
THE PAINTING!
ALEX:
BULLSHIT. ANYWAY, THE PAINTING'S OVERRATED . . .
BETTY:
OVERRATED? IT'S A MASTERPIECE!
ALEX:
A MASTERPIECE? HISTORICALLY IMPORTANT MAYBE—
BETTY:
OH, NOW YOU'RE JUDGING SEURAT, ARE YOU?
ALEX:
ALL IT IS IS PLEASANT, JUST LIKE GEORGE'S WORK:
BETTY:
IT'S JUST YOUR JEALOUSY OF GEORGE'S WORK:
ALEX:
NO NUANCE, NO RESONANCE, NO RELEVANCE—
BETTY:
THERE'S NUANCE AND THERE'S RESONANCE, THERE'S RELEVANCE—
ALEX:
THERE'S NOT MUCH POINT IN ARGUING.
BESIDES, IT'S ALL PROMOTION, BUT THEN—
BETTY:
THERE'S NOT MUCH POINT IN ARGUING.
YOU SAY IT'S ALL PROMOTION, BUT THEN—
GREENBERG:
IT'S ONLY NEW, THOUGH, FOR NOW
AND YESTERDAY'S FORGOTTEN.
TODAY IT'S ALL A MATTER OF PROMOTION—
REDMOND:
NOUVEAU.
AND YESTERDAY'S FORGOTTEN
AND YOU CAN'T TELL GOOD FROM ROTTEN
AND TODAY IT'S ALL A MATTER OF PROMOTION—
HARRIET:
YOU CAN'T DIVIDE ART TODAY.

GO WITH IT!
WHAT WILL THEY THINK OF NEXT?
BILLY:
   I'M NOT SURPRISED.
   WHAT WILL THEY THINK OF NEXT?
OTHERS:
   MOST ART TODAY
   IS A MATTER OF PROMOTION—
GEORGE:
   THE ART OF MAKING ART
   IS PUTTING IT TOGETHER—
ALL:
   THAT IS THE STATE OF THE
   ART . . .
   AND ART ISN'T EASY.
GEORGE:
   BIT BY BIT—
   LINK BY LINK—
   DRINK BY DRINK—
   MINK BY MINK—
   AND THAT
   IS THE STATE
   OF THE
ALL:
   ART.

(George frames the successfully completed picture with his hands, as at the end of Act One. As soon as he exits, however, the cut-outs collapse and disappear. Marie is over at the painting, holding court. With her are Harriet and Billy.)

GREENBERG: Ladies and gentlemen, dinner is served.(Most of the party exits.)
HARRIET: (To Marie.) Excuse me, could you please tell me: what is that square form up there? (Blair Daniels, an art critic, has been standing nearby.)
DANIELS: That is a baby carriage.
MARIE: Who told you that?!
DANIELS: I'm sorry to butt in. I'm Blair Daniels and I've been waiting for the opportunity to tell you how much I enjoyed seeing you on stage.
MARIE: Why, thank you. But, my dear, that is not a baby carriage. That is Louis's waffle stove.
DANIELS: Waffle stove? I've read all there is to read about this work, and there's never been any mention of waffle stove!
MARIE: I have a book, too. My mother's. It is a family legacy, as is this paint-ing. And my mother often spoke of Louis's waffle stove!
DANIELS: Louis. Yes, you mentioned him in your presentation.

MARIE: Family. You know, it is all you really have.

BILLY: You said that before.

MARIE: I say it often.

HARRIET: Excuse us. (*Harriet and Billy exit.*)

MARIE: You know, Miss Daniels, there are only two worthwhile things to leave behind when you depart this world: children and art. Isn't that correct?

DANIELS: I never quite thought of it that way. (*Elaine joins them.*)

MARIE: Do you know Elaine?

DANIELS: No. I don't believe we've met. Blair Daniels.

ELAINE: I've heard a lot about you.

MARIE: Elaine and George were married once. I was so excited. I though *they* might have a child. George and I are the only ones left, I'm afraid. (*Whispers.*) I want George to have a child—continue the line. You can understand that, can't you, Elaine?

ELAINE: Of course.

MARIE: Are you married, Miss Daniels?

DANIELS: Awfully nice to have met you.

ELAINE: Good-bye.

MARIE: Elaine, fix my chair so I can see Mama. (*She does. Elaine approaches George.*)

ELAINE: George. I think Marie is a little too tired for the party. She seems to be slipping a bit.

GEORGE: We better take her back to the hotel.

ELAINE: I'll take her back. You stay.

GEORGE: Nah, it's a perfect excuse for me to leave early.

ELAINE: George. Don't be silly! You're the toast of the party. You should feel wonderful.

GEORGE: Well, I don't feel wonderful.

ELAINE: Poor George. Well . . . tonight was a wonderful experience for Marie. I don't remember seeing her so happy. It was very good of you to include her.

GEORGE: She is something, isn't she?

ELAINE: Yes, she is . . .

(*The Elaine/George scene has been underscored with the chords from Act One. Marie has been staring up at the painting.*)

MARIE:
YOU WOULD HAVE LIKED HIM,
MAMA, YOU WOULD.
MAMA, HE MAKES THINGS—
MAMA, THEY'RE GOOD.
JUST AS YOU SAID FROM THE START:
CHILDREN AND ART . . .

(*Starts nodding off.*)
CHILDREN AND ART . . .

HE SHOULD BE HAPPY—
MAMA, HE'S BLUE.
WHAT DO I DO?

YOU SHOULD HAVE SEEN IT,
IT WAS A SIGHT!
MAMA, I MEAN IT—
ALL COLOR AND LIGHT—!
I DON'T UNDERSTAND WHAT IT WAS,
BUT, MAMA, THE THINGS THAT HE DOES—
THEY TWINKLE AND SHIMMER AND BUZZ—
YOU WOULD HAVE LIKED THEM . . .
IT . . .
HIM . . .

Henry . . . Henry?
GEORGE: (*Coming over.*) It's George, Grandmother.
MARIE: Of course it is. I thought you were your father for a moment. (*Indicating painting.*) Did I tell you who that was?
GEORGE: Of course. That's you mother.
MARIE: That is correct.
    ISN'T SHE BEAUTIFUL?
    THERE SHE IS—
        (*Pointing to different figures.*)
    THERE SHE IS, THERE SHE IS, THERE SHE IS—
    MAMA IS EVERYWHERE,
    HE MUST HAVE LOVED HER SO MUCH . . .
GEORGE: Is she really in all those places, Marie?
MARIE:
    THIS IS OUR FAMILY—
    THIS IS THE LOT.
    AFTER I GO, THIS IS
    ALL THAT YOU'VE GOT, HONEY—
GEORGE: Now, let's not . . .
MARIE: (*As George starts to protest.*)
    WASN'T SHE BEAUTIFUL, THOUGH
    YOU WOULD HAVE LIKED HER.
    MAMA DID THINGS NO ONE HAD DONE,
    MAMA WAS FUNNY,
    MAMA WAS FUN,
    MAMA SPENT MONEY

WHEN SHE HAD NONE.
MAMA SAID "HONEY,"
MUSTN'T BE BLUE.
IT'S NOT SO MUCH DO WHAT YOU LIKE
AS IT IS THAT YOU LIKE WHAT YOU DO.
MAMA SAID, "DARLING,"
DON'T MAKE SUCH A DRAMA.
A LITTLE LESS THINKING,
A LITTLE MORE FEELING —

GEORGE: Now, don't start . . .

MARIE: (*As George looks at her sharply.*)
I'M JUST QUOTING MAMA . . .
    (*Interrupting, indicates Louise.*)
THE CHILD IS SO SWEET . . .
    (*Indicates the Celestes at center.*)
AND THE GIRLS ARE SO RAPTUROUS . . .
ISN'T IT LOVELY HOW ARTISTS CAN CAPTURE US?

GEORGE: Yes, it is, Marie.

MARIE:
YOU WOULD HAVE LIKED HER —
HONEY, I'M WRONG,
YOU WOULD HAVE LOVED HER.

MAMA ENJOYED THINGS.
MAMA WAS SMART.
SEE HOW SHE SHIMMERS —
I MEAN FROM THE HEART.

I KNOW, HONEY, YOU DON'T AGREE,
    (*Indicates painting.*)
BUT THIS IS OUR FAMILY TREE.
JUST WAIT TILL WE'RE THERE, AND YOU'LL SEE —
LISTEN TO ME . . .
    (*Drifting off.*)
MAMA WAS SMART . . .
LISTEN TO MAMA . . .
CHILDREN AND ART . . .
CHILDREN AND ART . . .

(*She falls asleep and Elaine wheels her off. As they go:*)

MARIE: Goodnight, Mama.(*George looks at the painting for a moment.*)
GEORGE: Connect, George. Connect . . .

(George exits. The Painting flies out and the island is once again revealed, though this time it is barely recognizable because it is the present, and the trees are now replaced by high-rise buildings. Dennis is there, looking at his blueprints. George enters.)

GEORGE: Are you certain that this is the best place for the Chromolume.

DENNIS: George, this is the largest clearing on La Grand Jatte.

GEORGE: Where's the still?

DENNIS: It has been built and should arrive tomorrow morning a few hours before the Chromolume. I wanted it here today, but they don't make deliveries on Sunday.

GEORGE: And fresh water for the cooling system?

DENNIS: We can draw it from the Seine. As for the electricity—

GEORGE: Did you see this tree?

DENNIS: No.

GEORGE: It could be the one in the painting.

DENNIS: Yes. It could.

(George hands Dennis the camera and goes to the tree. Dennis takes a picture.)

GEORGE: At least something is recognizable . . .Now, about the electricity?

DENNIS: The wind generator's over there.

GEORGE: You have been efficient, as always.

DENNIS: Thank you.

GEORGE: I will miss working with you, Dennis.

DENNIS: Well, I can recommend some very capable people to help you with the Texas commission.

GEORGE: I turned it down.

DENNIS: What?

GEORGE: Dennis, why are you quitting?

DENNIS: I told you, I want—

GEORGE: I know what you told me! Why are you really leaving?

DENNIS: George. I love the Chromolumes. People really enjoy them. But I've helped you build the last five, and now I want to do something different.

GEORGE: I wish you had told me that in the first place.

DENNIS: I'm sorry.

GEORGE: Why do you think I turned down the commission? I don't want to do the same thing over and over again either.

DENNIS: There are other things you could do.

GEORGE: I know that. I just want to do something I care about.

DENNIS: Yeah . . . I see you brought the red book!

GEORGE: Since Marie died, I thought I would at least bring something of hers along.

DENNIS: Marie really wanted to make this trip.

GEORGE: I know.

DENNIS: I hope you don't mind, but I took a look at the book. It's very interesting.

GEORGE: It's just a grammar book, Dennis.

DENNIS: Not that part. The notes in the back. (*George picks up the book and begins leafing through it.*) Shall we wait for it to get dark? I'm not certain about the ambient light.

GEORGE: You go, Dennis. I'd like to be alone actually.

DENNIS: Are you sure?

GEORGE: Yeah. I'll see you back at the hotel.

DENNIS: George. I look forward to seeing what you come up with next.

GEORGE: (*Smiling.*) You're not the only one, Dennis.

DENNIS: So long.

GEORGE: Bye.

(*Dennis exits. Music under.*)

GEORGE: (*Leafing through the red book, reading.*)
"CHARLES HAS A BOOK . . ."
  (*Turns a page.*)
"CHARLES SHOWS THEM HIS CRAYONS . . ."
  (*Turns the book to read writing in the margin.*)
"GOOD FOR MARIE . . ."
  (*Smiles at the coincidence of the name, turns a page.*)
"CHARLES MISSES HIS BALL . . ."
GEORGE MISSES MARIE . . .
  (*Looks up.*)
GEORGE MISSES A LOT . . .
GEORGE IS ALONE.

GEORGE LOOKS AROUND.
HE SEES THE PARK.
IT IS DEPRESSING.
GEORGE LOOKS AHEAD.
GEORGE SEES THE DARK.
GEORGE IS AFRAID.
WHERE ARE THE PEOPLE
OUT STROLLING ON SUNDAY?

GEORGE LOOKS WITHIN:
GEORGE IS ADRIFT.
GEORGE GOES BY GUESSING.
GEORGE LOOKS BEHIND:
HE HAD A GIFT.

WHEN DID IT FADE?
YOU WANTED PEOPLE OUT
STROLLING ON SUNDAY—
SORRY, MARIE . . .

(*Looks again at the name in the book.*)

SEE GEORGE REMEMBER HOW GEORGE USED TO BE,
STRETCHING HIS VISION IN EVERY DIRECTION.
SEE GEORGE ATTEMPTING TO SEE A CONNECTION
WHEN ALL HE CAN SEE
IS MAYBE A TREE—
(*Humorously.*)
THE FAMILY TREE—
SORRY, MARIE . . .

GEORGE IS AFRAID.
GEORGE SEES THE PARK.
GEORGE SEES IT DYING.
GEORGE TOO MAY FADE,
LEAVING NO MARK,
JUST PASSING THROUGH.
JUST LIKE THE PEOPLE
OUT STROLLING ON SUNDAY . . .

GEORGE LOOKS AROUND.
GEORGE IS ALONE.
NO USE DENYING
GEORGE IS AGROUND.
GEORGE HAS OUTGROWN
WHAT HE CAN DO.
GEORGE WOULD HAVE LIKED TO SEE
PEOPLE OUT STROLLING ON SUNDAY . . .

(*Dot appears. George looks up and discovers Dot. He stands.*)

DOT: I almost did not recognize you without your beard. you have my book.
GEORGE: Your book?
DOT: Yes.
GEORGE: It is a little difficult to understand.
DOT: Well, I was teaching myself. My writing got much better. I worked very hard. I made certain that Marie learned right away.
GEORGE: Marie . . .
DOT: It is good to see you. Not that I ever forgot you, George. You gave me

so much.

GEORGE: What did I give you?

DOT: Oh, many things. You taught me concentration. At first I thought that meant just being still, but I was to understand it meant much more. You meant to tell me to be where I was—not some place in the past or the future. I worried too much about tomorrow. I thought the world could be perfect. I was wrong.

GEORGE: What else?

DOT: Oh, enough about me. What about you? Are you working on something new?

GEORGE: No. I am not working on anything new.

DOT: That is not like you, George.

GEORGE:
    I'VE NOTHING TO SAY.

DOT: You have many things . . .

GEORGE:
    WELL, NOTHING THAT'S NOT BEEN SAID.

DOT:
    SAID BY YOU, THOUGH, GEORGE . . .

GEORGE:
    I DO NOT KNOW WHERE TO GO.

DOT:
    AND NOR DID I.

GEORGE:
    I WANT TO MAKE THINGS THAT COUNT,
    THINGS THAT WILL BE NEW . . .

DOT:
    I DID WHAT I HAD TO DO:

GEORGE:
    WHAT AM I TO DO?

DOT:
    MOVE ON.

    STOP WORRYING WHERE YOU'RE GOING—
    MOVE ON.
    IF YOU CAN KNOW WHERE YOU'RE GOING,
    YOU'VE GONE.
    JUST KEEP MOVING ON.

    I CHOSE, AND MY WORLD WAS SHAKEN—
    SO WHAT?
    THE CHOICE MAY HAVE BEEN MISTAKEN,
    THE CHOOSING WAS NOT.
    YOU HAVE TO MOVE ON.

LOOK AT WHAT YOU WANT,
NOT AT WHERE YOU ARE,
NOT AT WHAT YOU'LL BE.
LOOK AT ALL THE THINGS YOU'VE DONE FOR ME:

OPENED UP MY EYES,
TAUGHT ME HOW TO SEE,
NOTICE EVERY TREE –

GEORGE:
 . . . NOTICE EVERY TREE . . .

DOT:
 UNDERSTAND THE LIGHT –

GEORGE:
 . . . UNDERSTAND THE LIGHT . . .

DOT:
 CONCENTRATE ON NOW –

GEORGE:
 I WANT TO MOVE ON.
 I WANT TO EXPLORE THE LIGHT.
 I WANT TO KNOW HOW TO GET THROUGH,
 THROUGH TO SOMETHING NEW,
 SOMETHING OF MY OWN –

BOTH:
 MOVE ON.
 MOVE ON.

DOT:
 STOP WORRYING IF YOUR VISION
 IS NEW.
 LET OTHERS MAKE THAT DECISION –
 THEY USUALLY DO.
 YOU KEEP MOVING ON.

(*Simultaneously.*)

DOT:
 LOOK AT WHAT YOU'VE
  DONE,
 THEN AT WHAT YOU
  WANT,
 NOT AT WHERE YOU ARE,
 WHAT YOU'LL BE.
 LOOK AT ALL THE THINGS
  YOU GAVE TO ME.

LET ME GIVE TO YOU
SOMETHING IN RETURN.
I WOULD BE SO PLEASED . . .
GEORGE: (*Looking around.*)
. . . SOMETHING IN THE
    LIGHT,
SOMETHING IN THE SKY,
IN THE GRASS,
UP BEHIND THE TREES . . .

THINGS I HADN'T LOOKED
    AT
TILL NOW:
FLOWER IN YOUR HAT.
AND YOUR SMILE.
GEORGE:
AND THE COLOR OF YOUR HAIR.
AND THE WAY YOU CATCH THE LIGHT.
AND THE CARE.
AND THE FEELING.
AND THE LIFE.
MOVING ON.
DOT:
WE'VE ALWAYS BELONGED
TOGETHER!
BOTH:
WE WILL ALWAYS BELONG
TOGETHER!
DOT:
JUST KEEP MOVING ON.

ANYTHING YOU DO,
LET IT COME FROM YOU.
THEN IT WILL BE NEW.
GIVE US MORE TO SEE . . .

You never cared what anyone thought. That upset me at the time because I wanted you to care what *I* thought.
GEORGE: I'm sure that I did.
DOT: I am sure that you did, too.
GEORGE: Dot. (*Indicates the book.*) Why did you write these words?
DOT: (*She comes over to him and looks in the book.*) They are your words, George. The words you uttered so often when you worked.
GEORGE: (*Reads slowly.*) Order.

(*Chord. Old Lady enters.*)

OLD LADY: George. Is that you? (*George turns to her. He looks back to Dot, who smiles, then back to the old lady.*)
GEORGE: Yes.
OLD LADY: Tell me! Is this place as you expected it?
GEORGE: What?
OLD LADY: The park, of course.
GEORGE: Somewhat.
OLD LADY: Go on.
GEORGE: Well, the greens are a little darker. The sky a little greyer. Mud tones in the water.
OLD LADY: (*Disappointed.*) Well, yes, I suppose—
GEORGE: But the air is rich and full of light.
OLD LADY: Good. (*Chord. As the Old Lady leaves, George reads the next word:*)
GEORGE: Design.

(*He raises his hand to the downstage right building and it begins to rise. Music vamp begins. One of the characters from the painting appears and begins to cross the stage.*)

GEORGE: Tension.

(*He raises two buildings stage right and left. More people appear and begin to promenade.*)

GEORGE: Composition. Balance.

(*Two more buildings rise. More people.*)

GEORGE: Light.

(*The large opaque building in the back rises.*)

GEORGE: Dot. I cannot read this word.
DOT: Harmony.

(*The company begins to sing "Sunday." George reads:*)

GEORGE: So much love in his words . . . forever with his colors . . . how George looks . . . he can look forever . . . what does he see? . . . his eyes so dark and shiny . . . so careful . . . so exact . . .

(*Dot takes George by the arm and they begin to stroll amongst the people. By the time we hear "Ordinary Sunday" the company has settled in the areas that they occupy in the painting. On the second "Sunday" they begin to exit very slowly. George remains on the apron, and Dot is the only one left in the park. The white canvas drop begins to descend. George looks in the book.)*

GEORGE: White. A blank page or canvas. His favorite. So many possibilities.

(George looks up and sees the canvas. Lights fade to black.)

END

The Death of Von Richthofen as Witnessed from Earth

a play with flying and songs

Des McAnuff

For R. E. Shenfield

The Death of von Richthofen As Witnessed From Earth was first performed at the Public Theatre in New York City on July 29, 1982 with the following cast:

Brent Barrett, Peggy Harmon, Marek Norman, Susan Berman, Karl Heist, Mark Petrakis, Michael Brian, Tad Ingram, John Vickery, Eric Elice, Jeffrey Jones, Robert Westernberg, Davis Gaines, Robert Joy, Martha Wingate, Bob Gunton, Ken Land, Sigrid Wurschmidt and Mark Linn-Baker.

Composer & Director: Des McAnuff
Choreography: Jennifer Muller
Scenery: Douglas W. Schmidt
Costumes: Patricia McGourty
Lighting: Richard Nelson
Sound: Bill Dreisbach
Orchestrations: Michael Starobin
Music Direction: Michael C. Roth

CHARACTERS:

R. Raymond-Barker, an English pilot
Robert Buie, a gunner
William Evans, a gunner
Wolfram von Richthofen, a virgin pilot, blond
Manfred von Richthofen, the Red Dragon, blond
Karl Bodenshatz, adjutant to the Red Dragon, blond
Hermann Goering, a German pilot, blond
A German Lance Corporal, a dispatch runner, dark
N.C.O. Secull, a piano player
Three Women, a cellist, a violinist, and a flautist

Act One contains twenty scenes and runs for seventy-five minutes. Act Two contains thirteen scenes and runs for fifty minutes.

The Space: Three areas, like three circus rings, one in between the other two.

The East, the first area, at one end of the field. Manfred von Richthofen's room at Cappy, France, by the air field of Jagdgeschwader I. Formerly an elegant bathroom in a decaying nineteenth-century summer house with velvet curtains, a marble basin, several heavy framed mirrors, a gigantic laundry basket, a toilet, a telephone, and a cast iron tub. A notary's desk, a German riding saddle, boots, uniforms, a hammock, sixty-one silver loving cups, and a stuffed Danish Wolfhound named "Moritz" have been added to the bathroom's decor. At the back of the bathroom are three twelve-foot louvered doors which lead to an empty makeshift bunkroom beyond. At the front of Richthofen's room a suspended window frame looks out onto No Man's Land.

No Man's Land, the second area, in the middle of the field, dividing East from West. Mire. Crosses planted for the dead and long since uprooted by constant shelling. Rubble, puddles, pot holes and craters have been left by the countless explosions and heavy rains. Empty helmets are strewn about. A burned-out tree stump, a broken rifle, and a few poles carrying tattered flags seem to be growing from the earth like a perverse garden. A stone path surrounds No Man's Land. It forms an oval around the field, passing out of view beyond the East and the West. Suspended above No Man's Land are several large props of aeroplanes, open fans like one might find in a tropical restaurant. Above them—the sky. In the midst of the fans floats a full-scale aeroplane, a Fokker Dreidecker I painted dull red. The numbers 425/17 are painted in white in the fuselage. It hovers twelve feet above No Man's Land.

The West, the third area at the opposite end of the field to Richthofen's room. The machine gun post of Gunners Robert Buie and William Evans of the 53rd Battery, 14th Battalion, Australian Field Artillery, near Bonnay. A rat-infested pit of slime. Sandbags and barbed wire surround bog. A Lewis gun stands erect at the center of the nest, beside it a searchlight and drums of ammunition. At the rear a tin top covers a dugout. Beyond this are the remains of an oak tree covered in rope like ship's rigging, which serves as a lookout post. Everything in the West is covered with mud.

ACT ONE

SCENE 1

(*No Man's Land and the West. 3:33 p.m., April 20th, 1918. Heavily overcast. Silence. A large explosion occurs behind the oak tree. Silence. A shell explodes in the bog. A shell explodes under a cross. Vickers thirty-caliber machine gun fire. Three white flares go off in the sky. Shells are breaking overhead. Human screaming and rifle fire. Indistinct words in several languages. Mortar. Smoke. Flashing light, the drone of several aeroplanes above. Lewis guns, Spandaus.*

A German Lance Corporal is standing in No Man's Land looking up at the sky watching the air battle. He is taking notes on a pad.

The sound of a Sopwith Camel diving toward earth on an obvious crash course emerges. The approaching scream of the machine terminates in the sound of a violent crash off to the south.

Music. Descending scales. The sun begins to shine. A man is falling from the sky, arms flailing, belly down, toward the bog. He wears goggles and the uniform of an Allied chaser pilot. He races helplessly toward certain death but he is English and does his best to overcome his sense of blind panic. His face is scorched. He speaks. The Lance Corporal watches him from the earth.)

RAYMOND-BARKER: Parachutes are forbidden according to the R.F.C., now the R.A.F., the War Office, King George the Fifth, Parliament, the Red Cross and my three aunts in Dover. The politicians claim we will desert our machines at the first sign of danger if parachutes are issued. I have never cared much for politics. (*He looks at his pocket watch. He begins to realize that he seems to have stopped falling and is magically floating in space.*) It's 3:33 p.m., April 20th, 1918. Major R. Raymond-Barker, third flight in the Third Squadron, in the Thirteenth Wing of the Third Brigade of the Third Army. Luckily, I'm not superstitious though I have just had a rather harrowing experience. I was puttering along thinking about flying home for tea time when my heavier-than-air machine was set upon by a red Fokker triplane. The cockpit burst into what we call a flamer. The compass and dash shat-

tered spraying liquid and fire and glass into my face. I had the simple choice
of incinerating in my seat or jumping from seven thousand feet without a
parachute. I'm afraid I soiled my pants just before I leapt and with my body
plummeting toward the earth at terminal velocity I watch my engine dive
ahead, dragged by the thrust of the engine into the earth before me. I reach
out for my own shadow, which races across the battlefield to greet me. Impact approaches but never quite seems to come so that, strangely, I feel I can
take my time, look about, fall forever. (*Major R. Raymond-Barker floats in
space where he proceeds to sing and dance on air. Meanwhile, Secull, the dead
Tommy that Raymond-Barker sings about, appears at a piano which floats in mid-
air above and beyond the machine gun nest in the West. Secull's uniform is in tat-
ters. He is a nasty little fellow with no teeth. Secull plays the piano and listens to R.
Raymond-Barker before joining him in two-part harmony.*)

ALL I WANTED WAS A CUP OF TEA

RAYMOND-BARKER: (*Continued.*)
   AT TERMINAL VELOCITY I CHANCED
   TO COME UPON A TOMMY HOLDING A MULE
   I WAS FALLING DOWN AND HE WAS FALLING UP,
   SWINGING ON A DONKEY'S TAIL.
   "HELLO."
   LOOKS AT ME AND GRINS, "TOO BAD YOU'RE FALLING IN."
   "I'VE JUST BEEN BLOWN BRIGHTLY OUT
   THE BLEEDING TEA POT." HE SAYS . . .
RAYMOND-BARKER & SECULL:
   SHOO, SHOO, SHOO, I'M A SUGAR CUBE
   FALLING FREELY IN SPACE.
   MILKED A MULE TO FEED MY COBBERS
   A PIPING CUP OF ASS MILK AND TEA, TEA,
   DEE, DEE, DEE, DEE, DEE, DEE, DEE.
   BET YOUR ASS THEY'D APPRECIATE
   SERVED WITH THE FRICASSE RAT.
   THE THIRTY POUND SHELL THAT FELL BENEATH THE VAT
   QUICKLY PUT AN END TO ALL OF THAT.
SECULL:
   STANLEY WAS A STEAMER AND HENRY WAS A DREAMER,
   BUT THE MAN WHO INVENTED THAT SHELL JUST PREVENTED
   AN ENGLISH TRADITIONAL
   TEA, DEE, DEE, DEE, DEE, DEE DEE, DEE DEE.
RAYMOND-BARKER & SECULL:
   TIP, TIP, TIP, TIP YOUR CAP FOR ME
   AND KEEP THAT KETTLE FIRE WARM

TELL MY CHUMS TO SAVE ME SOME
MY TEA, DEE, DEE, DEE DEE, DEE DEE, DEE DEE.
RAYMOND-BARKER: HE SAYS . . .
SECULL:
REMEMBER ME AS SECULL
I SERVE ME TEA WITH TREACLE
IF THE POT DON'T STAY HOT, YOU DRINK THE LOT.
SWEET REALITY – DEE DEE, DEE DEE.
RAYMOND-BARKER & SECULL:
OH ME, OH MY, OH ME, MY OLD MOTHER KNOWS.
IT DON'T TAKE MUCH TO PLEASE ME.
NO, I DON'T WANT NO SILVER TROPHY.
ALL I'M WANTING IS A CUP OF TEA.
ONE, TWO, THREE, DO, RE, ME.
QUITE THE VIEW FROM HERE WHAT SCENERY
WELL, HERE WE GO, MY GOODNESS ME.
WE'RE BUMP-TEE-DEE, DOWN-TEE-DEE,
BUMP-TEE-DEE, DOWN-TEE-DEE,
BUMP-TEE-DEE, ALL FALLING DOWN.
I DON'T WANT NO SILVER TROPHY
ALL I'M WANTING IS A CUP OF TEA

(*Secull and the piano begin to vanish.*)

RAYMOND-BARKER:
THE SKIES UP HERE, APPEAR TO CLEAR,
I CAN WATCH HIS FACE GO REELING PAST MY BODY
SAYS HE, "ALL I WANTED, ALL I WANTED
ALL I WANTED WAS A CUP OF TEA."

(*Three flares go off above, as Raymond-Barker falls face down and lands in the crater that his body makes upon impact. Explosions occur in the bog and overhead. Three women, dressed like peasants, appear along the road from the East on bicycles. They have musical instruments, paintings and canvasses strapped to their backs. They disappear behind the machine gun nest in the West.*)

SCENE 2

(*The West, 3:40 p.m., April 20th. The machine gun nest of Buie and Evans. Buie is hanging on to the Lewis gun. Evans's rump sticks in the middle of the nest as his head is embedded between two sandbags in the wall. Buie wears a combat helmet. Their khaki Anzac uniforms are covered in grease and mud.*)

BUIE: You can come out now, Swine. Your hide has been spared. Got a brother like you at home, Mister Inch. Wouldn't fish. Just drink. Wouldn't fight. Just drink. Equally disgusting. (*Buie kicks Evans's extended rump. Evans jumps to at-*

tention, looks around.)

EVANS: Hello, Buie. All over? (*Evans removes his ear plugs.*)

BUIE: You are a cowardly pig, Mister Inch.

EVANS: (*Nervously.*) If someone's going to be critical, someone else may be forced to leave the stuffing in his ears and remain deaf as a dead dog.

BUIE: You're about as useful as a dead dog, I must say.

EVANS: I'm not embarrassed. I love you, Buie.

BUIE: Button it.

EVANS: That was our seventh straight attack, Buie. I keep track. Seven days, seven attacks, still together. Yes, that little romper was number seven and take a crack at what happened to your colleague here.

BUIE: I'm not responding as you can see.

EVANS: I pissed my pants again, Buie, you hero. The sum of the number of attacks is equal to the sum of the number of pisses.

BUIE: One day you'll get your rump blown right off, Mister Inch.

EVANS: I won't mind, Buie. As long as it's not the precious noggin'. Anyway, I can't compete with your heroics. Standing bravely exposed by Lewis. How many did you kill, Buie?

BUIE: Button it.

EVANS: I will inform you then, Gunner Buie, you got off as many rounds as you've managed since we were transferred to the Lewis gun. That would be zero.

BUIE: I think she's jammed. And that is my hypothesis.

EVANS: Even given that N.C.O. Secull finds enough time away from making the tea to repair our gun, pray how do you propose to fire it, my pet fish?

BUIE: We've got the instructions, don't we?

EVANS: We are Vickers machine gunners, Buie, we are not schooled in the wonders of the automatic Lewis. And I will continue to protect my precious noggin' until we are taught.

BUIE: (*Opening the instruction manual.*) It's all down in print. Double A. sight, two ellipses for fast and slow speeds of the angular movement of the target. It's a cake.

EVANS: But we're not bakers, Buie. Think big, boy, our talents lie in greener pastures.

BUIE: I'm quite sure I've located the problem.

EVANS: That's highly unlikely. You should ask Secull to fix her up.

BUIE: I'll fix her up. A man's got no right to fire a gun he can't fix up. I've got me pride.

EVANS: Buie, you miss the whole point. What's needed here is not pride but logic. We'll never get in on the Music Hall Circuit if we don't get out of the war, we won't get out of the war without medals, we won't win medals without shooting Fritz and we can't shoot Fritz with a busted Lewis. But with medals, Buie, what a story we'll be, what a theatrical team we'll make.

BUIE: I said I'll fix her up.

EVANS: Evans, Buie, and Secull. Back from the War. I'll do singing and jokes and you can do sharpshooting and juggle live grenades for the necessary suspense. Secull on piano. We'll be famous, the Music Hall's darlings, I can see it now. We'll have a marvelous success in America. I've seen the maps. We'll play Rochester, Myrtle Beach, San Jose. (*Music.*)

BUIE: (*Looking up and not listening.*) Secull says it's going to rain some more.

EVANS: (*Looking up and not listening.*) The Boys from Down Under!

BUIE: Probably all night.

EVANS: What a thrill!

BUIE: What a mess. (*A bomb lands right beside the bunker. Evans immediately buries his head between the sandbags so that once again his rump sticks out into the center of the nest. Buie stays huddled at the Lewis gun, reading the instruction book, terrified.*)

SCENE 3

(*The East. No Man's Land becomes the airfield of the Flying Circus. 4:10 p.m., April 20th. Wolfram stands on the airfield, outside the window to Richthofen's room, looking up at the sky to the West. He wears boots and a long black leather coat that reaches to his ankles. Richthofen is flying above No Man's Land toward the airfield and home. The Three Peasant Women are watching Richthofen's aeroplane from the West.*)

OUR RED KNIGHT

WOLFRAM:
IF YOU SIGHT ONE BIRD – RED WITH TRIPLE WINGS
SHOW HIM YOUR TAIL OR TURN TO FIGHT.
FIND YOURSELF STARING STRAIGHT INTO HIS FACE.
REST DEEP ASSURED IT'S YOUR LAST SIGHT.
WHEN YOU SEE ALL RED – LIFE SLIPS THROUGH YOUR HANDS
SAND THROUGH YOUR FINGERS, BROKEN GLASS.
FOOLS FACE HIM, GODS CHASE HIM,
VICTIMS FALL PREY, SURVIVORS SAY,
DOWN TO EARTH WE WATCHED THEM FALLING.
FALL IN. FALL IN.

CLAWS MADE OF IVORY, EYES – ATOMIC BLUE,
BLACK CROSSED AND NUMBERED IN BOLD WHITE.
TUBING OF SILVER, TEETH – A RAZOR'S EDGE,
BLOOD RED THE BRAIN OF OUR RED KNIGHT.
THE EARTH IS ABOVE AND BELOW AND ALL AROUND,

DANCE WITH HIM, WON'T YOU, HEAR HIS GUNS.
OUTRACE HIM, EMBRACE HIM,
TRY AS YOU MAY, HE'LL HAVE HIS WAY,
DOWN TO EARTH HE'LL WATCH YOU FALLING.
FALL IN. FALL IN.

WOLFRAM & THE WOMEN:

EACH KILL–A NUMBER, EACH–A MIRACLE,
ONE SACRIFICE PER SACRED FLIGHT.
EACH DEATH A GLORY, EACH A PRIVILEGE,
DIE BY THE HAND OF OUR RED KNIGHT.
WATCH FOR THE HIGH PRIEST, WATCH HIM CHANGE HIS
    SHAPE,
TURN A MAN FROM A DRAGONFLY.
WORSHIP HIM, WAIT ON HIM.
DROP TO YOUR KNEES, SEE THROUGH THE TREES,
DOWN TO EARTH WE WATCH HIM FALLING.
FALL IN. FALL IN. FALL IN.

(*The women disappear in the West. Richthofen's aeroplane floats down to earth and lands on the airfield in the East. Wolfram moves to greet him. Richthofen looks down from the cockpit. They are obviously being watched by other pilots.*)

RICHTHOFEN: I've told you to watch the others, cousin. I don't like to be greeted after a battle. It's bad luck. And I find it maudlin. I hope you haven't brought me another apple.

WOLFRAM: No, Rittmeister.

RICHTHOFEN: Then you may be learning after all.

WOLFRAM: I come to you for justice.

RICHTHOFEN: (*Removing his goggles.*) Justice?

WOLFRAM: Justice, cousin. You've kept me in training for longer than any other chaser pilot, checking and rechecking my reflex. I'm becoming an automaton. You have only to look at my chart. I've logged eight entire hours of solo flight. I'm ready to take my place in the Flying Circus.

RICHTHOFEN: Bodenshatz saw a woman going into your room last night.

WOLFRAM: Perhaps the Oberleutnant was–

RICHTHOFEN: Was she from the town?

WOLFRAM: I believe they were French, Rittmeister.

RICHTHOFEN: They? How many were there? (*Pause.*)

WOLFRAM: I believe there were three, Rittmeister.

RICHTHOFEN: A chaser pilot has to be certain of his mathematics.

WOLFRAM: There were three, Rittmeister.

RICHTHOFEN: (*Looking out at the other pilots.*) There is only one unwritten rule here–celibacy. We save our lovemaking for our only mistresses, the English scouts in the sky. All of our will and desire is focused on them. (*Wolfram begins to defend himself.*) You haven't learned. Perhaps that is why you're still standing on the ground. (*Richthofen climbs out from the cockpit of his machine and dismounts. He is dressed in full flight gear.*)

WOLFRAM: (*Quietly and urgently.*) Some of the others landed before you. There is a rumor that you scored two more victories on this sortie.

RICHTHOFEN: It's no rumor. But I promised mother I'd never discuss my kills with relations.

WOLFRAM: That makes eighty.

RICHTHOFEN: I'm glad to see that your mathematics are improving.

WOLFRAM: They say you will retire at eighty. (*A pause.*)

RICHTHOFEN: Who told you that?

WOLFRAM: There are rumors.

RICHTHOFEN: (*Begins to leave.*) Go away, Wolfram.

WOLFRAM: (*Announcing to the whole airfield.*) I want to fly with you, cousin. I am waiting to spread my wings in the Geschwader.

RICHTHOFEN: (*Turning back.*) Wolfram. Did your mother advise you to emulate me?

WOLFRAM: Yes, Rittmeister.

RICHTHOFEN: I'm flattered. Did she also suggest that you wear my clothes?

WOLFRAM: No, Rittmeister.

RICHTHOFEN: Then why are you wearing my coat?

WOLFRAM: (*Privately.*) They stole my clothes while I was at the showers. The other pilots. To mock me. To degrade me. I had to borrow your coat.

RICHTHOFEN: (*Looking out at the other pilots, amused.*) You'll live longer if you can learn to develop a sense of humor.

WOLFRAM: (*Bitterly.*) They are telling me that I have no use for the uniform of a chaser pilot. They've insulted my pride, my manhood.

RICHTHOFEN: (*Quietly.*) You must become much more than a man. You must become a machine. The machines survive, the rest die. The silk scarf is nothing more than lubrication, grease so that the machine can turn its head quickly in a flight; the goggles are to protect the tissue that forms that delicate pair of sights; the leather is to keep the moving parts insulated. The uniform is not a matter of pride, it's a mechanical detail. Give me the coat, Wolfram.

WOLFRAM: I feel disgraced.

RICHTHOFEN: Death is the only disgrace. And you can't afford feelings. Not embarrassment. Never humiliation. You must concentrate outward, ever outward. You can kill in the nude. Give me the coat, Wolfram.

WOLFRAM: They left me nothing but my boots and . . .

RICHTHOFEN: The coat. (*Richthofen waits for a moment and turns to walk away.*)

WOLFRAM: Yes, Rittmeister. (*Wolfram removes the coat. He is wearing a woman's dress. It doesn't look ridiculous and Richthofen doesn't laugh. He looks out to the field where the other pilots are obviously laughing.*)

RICHTHOFEN: Come to see me in an hour and we'll discuss your first sortie.

WOLFRAM: Yes, Rittmeister.

RICHTHOFEN: And Wolfram. You'd might as well smile. (*Richthofen is gone.*

Wolfram walks nobly off the field. The Fokker triplane floats back into the air and disappears.)

SCENE 4

(The West. 4:17 p.m., April 20th. The machine gun nest of Buie and Evans. Buie is reading the manual by the Lewis gun. Evans is in his undershorts. He is hanging his trousers up to dry.)

EVANS: *(Feeling his wet pants.)* Prolonged fear is bad for the bladder, do you find that, Buie? I do, however, wish we had a kick to celebrate this, our eight attacks in succession. Warm our veins in the Great War. Buie?

BUIE: Where'd you hide it, devil?

EVANS: Out in the bog.

BUIE: Secull'll catch you.

EVANS: You won't tell, will you? Three little bottles'll be buried under a certain cross no doubt as I hid 'em there properly myself.

BUIE: You're going for it, I suppose.

EVANS: I thought I would bribe you.

BUIE: You can't bribe an abstainer with spirits.

EVANS: I'll give you the tin of beets from the Red Cross.

BUIE: You ate the beets.

EVANS: But you're our hero. Standing by your post, shells exploding everywhere, Australian fisherman's son, little Bobby Buie from the Hawkesberry, the hunter with the jammed gun against the entire German Army. He doesn't need bribes. He'll dash out, get the steam for his cobber.

BUIE: Never will.

EVANS: Buie. Please.

BUIE: *(With the manual.)* I've got to read while there's still light. You go.

EVANS: I can't.

BUIE: Why not?

EVANS: I'm suffering from severe terror of the vicious Huns.

BUIE: Then you'll do without.

EVANS: I'll do your chores. I'll feed the mule. *(Evans is climbing the tree and taking a feed bag from a branch.)*

BUIE: Secull's fed it.

EVANS: I can point the secret spot out to you. Third grave marker in. You'll impress me if you can get the steam, go on, dig it up. Good practice for our medals. I'll cover for you. I need the steam, Buie. Please.

BUIE: Mister Inch, the Australian Army resents your interrupting their very important document on modern warfare.

EVANS: *(Sitting up in the branches looking down behind the tree.)* Did you move the mule?

BUIE: It's tethered to the tree.

EVANS: It's not there. (*Evans squints. He puts on his specs which he keeps wrapped in a dry pair of underpants.*)

BUIE: It's a wonder we can be winning this war with drunken myopics for gunners.

EVANS: (*Looking.*) Where's Secull?

BUIE: Making our tea like a good mother.

EVANS: He was trying to get some ass milk out of the mule for our tea.

BUIE: You don't get ass milk from mules.

EVANS: Secull says it's a donkey. You know how stubborn he is.

BUIE: It's a mule.

EVANS: Well, it's gone. The mule's gone. There's just a big hole. I think I'm going to be sick. (*Buie climbs up the tree to join Evans. A pause.*)

BUIE: I wonder where Secull went.

EVANS: He went up in smoke, that's where he went.

BUIE: He was milking the mule?

EVANS: I told you.

BUIE: I thought you were joking.

EVANS: (*Giggling in horror.*) We didn't even need a mule.

BUIE: What a stupid time to get yourself killed, trying to milk a mule. And he was our leader Secull. It's embarrassing. There's no blood, no body, no mule.

EVANS: No more of his fucking tea anyway.

BUIE: It's funny being dead and leaving nothing to bury.

EVANS: Secull will win his medal now. And him with no place to pin it. That's justice.

BUIE: It's April twenty, isn't it, Inch? Secull's death day. I should write that down. (*They sit in the branches of the tree, staring out.*)

SCENE 5

(*The East. 4:28 p.m., April 20th. Richthofen's room. Music. The phonograph is playing. Richthofen has just entered the room, still in his flight gear. There is an unopened gift-wrapped package on the desk. Richthofen picks it up, reads the card and walks to the window. He slowly opens the package. He looks up and smiles like a demon.*)

SPEED

RICHTHOFEN:
SPEED! EVERYTHING FLIES, THE MOON CROSSES THE SKIES,
A LOST MIRACLE IN HEAVIER-THAN-AIR DESIGNING.
SPEED! EVERYTHING SPINS, AN EARTH RIDER BEGINS.
TO DREAM SPHERICAL, ELECTRIC JOURNEY, SHIPS UN-
   EARTHLY.
SPEED! ANCIENT OCCUPATION, HELD BY DEMONS.
SPEED! LUNAR INVITATION, "RIDE ME, FLY ME

OFF INTO THE CENTURY OF THE SUN."
AND HOW CONVENIENTLY SIMPLE SPEED BECOMES.

SPEED! EVERYTHING MOVES. WE FINALLY CHOOSE DIRECTION
RIDING ON OUR TUBULAR CONTRAPTIONS.
SPEED! YES, EVERYTHING MOVES BUT ANIMALS WALK,
AND LUNATICS FLY AND LUNATICS DREAM
THAT ANIMALS TALK AND DREAMERS REMOVE
THEIR HORNS AND THEIR HOOVES AND LUNATICS PROVE
THAT ANIMALS FLY, I'M FLYING FROM WHERE
THE SANE FOLK ASK WHAT FLYING IMPROVES.
EVERYTHING MOVES. WE RIGHTFULLY CHOOSE DIRECTION
STRAIGHT FROM HEAVENLY PREDESTINATION.

SPEED! MINIATURE GOD, FACE MINIATURE GOD
SPACE-TUMBLE, TWISTING,
CHASE THE MOON WITH DREAMS PERSISTING.

SPEED! ANCIENT OCCUPATION HELD BY DREAMERS
SPEED! FLYING IN FORMATION, SLIDING, GLIDING.
OFF INTO THE CENTURY OF THE SUN
AND HOW INGENIOUSLY SIMPLE SPEED BECOMES.
HOW CONVENIENTLY SIMPLE WITH THE MOON
AS OUR EXAMPLE, FLYING EASILY,
REMINDS US HOW IT'S DONE.

(*Karl Bodenshatz, the Adjutant of Jadgeschwader I, enters Richthofen's room carrying a tray with roast duckling under glass and a bottle of cognac. He sets down the tray and arranges the meal. In Richthofen's hand is the scale model of a Fokker Dreidecker, painted red. Gift wrapping lies at his feet.*)

RICHTHOFEN: (*Looking at the model aeroplane.*) Do you suppose that the little man inside the cockpit with no face is meant to be me?
BODENSHATZ: It's only a toy machine, Rittmeister. It's meant for fighting boredom on rainy days, not for fighting the English on sunny ones.
RICHTHOFEN: Do you think it's meant as a token of good luck?
BODENSHATZ: Yes. It's unlikely that you'll die in it, Rittmeister, so it must be good luck.
RICHTHOFEN: They send me gifts as if my kills were birthdays. Why not another stupid loving cup? Has Berlin finally run out of silver?
BODENSHATZ: (*Quietly.*) Field Marshall von Ludendorff expects news of your decision tonight, Rittmeister.
RICHTHOFEN: I never promised him that I'd retire at eighty.
BODENSHATZ: You said that you would seriously consider it. Von Ludendorff

wants you alive.

RICHTHOFEN: I don't appear to be dead.

BODENSHATZ: You've been brought down and wounded once. That would seem to indicate a certain . . . vulnerability. (*Bodenshatz ritualistically helps Richthofen out of his flight gear.*)

RICHTHOFEN: Karl. Why do you suppose these old men are so passionate about keeping me alive?

BODENSHATZ: The death of the Red Dragon would utterly demoralize the Fatherland. You are a symbol of luck to the people.

RICHTHOFEN: Believing in luck is a diversion.

BODENSHATZ: If luck is so unimportant, excuse me, Rittmeister, why are we always discussing it?

RICHTHOFEN: I didn't say it was unimportant. I said it was a diversion. It is very important that the new pilots believe in my luck. It persuades them to believe that they too can survive the odds. The luck is irrelevant. The belief is essential.

BODENSHATZ: And if you should die?

RICHTHOFEN: They'll simply believe I've lost my luck. (*They smile.*)

BODENSHATZ: (*Sharply.*) What about the rest of the people?

RICHTHOFEN: I don't have to look into the faces of the rest of the people.

BODENSHATZ: Nevertheless, they are there . . . in decreasing numbers.

RICHTHOFEN: You are naive, Karl. Von Ludendorff knows that our last great offensive has stalled and the war is lost. It's politics. If I die during the final stage of the campaign it will be one more defeat for him to cope with in the aftermath. They're all idiots.

BODENSHATZ: Be careful.

RICHTHOFEN: You're not Judas, are you, Karl? And I certainly couldn't be Christ. According to the English He's flying for them.

BODENSHATZ: Anthony Fokker made the model with his loving hands.

RICHTHOFEN: The Kaiser kissed the wing tips.

BODENSHATZ: You must answer them, Rittmeister.

RICHTHOFEN: Curse for me, Karl.

BODENSHATZ: Shiesee!

RICHTHOFEN: Have the kills been confirmed from the ground?

BODENSHATZ: The seventy-ninth is in. We're still waiting for a confirmation on the eightieth.

RICHTHOFEN: What you are drinking?

BODENSHATZ: I confiscated a bottle of cognac from your cousin. It will etherize your mind, extract the pain from your wound.

RICHTHOFEN: I'm not in pain and I'm not drinking, thank you.

BODENSHATZ: And you're not eating, thank you.

RICHTHOFEN: (*Impatiently.*) Then eat for me, Karl.

BODENSHATZ: (*Sits to eat.*) Our leaders have been waiting since before the rains hoping for you to fly to bag your eightieth lord before being wasted by some bright, young Englishman. You must answer them tonight, Manfred. (*Pause.*)

RICHTHOFEN: They never asked Oswald Boelcke to retire.

BODENSHATZ: What would Boelcke have done?

RICHTHOFEN: Summon his corpse from the grave and I'll ask his advice.

BODENSHATZ: You wouldn't listen. He had only forty kills . . . you have eighty.

RICHTHOFEN: Eighty. It's a nice round number.

BODENSHATZ: Two Boelcke's in one.

RICHTHOFEN: What does Ludendorff suggest?

BODENSHATZ: That you become an inspector until the war has ended.

RICHTHOFEN: With a bloated backside at a desk. No offense to you, Karl, your backside is probably perfect.

BODENSHATZ: I remain your faithful adjutant, regardless. I'm ready to record your every thought. (*Bodenshatz sits at the desk.*)

RICHTHOFEN: (*Dictates.*) Dear Field Marshall, I, Manfred von Richthofen . . . ace of aces, am a well oiled, highly accurate, synchronized weapon of German innovation, an almost unstoppable killing machine . . . help me, Karl.

BODENSHATZ: Over the last three years, stubs that first appeared on my hips have grown into wings. I have no choice but to fly. I am now an aeroplane. (*They smile.*) Ludendorff may not understand.

RICHTHOFEN: Then what do you suggest?

BODENSHATZ: I'll cut your hair.

RICHTHOFEN: Answer please.

BODENSHATZ: (*Quietly.*) You cannot leave your historic decision to me. If you want advice, you'd better look to another hunter. As you know, I'm not a hunter. (*Richthofen walks to the stuffed Danish Wolfhound. He strokes it.*)

RICHTHOFEN: Then I will have to ask my faithful Danish friend, a genuine hunter, the last hunter. Moritz! If you think I should retire from the air I want you to bark three times. (*He waits. Silence.*)

SCENE 6

(*No Man's Land and the West. 4:45 p.m., April 20th. Music. Raymond-Barker is lying half out of a crater where he has landed after having fallen from 7,000 feet. Above and beyond the oak tree in the West floats the late N.C.O. Secull on piano. He retains his own body but he has temporarily acquired the head of a mule. Buie and Evans, in the machine gun nest, seem to hear and see nothing.*)

SWEET ETERNITY

RAYMOND-BARKER: (*Quietly.*)
I WAS FALLING DOWN AND HE WAS FALLING UP
HE COULD HAVE LANDED MILES FROM ME.
SECULL AND I AND THE MULE IN THE SKY.

SAY "GOOD EVENING" TO MORTALITY.
THERE'S NO TIME FOR ALIBI WHEN YOU'RE DROPPING
EARTHBOUND FROM THE SKY.
JUST SAVE AN UNMARKED GRAVE TO BURY
ME AND THE MULE AND SECULL THE FOOL.
WHAT GOES UP COMES DOWN AS A RULE.
'SCUSE ME, I DROPPED IN TO SEE
MY SWEET ETERNITY, DEE DEE, DEE DEE.

(*Secull disappears. The piano music continues. Raymond-Barker whistles along softly. Buie peers out into No Man's Land and listens. The whistling stops. Distant shelling.*)

EVANS: It makes you sorrily aware of your own mortality, doesn't it? To think a big mule like that dead.

BUIE: Did you hear that?

EVANS: We are all of us very cheap.

BUIE: Listen up. Somebody's out there.

EVANS: Nonsense. I refuse to be terrorized by your over-active imagination.

BUIE: He could have his sights trained on your noggin' right this very instant, Mister Inch. (*Evans crouches, feels his temple, puts on his helmet and peers out.*)

EVANS: (*Quietly.*) The bastard. Where is he?

BUIE: I can smell him.

EVANS: It's the wind.

BUIE: It's not. It's Fritz. We're being stalked. And no Secull to tell us what's to be done.

EVANS: In the navy you get a rum ration.

BUIE: What do you think?

EVANS: Should have been a sailor.

BUIE: I'll go. (*Buie starts to climb over the sand bags. Evans stops him.*)

EVANS: Buie! If it is Fritz and he guts you I could be alone all night.

BUIE: Not to worry, Mister Inch. Back in a nip.

EVANS: Well, I won't watch. I'm not watching, Buie! (*Evans buries his head in the sandbags. Buie dashes into No Man's Land, knife in teeth. He stops a few feet from Raymond-Barker's body, puts his knife away and stares. Buie approaches the body slowly, with his hand extended and bends to feel for breath.*)

BUIE: Inch! He's dead. It's alright.

EVANS: What?

BUIE: He's not breathing. It's a corpse.

EVANS: Is it a Fritz?

BUIE: No. It's one of us. It's a flyer.

EVANS: What's he doing?

BUIE: Just lying there. He's dead. (*Buie bends down and reads Raymond-Barker's tag around his neck.*) It's R. Raymond-Barker. Major.

EVANS: Well, whoever he is, don't go bringing him in here.

BUIE: He's all bloody inside the suit. He's broken all his bones. The suit's holding him together. It's awful. You should see him. He looks like a bust doll.

EVANS: See if he's got any sweets.

BUIE: Flyers don't eat sweets.

EVANS: What's he got?

BUIE: A nice scarf. Real silk. With "R" on it.

EVANS: Take it.

BUIE: No. We should bury him.

EVANS: Buie. Take the scarf. Souvies.

BUIE: It won't rat him. It's not dignified. He's not very old. He's got a nice moustache. It's a shame.

EVANS: It is a shame.

BUIE: Damn shame.

EVANS: Shame, that it is. Buie, my cobbler, I hate to ask but while you're up would you mind making a trip to the bank?

BUIE: You're a disgrace, Mister Inch. I could be killed out here.

EVANS: It's right there. Third marker in. Go on, fetch the steam. ((*Buie follows instructions.*)

BUIE: That's your problem right there. No respect for the dead.

EVANS: That's the spot. (*Buie digs into No Man's Land.*)

BUIE: The first one's broke.

EVANS: No. Keep digging.

BUIE: The second one's broke. The bombs seem to have found your secret wine cellar.

EVANS: Pray to God. Dig. One to go. One left. Dig.

BUIE: You're in luck. One whole.

EVANS: I'll pour it directly on the brain. Bring it here. We've wasted enough time with politics. (*Buie trots over to the nest and scrambles over the sandbags. They look at each other. Buie gives Evans the bottle. They look out at the body. Evans drinks.*)

BUIE: I know how he got there. He fell from the sky. He was probably still living when he hit the earth.

EVANS: To be frank, if I might, I'm not fussy about this situation, Buie. No Secull. Him out there dead. Me getting drunk. You with our jammed Lewis. It's a very ugly night. We're a long way from getting the Music Hall off the ground, I'd be forced to say, Buie. (*Buie takes his position at his post behind the Lewis gun.*)

BUIE: I'd love to get one of those things up there, out of the muck. It makes you angry just to watch them. Like something out of the future. I'd love to kill a flying machine, wouldn't you, Inch? Unnatural bastards. (*Buie looks through the gunsight.*)

SCENE 7

(The East. 4:55 p.m., April 20th. Richthofen is in the far corner of the room, stand-ing on his head, apparently in some state of meditation. Bodenshatz is speaking into a telephone.)

BODENSHATZ: He said to tell you that he hasn't made up his mind, Field Marshall. The wound is bothering him now, he's doing the exercises. I'll call you as soon as he comes to a decision, sir. No, he's not in the mood for a party. Has a confirmation come in on his eightieth kill? . . . Good . . . No need to send it over . . . No, please don't send Hermann. I don't think the Rittmeister even likes Hermann, sir. He hardly knows him. Hello? Field Marshall? Oh. Hello, Hermann. I can't talk to you just now . . . please don't bother . . . Leck mich am arsch, Hermann. *(Bodenshatz stares at the receiver.)*

SCENE 8

(The West. 5:05 p.m., April 20th. The machine gun nest of Buie and Evans. Evans is out of sight in the dugout. Buie is sitting bolt upright, fast asleep at the Lewis gun. The Three Peasant Women sit in the oak tree. They play orchestral instruments: cello, violin, and flute. Secull's silhouette floats in the background. Buie is dreaming.)

TAKE WHAT YOU CAN

THE WOMEN:
68, 69, 70, 71, 72, 73, 74
75, 76, 77, 78, 79, 80 . . .

TAKE WHAT YOU CAN, THE SKY IS FALLING.
NECK DEEP HIGH IN THE MUD I'M CRAWLING.
IF I HAD A NAME I'VE FORGOTTEN IT NOW.
YOU MAKE ONE TO SUIT WHEN THE BOYS COME CALLING.

TAKE WHAT YOU CAN THE LITTLE THING'S CRYING.
IMAGINARY PORK IN THE PAN IS FRYING.
NEVER SEEN THE SEA AND I'LL NEVER SEE IT NOW.
TELL ME WHAT YOU'RE SELLING AND I'LL TELL YOU WHAT
I'M BUYING.

I LEARNED TO COUNT MY WAY TO EIGHTY – TO EIGHTY.
THOSE NUMBERS ALL SEEM ENDLESS NOW – THOSE NUMBERS
SEEM NEEDLESS.
ONE OF THESE AND HALF OF THOSE, FLEA INFESTED CLOTHES
CONCEALING WHAT YOU'RE STEALING.

TAKE WHAT YOU CAN AND IGNORE THE WRITING.
SNATCH IT WHEN WET SO FINGER IT WELL.
CARRY IT HOME IF IT LOOKS INVITING.

I LEARNED TO DRESS MY HAIR WITH FLOWERS, – FOR HOURS.
READ NEW CENTURY PHILOSOPHY – THOSE NUMBERS SEEM
  NEEDLESS
BY CHEMISTRY, THROUGH INDUSTRY, WE'LL GROW,
YOU KNOW I'VE SEEN THEM IN THEIR DREAM MACHINES.

CLAP, CLAP, CLAP FOR THE HORSELESS CARRIAGE.
ROOT, ROOT, ROOT TO ARRANGE YOUR OWN MARRIAGE.
NOTHING LIKE A WAR KEEPS THE POPULATION DOWN.
THERE'S PLENTY OF BOYS SO DON'T DISPARAGE.

TAKE WHAT YOU CAN THE SKY IS FALLING.
NECK DEEP HIGH IN THE MUD I'M CRAWLING.
IF I HAD A NAME I'VE FORGOTTEN IT NOW.
THEY MAKE ONE TO SUIT WHEN THE GRAVE COMES CALLING.
TAKE WHAT YOU CAN, WHAT CAN YOU TAKE,
WHAT CAN YOU TAKE, WHAT YOU CAN.

(*No Man's Land. The Lance Corporal is sitting cross-legged in the mud, roasting a piece of meat over a small open fire which he shelters from the rain. The corpse of Raymond-Barker is visible nearby.*)

IF I HAVE THE WILL

LANCE CORPORAL:
  IF I HAVE THE WILL TO SIT HERE ALONE ON MY BIRTHDAY.
  WITH WHO KNOWS WHAT IN THE DARK.
  BUT ONE IDEA COMES
  MY MOTHER GIVES BIRTH TO A WOLF.
  TWENTY-NINE YEARS AGO TODAY, PLENTY.
  APRIL TWENTY.

  IF I HAVE THE WILL TO SIT HERE ALL NIGHT ON MY BIRTHDAY
  WITH WHAT KNOWS WHO IN THE RAIN.
  WITH THAT ONE LYING THERE
  WHO CAME FALLING FROM THE SKY.

  TWENTY-NINE YEARS AGO TODAY. I'M HUNGRY.
  APRIL TWENTY. HAPPY BIRTHDAY TO ME.
  HAPPY GERMANY!

(The West. While the Lance Corporal is singing in No Man's Land, the Cellist slings her instrument on her back and climbs down into the machine gun nest where Buie sleeps. She frisks him, picks up, examines and discards the empty tin of beets, creeps into the dugout and reappears carrying Evans's bottle of wine. The Flautist and the Violinist climb quietly down from the tree but as they sneak away one of them kicks over Buie's rifle by the dugout. Buie opens his eyes. He is confused. The Women freeze. He turns to see them, picks up his rifle, and aims it at them. The Cellist stares him down. He can't pull the trigger. He shakes. The Women simply walk away. They disappear around the tree as the Lance Corporal's song ends.)

BUIE: *(In desperation.)* Hi! Evans! Evans! Evans! We got rats. Help me, Evans, we're being ratted. *(Evans leaps out of the dugout. Buie aims the rifle after the Women and climbs the tree.)*

EVANS: Where?

BUIE: I couldn't get a shot in.

EVANS: Buie!

BUIE: I tried. They were standing there . . . they were too quick . . . professionals.

EVANS: You missed your chance for action. God forgive you.

BUIE: They just took your wine.

EVANS: They took my wine. They took my wine? Oh, my God. The nerve of these people.

BUIE: It was three women.

EVANS: And me with this sudden thirst.

BUIE: One second earlier, I would have had her, straight between the eyes. *(Pause. Evans looks warily at Buie.)*

EVANS: Well, we could be logical. If you had fired a shot we would have attracted attention down the line, got a new N.C.O. and I wouldn't have been able to drink the wine anyway. Three lives would have gone to waste. There you go. That's logic. You should have talked them into sharing.

BUIE: They should be shot. It makes me tired, stealing from us, it's not Christian.

EVANS: They were just starving, Buie, that's all. Lost. Starving to death. Anyway, I'm the alcoholic, love, it was my wine.

BUIE: She was lucky, Inch. One more step and her brains were mashed potatoes.

EVANS: *(Trying to be cheerful.)* Very poetic, Buie, my mule's ass. Unfortunately, I can't be drunk so as to appreciate it fully. However, I could eat some mashed potatoes.

BUIE: They should move the peasants out of the road if they want to have a war.

EVANS: Oh, you'll hit something yet, Buie, don't you worry. *(Buie turns his head sharply and stares at Evans.)*

SCENE 9

(The East. 5:30 p.m., April 20th. Richthofen's room. Bodenshatz paces. Richthofen has mounted the riding saddle that is slung over a wooden horse in the room. He hunches in pain like a wounded highwayman, his feet in the stirrups, his hand to his head, a blanket around his shoulders. Rain on the roof.)

BODENSHATZ: *(Efficiently.)* Kill seventy-eight. Concentrate.

RICHTHOFEN: Confirmed. April 7. Spad 5.7. Single seater, R.A.F. North of Villiers – Brettoneaux. Pilot killed.

BODENSHATZ: Concentrate your attention outward, keep your head still. Kill seventy-nine.

RICHTHOFEN: *(Faster.)* Confirmed. April 20. S.E. 5.A. Single seater, R.A.F. Southwest of Bois-de-Hamel. Pilot killed.

BODENSHATZ: The pain is now gone, Rittmeister. Kill eighty.

RICHTHOFEN: *(At fever pitch.)* Not yet confirmed. April 20. Sopwith Camel. Single seater, R.A.F. Between the lines at Bonnay. Pilot jumped in flames. Assumed dead.

BODENSHATZ: The pain has now gone, Manfred.

RICHTHOFEN: It has not gone, you stupid man.

BODENSHATZ: List all of the dogs you've owned. Or medals you've won, school teachers.

RICHTHOFEN: It doesn't help.

BODENSHATZ: Give me a list of sweethearts.

RICHTHOFEN: The fragment of the bullet is alive inside my skull. And when it gets restless it pries loose from the notch where it lives and rolls deeper into my brain.

BODENSHATZ: Tell me the story of the accident.

RICHTHOFEN: I can control the pain.

BODENSHATZ: You're crying.

RICHTHOFEN: I am not crying.

BODENSHATZ: Then tell me the story again. Or could it be too painful, Manfred? *(Pause.)*

RICHTHOFEN: *(Quietly.)* I let him shoot, for at a distance of 300 yards even the best marksman is helpless. Now he flies toward me and I hope that I will succeed in getting him to open fire. I haven't even released my safety catches. Suddenly something strikes me in the head. My arms go limp; my legs flop loosely; I am completely blind. I am diving helplessly, being sucked into the earth. At this moment, I realize that this is how it feels to be shot down; to die. I tear off my goggles. I concentrate all of my energy and say aloud, "I must see, I must see, I must see." Gradually I discern black and white shapes through the red of the blood and . . . Karl. The pain is gone. *(Pause. It is quiet.)*

BODENSHATZ: Your miracles are recurring.

RICHTHOFEN: There are no miracles. There's only luck. Perhaps I was only pretending then.

BODENSHATZ: (*With the ice pack.*) Perhaps you are only pretending now. I'll rub your back.

RICHTHOFEN: You're very kind, Karl. You ooze kindness and concern.

BODENSHATZ: I used to admire your boyish looks. Your complexion is degenerating at an alarming rate.

RICHTHOFEN: If I'd known I would live this long I'd have taken better care of myself.

BODENSHATZ: You don't look twenty-five, Manfred.

RICHTHOFEN: My hands are still young.

BODENSHATZ: Stubby fingers. Like an old woman's. It feels as if your back has been stuffed with marbles. You wouldn't allow any of your pilots to fly in your present condition. You need a holiday. Go to the Black Forest. Hunt quail. Quail don't shoot back. Make the decision about your future there. Go tomorrow.

RICHTHOFEN: I've promised Wolfram to take him on his first sortie tomorrow.

BODENSHATZ: I've never known the Red Dragon to allow his emotions to become entangled in the machinery of war.

RICHTHOFEN: I owe it to my family to accompany Wolfram on his first mission.

BODENSHATZ: You owe it to Germany to rest . . . immediately. Wolfram can wait. Wolfram can go with someone else. Please, Rittmeister. The perfect machine used to know when to rest.

RICHTHOFEN: And is the Black Forest really the garden of youth?

BODENSHATZ: That depends on whether or not you believe in Teutonic folklore.

RICHTHOFEN: Oberleutnant Bodenshatz.

BODENSHATZ: (*Snapping to attention.*) Yes, Rittmeister.

RICHTHOFEN: Bring Wolfram in.

SCENE 10

(*The West. 5:40 p.m., April 20th. The machine gun nest of Buie and Evans. Buie is tinkering with the gun.*)

EVANS: It's suspiciously light.

BUIE: It's not suspicious. It's just the fire reflecting on the clouds.

EVANS: It's curiously light. And of course we know why. Fritz has invented a way of keeping it light all the time. Don't you doubt it. The moon out now. The sun out at midnight. Fritz, tipping the world right off its axis. We've got him now. He's desperate. And I'm hungry.

BUIE: Try counting to yourself.

EVANS: This predicament is what we get for eating our supper for lunch. Intense hunger. I'll bet this makes a very nice picture, us sitting here, winning the war, eating oxygen for supper. (*Buie keeps working on the gun.*)

SCENE 11

(*The East. 5:42 p.m., April 20th. Wolfram has joined Bodenshatz and Richthofen. Wolfram is in full uniform. Richthofen holds his walking stick.*)

RICHTHOFEN: I will be taking a holiday in the morning. At dawn I'll be traveling east to the Black Forest where I will hunt quail with Moritz. I will return to active duty in nine days. Active duty. Make a note of that, Karl.

BODENSHATZ: Yes, Rittmeister.

RICHTHOFEN: This leaves you with a decision, Wolfram. Consider that it could easily be the last decision you ever make. You can go up under Reinhardt's supervision in the morning and take your first sortie without me . . . or you can wait for my return, cousin. You can wait for me. It's no disgrace, Wolfram. Do you understand me?

WOLFRAM: I have always dreamed of flying my maiden in the formation of the dragon, in the left front flank, with my famous cousin at the apex.

RICHTHOFEN: (*Smiles.*) Yes, Wolfram.

WOLFRAM: It will be a great disappointment not to have you there. (*Pause.*)

RICHTHOFEN: They you'll fly with Reinhardt.

WOLFRAM: Yes, Rittmeister.

RICHTHOFEN: It doesn't matter, Wolfram. We'll fly together when I return, won't we?

WOLFRAM: Thank you, cousin.

RICHTHOFEN: If you're still alive. These are your instructions. One. Avoid encounters. Remain a thousand meters above the air battle no matter how anxious you become about the fighting. Two. In the event of an unwanted encounter with a pilot of greater skill, avoid trying to outmaneuver him with aerobatic tricks. You'll only lose altitude and be inaccurate. Three. In the unlikely event of an encounter with a pilot of lesser skill be careful not to chase your prey low over enemy lines. This is particularly easy to do when an east wind is blowing. You will find yourself vulnerable to ground fire. The practice can be considered completely insane, consciously suicidal. (*Richthofen sits on the cot and covers his forehead. He is in pain. Wolfram and Bodenshatz start toward him. Bodenshatz intercepts Wolfram and ushers him out.*)

SCENE 12

(*The West. 6:05 p.m., April 20th. The machine gun nest of Buie and Evans. Buie sits on the tin roof and reads the manual. Evans tosses bullets into a tin drum. Music. The late N.C.O. Secull floats undetected at the piano in the background. The Women sing in the distance.*)

I'VE GOT A GIRL

BUIE & EVANS (with the WOMEN):
YOU FROM ME. I CAN'T TELL YOU FROM ME. ME FROM YOU.
I CAN'T TELL ME FROM YOU. YOU FROM ME FROM YOU.

BUIE:
IS TODAY SATURDAY? FOUR O'CLOCK? IS IT SPRING?
I KEEP LOSING SATURDAY. SUN WENT DOWN, MUST BE DARK.
MAYBE IT'S SATURDAY. SATURDAY NIGHT!

(Buie and Evans do a music hall dance on the tin roof, with Secull harmonizing and playing piano. Buie proficiently juggles three grenades.)

EVANS (with SECULL):
I'VE GOT A GIRL, SHE IS A DANCER.
SHE KNOWS HOW TO TWIRL A QUESTION AND ANSWER.
WHILE SHE'S FAR AWAY MY LETTERS ENTRANCE HER
SHE'D LIKE TO BE DOWN HERE WITH ME. SHE'S ECSTASY.
SENT ME A STOCKING AND HER OLD SILK PANTS.
I PUT THEM ON MY FRIEND AND ASKED HIM TO DANCE.
YOU'D BETTER DANCE.

BUIE (with SECULL):
I'VE GOT A CHUM AS SHORT AS ME MOTHER.
HE SITS ON HIS BUM AND DRINKS LIKE ME BROTHER.
THEY GAVE HIM A MULE BUT HE'D HAVE NO OTHER.
THEY OUGHT TO KILLED HIM LONG AGO; HE'S RUDE YOU
    KNOW.
GIVE HIM A RIFLE AND HE'S ON HIS KNEES.
HANDING IT BACK AND PRETENDING TO SNEEZE.

BUIE & EVANS:
WHAT'S THE USE WITH A GUNNER.
IF THE GUNNER DON'T GUN?
WHAT'S THE USE WITH A TIN OF BEETS
IF YOU'VE EATEN EVERY ONE?

HE WAS BORN IN THE AGE OF VICTORIA
WHEN MANNERS WERE TRULY FINE (FINER BLESS ME).
NOW YOU CAN'T TELL THE CLERKS FROM THE COUNTS
WHAT IS YOURS AND WHAT IS MINE IS YOURS OR . . .
ME I'VE TRAVELLED FROM PERTH TO PRETORIA
I STILL GET SHIVERS IN MY SPINE

BECAUSE THEY'RE FLYING, FLYING.
THEY'RE FLYING, FLYING.

FLY! YES I'M WATCHING YOU.
FLY! AND I'M NOT IMPRESSED.
FLY! THROWING STONES AT BIRDS.
GET YOUR SLING AND PEBBLE AND LINE THE BASTARD UP.
CATCH HIM WHILE HE'S DOZING OFF OR DRINKING FROM A
   CUP
KEEP YOUR FINGERS STEADY, HIT HIM WHEN YOU'RE READY.
   NOW.

FLY! WHAT THEY DO UP THERE?
FLY! THEY JUST SIT AND STARE.
FLY! COFFINS IN THE AIR.
GIVE HIM WHAT HE'S WANTING IF HE'S GOING TO MUCK
   AROUND.
HE'S THINKING WHAT HE'S SMASHING, LOVE TO BRING HIM
   CRASHING DOWN.

FLY! FASTENED ON THE GROUND.
FLY! MAKE THAT NASTY SOUND.
FLY! LOVE TO BRING ONE DOWN.
WHAT THEY THINK THEY'RE DOING
UP THERE JUST ABUSING ME.

SCENE 13

(*The East. 6:15 p.m., April 20th. Richthofen's room. Richthofen is in the tub. He is sitting, naked in ice cold bath water, asleep. His skin is blue. The closed louvered doors are illuminated from beyond. Two men's shadows move back and forth across the doors; Bodenshatz and a larger man. They speak in hushed voices.*)

GOERING: He's only agreed to a holiday.
BODENSHATZ: Yes.
GOERING: He intends to keep flying in spite of his agreement?
BODENSHATZ: He may change his mind.
GOERING: Von Ludendorff thought that I might be able to talk with him, how shall I say, more intimately.
BODENSHATZ: He hardly knows you, Oberleutnant.
GOERING: No offense. But I'm a flyer, Oberleutnant. He's at a turning point. All of his colleagues are dead.
BODENSHATZ: He doesn't want visitors.
GOERING: Everyone agrees that he must be kept alive at all cost. The value of

his life is immeasurable.

BODENSHATZ: Yes. But I've already talked to him.

GOERING: And you failed.

BODENSHATZ: I did my best.

GOERING: I rode through the rain with the confirmation of his eightieth miracle. I feel a responsibility to see him.

BODENSHATZ: Please. You'll make it worse. Leave him. (*Bodenshatz peers in on Richthofen. Goering's shadow remains.*)

GOERING: Trust me. (*Richthofen stirs.*)

BODENSHATZ: Quiet.

RICHTHOFEN: Karl! Karl! More ice! (*Bodenshatz carrying a bucket steps into the room, closes the door, locks it, and pours the bucket of ice into the tub.*)

BODENSHATZ: You've had six buckets already, Rittmeister.

RICHTHOFEN: And I'll bathe in ice water every day that I'm in the Black Forest.

BODENSHATZ: I feel like some exotic torturer.

RICHTHOFEN: Ice grooms muscles, sharpens nerves, cools the blood. Do you know of the Eskimos? (*Richthofen doesn't notice that a door is slowly opening. Goering stands in the shadows.*)

BODENSHATZ: You'll catch your death.

GOERING: Did I miss the party? (*Goering steps into the light, with his leather rain cape dripping wet. He carries a bottle of French wine in one hand and two wine glasses in the other. He wears one of those stupid little paper party hats. Grins.*)

RICHTHOFEN: There isn't any party.

GOERING: Sorry, I didn't mean to interrupt. But no need to be modest. Continue, Rittmeister. Keep scrubbing.

BODENSHATZ: I know I locked that door, Rittmeister, honestly.

GOERING: I hope I'm not in the way.

RICHTHOFEN: Am I being congratulated, Hermann?

GOERING: Yes! Happy eightieth! May all of your kills be—

RICHTHOFEN: Foreigners?

GOERING: I was going to say "merciless."

RICHTHOFEN: Surely that is understood.

BODENSHATZ: The catch must be rusted through on the lock. Shall I throw him out?

RICHTHOFEN: In a moment. (*Goering takes the bucket from Bodenshatz, dips it into the bathwater and scoops up some ice. He places the bottle in the bucket.*)

GOERING: French wine. It's very poor, I'm afraid, tending toward the flat side at room temperature, but the best on the black. Oh, sorry. (*Goering drops a cube of ice back into the tub.*) Don't want to steal all of your ice. By the way, isn't that a bit chilly?

RICHTHOFEN: How did you manage to get away? (*Goering removes his cape. Underneath he wears his full dress uniform with his Ordre pour le Merite pinned conspicuously to the center of his chest. A pendant hangs around his neck with a large opal that matches his eyes.*)

GOERING: I borrowed a motorcycle, rode through the rain as soon as I heard. Incredible. Eighty kills. Our leader, our teacher, our ace of aces. Wouldn't miss the party.

RICHTHOFEN: There's no party.

GOERING: There should be.

RICHTHOFEN: Well, there isn't!

GOERING: I was sorry to hear your dog died.

RICHTHOFEN: He didn't die. He's sitting right there. Moritz isn't dead. He's simply waiting. (*Goering looks around at the stuffed Danish Wolfhound. It looks back.*)

GOERING: You're looking very well.

RICHTHOFEN: Thank you. You're looking healthy, a bit fat. (*Pause.*)

GOERING: Have I picked a bad time?

RICHTHOFEN: I'm not drinking.

GOERING: Well, you wouldn't toast yourself, would you? We'll do it. This fellow and I, won't we? Two glasses, one each. This gentleman.

RICHTHOFEN: Don't you know Hermann, Karl?

BODENSHATZ: Yes, I saw him outside. I tried to prevent him from bothering you.

RICHTHOFEN: Hermann is Staffelfuhrer at Jasta Twenty Six.

GOERING: Twenty One!

BODENSHATZ: We've met before.

GOERING: Yes. I'd simply forgotten your name. Cheers.

RICHTHOFEN: Since we have the luxury of deserting our comrades to attend imaginary parties we couldn't be losing the war, could we, Hermann?

GOERING: I've been grounded by God; a victim of the great proverbial flood. The German Navy is better equipped to maneuver about our airfield. I tried to soak up the water with a sponge but I was persuaded to leave the job to God and the sun.

RICHTHOFEN: And God has shown that he favors Goering over the English by granting him the lives of sixteen English flyers.

GOERING: (*Quietly.*) Seventeen. I landed in a field beside the last one. He died in my arms. Bad luck to face the corpse. I knew it would bring something. Rain. No English scouts for me until our airfield dries. Unless, of course, I can borrow your machine, Rittmeister.

RICHTHOFEN: You can call me Manfred now that you're saying goodbye. I'm feeling very informal tonight.

GOERING: Thank you, Manfred.

RICHTHOFEN: And now that the imaginary party is over I'll finish my bath. Chaser pilots should keep their eyes open under water for thirty seconds, three times a day. There's some free advice. Goodbye, Hermann. (*Richthofen's head disappears under the water and out of ear shot.*)

BODENSHATZ: You'd better go.

GOERING: I sense that he needs to talk to me.

BODENSHATZ: Leave it alone. You'll make it worse. (*Richthofen emerges from under water.*)

RICHTHOFEN: When I open my eyes I can see my toes clearly under water. I feel like a submarine.

GOERING: Tell me about this record kill, please. I can't wait another second for your delicious description.

RICHTHOFEN: Are you still here, Hermann? Hermann's cape, Karl.

GOERING: I came to hear the story of your glorious eightieth kill. I came a long way in the rain, Manfred.

RICHTHOFEN: And you've got a long way to go back so you'd better get started, hadn't you? (*Richthofen submerges.*)

BODENSHATZ: You're embarrassing me.

GOERING: He must talk to me.

BODENSHATZ: He'll be furious.

GOERING: Give me my chance to persuade him. (*Richthofen emerges.*)

RICHTHOFEN: (*Gasping.*) Don't be boring, Hermann. (*Goering produces papers from his satchel.*)

GOERING: I was attending a meeting with Field Marshall von Ludendorff when we received confirmation of your eightieth kill. Some dispatch runner saw it. Exciting. I rushed over with the confirmation. I'm a glutton for hearing good news.

RICHTHOFEN: Do you think if we let Hermann present us with the confirmation he'll go home, Karl?

BODENSHATZ: Definitely, Rittmeister.

GOERING: I'm sorry, if I'm being troublesome, I'll—

RICHTHOFEN: Please, Hermann, read the witness report and go home before I drown myself. Read.

GOERING: (*Reads.*) 3:33 p.m., April 20, 1918. Saw all red Fokker Dreidecker shoot down enemy machine in flames between the lines at Bonnay; pilot killed. Upon examination of the wreckage the aeroplane was identified as a French Spad. The aero—

RICHTHOFEN: It wasn't a Spad. It was a Sopwith Camel. (*An awkward pause.*)

GOERING: Ah. The witness must have been mistaken. It doesn't—

RICHTHOFEN: Let me see that. (*Goering hands him the witness report.*)

BODENSHATZ: It's only a technicality, Rittmeister.

RICHTHOFEN: I know it was a Sopwith Camel. Which idiot made this report? Who is the witness?

GOERING: One of Ludendorff's dispatch runners witnessed the kill from the earth. A Lance Corporal. A nobody.

RICHTHOFEN: It wasn't a Spad. I'm sure it was a Sopwith Camel.

BODENSHATZ: Rittmeister, a man of your reputation doesn't need witness reports. (*Richthofen jumps out of the tub. Goering and Bodenshatz furiously dry him with towels.*)

RICHTHOFEN: Boots! Trousers! Jacket!

GOERING: I'm sure Berlin will accept your word.

RICHTHOFEN: I don't want them to accept my word.

BODENSHATZ: You really shouldn't go out, Rittmeister. You fly for your holiday in the—

RICHTHOFEN: There will be no holiday until I have a piece of kill eighty tucked
safely inside my breast pocket.

GOERING & BODENSHATZ: Yes, Rittmeister. (*They dress him.*)

SCENE 14

(*No Man's Land. 6:30 p.m., April 20th. Battle sounds. Rain. The Three Women
pedal back to the East on their bicycles, with their paintings, and musical instruments
strapped to their backs. The Lance Corporal leaps out of the shell hole where he's been
hiding; and stands directly in the Women's path. The three of them plough into him
and there is a small accident.*)

LANCE CORPORAL: You're not gypsies. You're German women, aren't you? I'm
sorry. It's just that we don't want gypsy tricksters in Germany. But you're
real Germans, aren't you? Are you injured? You're escaped prisoners return-
ing to the Fatherland. Where is your home? Of course you cannot speak,
you've been tortured by the French. They've removed your tongues. Forgive
me. I won't humiliate you by asking questions. (*The Lance Corporal rummages
through their belongings. He finds the bottle of wine and keeps it.*) You're noble
women, I can see that. Artists. Musicians. And mothers as well, no doubt.
Allow me to say that you ladies are the backbone of Germany. Do you play
Wagner? Never mind. Follow the road into the East until you come to a
hotel where an eagle stands on a sign post. Field Marshall von Ludendorff
will take care of you, I can promise. I delivered a report there earlier. It seemed to cause a lot of excitement. There was talk of a party. Perhaps you'll
entertain. I'd escort you myself but I'm expecting a visitor here tonight. I
have to wait for him. I wish you could play me a birthday song. No time. On
another birthday, perhaps. Go now. Thank you for my birthday gift.
Ladies. (*He drinks out of the wine bottle. The Women mount their bicycles and
ride out of sight in the East. The Lance Corporal walks to his shell hole. Music.
The late Raymond-Barker and N.C.O. Secull appear together, floating in space
above No Man's Land.*)

ENGLAND – THE U.K.

RAYMOND-BARKER & SECULL:
WHAT IS HEAVEN LIKE YOU ASK.
DO ANGELS SING AND PLAY?
HOW'S THE WEATHER? ARE DOGS ALLOWED THERE?
HOW DOES GOD DESCRIBE HIS KINGDOM?

HE HAS THIS TO SAY. –
IT RESEMBLES (AND VERY CLOSELY)
ENGLAND, THE U.K.

IT'S FOGGY AND DIM AND THE HEDGES ARE TRIM.
YES, IT'S VERY LIKE MERRY ENGLAND.
A PUB ON EVERY CLOUD.
ARE THE LADIES ALLOWED?
YES, EXCEPT ON SUNDAY.
BUT EVEN THEN WITH GENTLEMEN.
AND THERE'S A LAD FOR EVERY LASSIE.
HEAVEN HAS ITS PARLIAMENT
WHERE THE M.P.'S ALL AGREE.
THE HOUSE OF LORDS ONLY HAS ONE MEMBER.
HERE A SOUL WHO'S CIVILIZED
ENJOYS ETERNITY.
YET STRANGELY THERE IS ANOTHER
HEAVEN LIKE DEUTSCHLAND.
WELL, BLESS ME.

(*The Lance Corporal reappears, popping up out of his shell hole and looking off to the East.*)

LANCE CORPORAL:
STAND UP. THE FATHERLAND WILL COUNT
ON YOU MY SON.
STAND UP FOR THE FATHERLAND
AND NEVER REST UNTIL THE WAR IS WON
AND EVERYONE IS ONE.

RAYMOND-BARKER & SECULL: (*Floating above, facing the East.*)
EVERY SOLDIER'S WELCOME HERE
THE MEEK AND THE COWARDLY.
PICTURE YOUR PERFECT, PRIVATE HEAVEN.
WHAT'S IT LIKE YOU WANT TO ASK,
JUST STEP ACROSS AND SEE.
FIND AND FOLLOW YOUR FAVORITE HERO.
IT'S HEAVEN – THE U.K.,
IT'S LIKE FRANCE AND JAPAN,
IT'S LIKE SPAIN AND DEUTSCHLAND.
IT'S O.K., IT'S O.K., IT'S O.K.

SCENE 15

(The East. 6:45 p.m., April 20th. The basket of an observation balloon. The sound of wind. Goering and Richthofen are standing in the balloon basket which rises rapidly into the air. Goering and Richthofen wear military hats and leather rain capes and look to the West through field glasses. The balloon basket continues to rise until Goering pulls on a guideline and the basket stops and hangs in the air.)

GOERING: *(Looking through field glasses.)* He thinks we're homosexuals.

RICHTHOFEN: *(Looking to Goering.)* Who does?

GOERING: Karl Bodenshatz.

RICHTHOFEN: That's preposterous.

GOERING: I could see it in his eyes when I was drying your skin. Not everyone in the world can understand the love one man can feel for another, great man. The feeling is above sexuality.

RICHTHOFEN: Bodenshatz knows that I like French women.

GOERING: Men all over Germany feel this way about you.

RICHTHOFEN: And the women?

GOERING: I don't understand.

RICHTHOFEN: The women are smarter than the men. They're not so easily duped.

GOERING: But this one man that shines, stands out from the crowd . . .

RICHTHOFEN: The only way for you to stand out from the crowd, Hermann, would be to dress everyone in the crowd the same.

GOERING: I wasn't thinking of myself. I could serve a man like you.

RICHTHOFEN: Search. Don't talk. Observe. What do you see?

GOERING: Yes, it's quite light out, isn't it? I feel this is all my fault.

RICHTHOFEN: What do you see?

GOERING: A burned out farmhouse.

RICHTHOFEN: Yes. Beyond that.

GOERING: Part of a church steeple.

RICHTHOFEN: That's the sector. Bonnay.

GOERING: Barbed wire. Tree stumps. Bodies. I think I can even see dead bodies. I have good eyes.

RICHTHOFEN: Do you see a bunker with a tin roof?

GOERING: Yes.

RICHTHOFEN: Look northeast of the bunker.

GOERING: Wreckage.

RICHTHOFEN: Yes.

GOERING: Do you find me attractive?

RICHTHOFEN: Pardon.

GOERING: Do you find my subservience attractive?

RICHTHOFEN: Hermann. *(Pause.)* You're not a French woman, are you?

GOERING: My eyes are very good. It is the wreckage of an aeroplane.

RICHTHOFEN: Yes.

GOERING: A Sopwith Camel.

RICHTHOFEN: Are you certain?

GOERING: Absolutely. I have very good eyes.

RICHTHOFEN: It's definitely not a French Spad?

GOERING: It's a Sopwith Camel. Your eightieth kill.

RICHTHOFEN: But you cannot be certain, Hermann. To be certain one would have to examine the machine. And I will be certain. Take me down. (*The balloon basket descends.*)

SCENE 16

(*The West. 7:35 p.m., April 20th. The machine gun nest of Buie and Evans. They sit looking out. Buie has field glasses.*)

BUIE: Did you see the balloons? Hundreds of 'em. Up at sunset. I'd have liked to pop them all, pop, pop, pop, just like that if Lewis wasn't bust.

EVANS: I didn't see any balloons.

BUIE: Put on your specs.

EVANS: I like you better when I'm blind, Buie. You're less scary somehow with just the voice. (*Buie points the beam of their searchlight at the body of Raymond-Barker in No Man's Land.*)

BUIE: What're we going to do about him?

EVANS: What?

BUIE: The flyer. We can't just leave him there. It's not nice.

EVANS: How can you be sure he's still there?

BUIE: 'Course he's still there. Where could he go? Dead people do not as a rule go for walks.

EVANS: Maybe he's gone to heaven.

BUIE: I'd suggest two minutes of silence if you could stay shut up for that long. 'Course you won't.

EVANS: Right. We ought to pay last respects.

BUIE: Well, go on. Make him a speech. Then we'll dispose of the human remains. (*Evans, delighted, prepares a major address.*)

EVANS: Well, we didn't know him, did we, really till after he fell from the sky so there's that. He was a flyer. R. Raymond-whoever. But we feel bad about it and so on behalf of King George and God and everybody—

BUIE: What a stinker.

EVANS: All right, you do it if it's such a stinker. Go on. Do it.

BUIE: No, you're best. Just get on with it, Reverend your grace.

EVANS: Well, we're sorry, that's all. And Buie here, he's going to kill a Fritz flyer for revenge and make us heroes so there's that.

BUIE: Don't make promises. Just tell him we're going to bury him proper.

EVANS: Well, that sounds like a promise. And he can't hear me, stupid.

BUIE: I know.

EVANS: (*Angrily.*) Amen.

BUIE: (*Angrily.*) Amen. (*Pause.*)

EVANS: So what'd you think of his eulogy?

BUIE: It was a bit vague.

EVANS: Well, of course it was vague. I didn't even know him, did I? So I didn't have much to work with. Now, Secull I could do. Although, frankly speaking, I always thought Secull was lying about playing the piano. I shall miss him on the great stage. Now we're a duet, you and me. (*The sound of Secull playing piano.*)

BUIE: I wish I was home catching fish.

EVANS: Oh, you'll have to do better than that. You've got to have big dreams, Buie.

BUIE: We should bury the flyer.

EVANS: He'll just get blown up again. Just leave him be.

BUIE: Somebody's got to do it.

EVANS: I don't mind burying them once. It's the bombs coming along and digging them back up that I resent. I had to bury Maxwell five times before he'd stay in the ground.

BUIE: I'll do it alone if you won't help.

EVANS: Wait. It's too light yet. There's a storm coming. Big. We'll go out in the storm under cover, dig it, drop it, fill it in. Are you satisfied now?

BUIE: Of course not. (*A bomb lands behind the oak tree. Evans ducks. Buie looks out at the corpse of Raymond-Barker.*)

SCENE 17

(*The East. 7:50 p.m., April 20th. Richthofen's room. Goering is cranking Richthofen's phonograph. Bodenshatz sits and watches. The three women's voices come from the phonograph. Goering hums along.*)

SAVE THE LAST DANCE

THE THREE WOMEN: (*On the phonograph.*)
JUST LISTEN TO THIS UNIQUE DEMONSTRATION
FROM THE PEOPLE AT KRUPP PHONOGRAPH, BERLIN.
BEFORE YOU EVEN KNOW IT, YOU'RE SINGING WITH A SWEET
SYMPHONY. HI SINGER! TRY SINGING TO THIS!

GOERING: (*Sings with the women's voices on the phonograph.*)
EVEN THE KAISER CALLS YOUR NAME
THE PHONO GOES ROUND AND AROUND AGAIN.
BUT NOTHING MEANS NOTHING. IF YOU DON'T GIVE IT ALL
    FOR LOVE.

EVEN YOUR LIFE FOR LOVE.

CROWDS OF A MILLION SMILE AT YOU.
YOU'D LOVE TO SMILE BACK BUT THERE'S TOO MUCH TO DO.
IT'S EASY TO STUMBLE, IT'S EASY TO FALL
IF YOU DON'T HAVE A LOVE FOR IT ALL.

(*Music from the phonograph continues.*)

BODENSHATZ: You sing very well.
GOERING: I was a choir boy.
BODENSHATZ: You remind me . . .
GOERING: Of what?
BODENSHATZ: Of how long it's been since I've danced.
GOERING: I'm sorry.
BODENSHATZ: No, no. It's been years, that's all.
GOERING: How would you like to dance?
BODENSHATZ: With who?
GOERING: The Rittmeister will be out searching for another hour or two.
BODENSHATZ: Dance with you?
GOERING: You're perfectly safe with me. Come. Do you waltz, Oberleutnant?
BODENSHATZ: I don't know, I—
GOERING: Come. (*They waltz about the room. Goering leads.*)
BODENSHATZ: I feel so clumsy with you. You dance so very well. (*Bodenshatz closes his eyes. They dance.*)
GOERING: We must reach him. We must get results.
BODENSHATZ: What does von Ludendorff suggest we do?
GOERING & BODENSHATZ: (*With the women's voices.*)
YOU JOIN THE PARTY LATE IN THE NIGHT.
FROM UPSTAIRS IN THE BEDROOM WHERE YOU'VE WON THE
FIGHT.
COMES A VOICE SOFTLY,
SAVE THE LAST DANCE FOR ME.
SAVE THE LAST DANCE FOR ME.

(*Bodenshatz and Goering are still dancing when the phonograph stops.*)

SCENE 18

(*No Man's Land. 9:00 p.m., April 20th. Rain. Darkness. Rumbles of thunder. Distant shelling. Richthofen appears out of the East pushing a motorcycle out of the roadway and into the bog of No Man's Land. He leans the motorcycle on the kickstand and looks to the North. The Lance Corporal pokes his head out of his shell hole, unnoticed by Richthofen, holding a piece of meat in one hand and the wine bottle that he has stolen from the women in the other. Richthofen carries his walking stick.*)

LANCE CORPORAL: Can I help you?

RICHTHOFEN: (*Wheeling around.*) Stand away! Where did you come from? At ease.

LANCE CORPORAL: I'm very honored.

RICHTHOFEN: Why are you here?

LANCE CORPORAL: I'm German.

RICHTHOFEN: You sound Austrian. Come here where I can see you.

LANCE CORPORAL: Sixteenth Bavarian Reserve Infantry under Field Marshal von Ludendorff. (*A shell lands nearby.*)

RICHTHOFEN: You'd better move along. We're gassing this sector before morning.

LANCE CORPORAL: Let me stay and assist you. What are you looking for?

RICHTHOFEN: Where are your comrades?

LANCE CORPORAL: I have no comrades. I'm a lone wolf.

RICHTHOFEN: State your rank.

LANCE CORPORAL: I'm a solo dispatch runner, a Lance Corporal. I was starving in the trenches. I've been hunting for food. All I could find was part of a dead mule. I've cooked it nicely but it turns my stomach. Would you like some of my wine. It's my birthday. I'd be honored to have you at my party.

RICHTHOFEN: Happy birthday. Move along now. (*Rifle fire.*)

LANCE CORPORAL: Thank you, Baron. (*He starts to go. Richthofen stops him.*)

RICHTHOFEN: How do you know who I am?

LANCE CORPORAL: Every German knows you, Baron. Photographs of the Red Knight are all over the newspapers.

RICHTHOFEN: How long have you been here?

LANCE CORPORAL: Just a few moments. Only the rats come out at night. It's very dangerous. (*Richthofen takes the Lance Corporal by the arm and points to the North.*)

RICHTHOFEN: Tell me. What's that pile of rubble? Over there, Corporal, you can see it, can't you?

LANCE CORPORAL: Ah, yes. Once it was an enemy flying machine. It's quite fresh. Did you shoot it down?

RICHTHOFEN: How do you know it's an enemy machine? It could be almost anything, couldn't it? (*The Lance Corporal magically produces a British flying insignia and unfolds it.*)

LANCE CORPORAL: (*Giving Richthofen the insignia.*) I tore this from the wing. I hope it's permitted. It's just a memento. I don't want any trouble.

RICHTHOFEN: What type of machine was it?

LANCE CORPORAL: I'm no expert.

RICHTHOFEN: In your humble opinion.

LANCE CORPORAL: I could only guess. My guess would be a Sopwith Camel. That's a name I know.

RICHTHOFEN: Excellent. If you know it's a Sopwith Camel, why did you report it as a Spad?

LANCE CORPORAL: I don't understand.

RICHTHOFEN: Of course you understand. A certain Lance Corporal misreported this kill. That would be you, wouldn't it? How did you know it was my kill?

LANCE CORPORAL: I didn't know. I asked you.

RICHTHOFEN: You watched the air fight, examined the wreckage, misresported the kill. Why?

LANCE CORPORAL: Is a "Spad" a type of enemy flying machine?

RICHTHOFEN: Why did you lie?

LANCE CORPORAL: (*Hurt.*) You think I lied, Baron?

RICHTHOFEN: Of course you lied.

LANCE CORPORAL: I would never lie to you. Look! Look at this! I have the real trophy for you. (*He bends down into a shell hole and pulls up the corpse of Raymond-Barker by the scruff of the neck. He crouches beside the body holding it up like a marionette.*) This one must have jumped from the machine. His body made this crater. I would have given anything to have been your witness. But I was not. I can hardly believe that you're here with me. I shouldn't say this but you're really quite beautiful. I would never rob you of this victory.

RICHTHOFEN: (*Turning away.*) I didn't get to see his face in the air.

LANCE CORPORAL: (*Holding back Raymond-Barker's head.*) There's something wrong with his face?

RICHTHOFEN: He looks like someone I know.

LANCE CORPORAL: A friend?

RICHTHOFEN: A cousin.

LANCE CORPORAL: A flyer?

RICHTHOFEN: He takes his first flight in the morning.

LANCE CORPORAL: Perhaps now there will be two Red Knights.

RICHTHOFEN: Perhaps one day there will be none. One day we will fly without bullets and machines. In the new age we will fly like birds. In the meantime, here we are, scavengers combing the mud for pieces of meat.

LANCE CORPORAL: Perhaps the Red Knight will usher in the new age.

RICHTHOFEN: (*With self-disgust.*) The Red Knight is too busy chasing victories in the rain, quarreling over a fool's mistake. Corporal, I don't want to have you arrested. I'm prepared to forget about this if you'll simply admit to your mistake.

LANCE CORPORAL: (*Dropping the body back in the crater.*) Whoever misreported your victory did it intentionally.

RICHTHOFEN: What do you mean?

LANCE CORPORAL: They recognized your machine, misreported the kill, knew that you would come here to confirm it in your rage, waited for you. Your habits are public domain.

RICHTHOFEN: Who would do this?

LANCE CORPORAL: Any one of the thousands of Germans who are cursed with cowardly generals and politicians. Hundreds of soldiers kill themselves in the trenches each day, knowing the war is lost, less afraid of dying than living in a defeated Germany, not even daring to dream of the new age you speak of.

RICHTHOFEN: Why would this person want me to come here?

LANCE CORPORAL: (*Inspired.*) To meet with you. To encourage you to prepare yourself. To implore you to read Hegel, Nietzsche, Schopenhauer. To remind you that you are a Prussian, a baron, our hero, our Siegfried. To inform you that we are hungry. To teach you that you are the only hope for leadership when this war ends and the real war in Germany begins. To beg you to save yourself for the sake of your higher duties.

RICHTHOFEN: But the real question, Corporal, is where is this person now? (*Pause.*)

LANCE CORPORAL: How would I know?

RICHTHOFEN: You would know because you, Corporal, are the person.

LANCE CORPORAL: If my mission was such a great one I would surely take full credit.

RICHTHOFEN: (*Smiling.*) Why should I believe you?

LANCE CORPORAL: (*Smiling.*) Why should I lie? (*Richthofen begins to leave. The Lance Corporal takes the silk scarf from the body of Raymond-Barker.*) Wait. Take this as a souvenir. It has the letter "R" embroidered on it.

RICHTHOFEN: No. If you fly with a piece of your victim's clothing, the dead flyer will haunt you in the cockpit. (*Richthofen pushes the motorcycle.*)

LANCE CORPORAL: Give the scarf to your cousin. Teach him to rise above superstition. Take the scarf.

RICHTHOFEN: No. The scarf is bad luck. But I'll hang the English insignia on my wall to remember you by. Good hunting, Corporal. (*Richthofen disappears into the East pushing the motorcycle. As soon as he's out of sight there is the sound of an engine starting and moving off into the East. The Lance Corporal is left holding the scarf.*)

IF I HAVE THE WILL (REPRISE)

LANCE CORPORAL:
BUT ONE IDEA COMES.
MY MOTHER GIVES BIRTH TO A WOLF.
TWENTY-NINE YEARS AGO.
THE INVISIBLE WOMEN:
HAPPY GERMANY

(*The Lance Corporal sets the half-full wine bottle down by the body, tosses the scarf across his shoulder and starts off into the East following Richthofen on foot.*)

SCENE 19

(*No Man's Land. 9:35 p.m., April 20th. The storm passes directly overhead. Heavy thunder. Buie and Evans clamber over the sandbags and out of the machine gun nest in the West and cross into No Man's Land with shovels. They creep over the body of Raymond-Barker.*)

EVANS: Not half awake. Fucking rain.

BUIE: Look at him now, all stiffened out and bloated.

EVANS: (*Finding a crater.*) What luck. A marvel. A miracle. What have I found Buie! God himself has dug us a nice grave. Buie, it's our lucky day. (*Thunder, they duck, reappear.*)

BUIE: Where's the silk scarf, then? Did you rat him without me looking?

EVANS: For a scarf?

BUIE: Well, you're a sneaky little devil, we know that.

EVANS: I didn't.

BUIE: Someone did.

EVANS: Let's stuff Mr. Raymond in the hole, digger, it's teeming mules. (*They pick up the body and drop it into the crater which is about three feet deep. They begin to cover the body with dirt. Meanwhile, Richthofen has reappeared on another part of the roadway, travelling to the East on the motorcycle. He stops, takes out a map and unfolds the British insignia which the Lance Corporal has given him. Music. Buie and Evans bury the body in No Man's Land. Simultaneously Richthofen makes his decision on the roadway. They are in separate locations.*)

HERE WE ARE

RICHTHOFEN:
WHAT AM I TO DO WITH YOU?
THE SAME OLD HABITS.
WHAT AM I TO DO WITH YOU?
LATELY I'VE BEEN STANDING IN MY OWN WAY,
BOUND ADDICTIVELY.
THESE OLD OPINIONS MAKE NO SENSE
I'VE LOST MY CONFIDENCE.

(*No Man's Land. Buie and Evans are digging. The music continues.*)

BUIE: (*Stopping.*) Evans. Do me a favor. Cover his face with the dirt.

EVANS: (*Stopping.*) Why me?

BUIE: Why not you?

EVANS: I did his feet. (*They each have a shovel full of dirt. They look down at the corpse.*)

BUIE: I'd rather not do his face, do you mind? It's kind of private and you did do the eulogy, Inch.

EVANS: Right. So you do this.

BUIE: One of us has to.

EVANS: If you can't throw dirt in the face of a corpse how do you ever hope to kill anybody? You do it, Buie. Do it. Do it. (*Buie throws a shovelful on the face of Raymond-Barker.*)

HERE WE ARE (*Continued.*)

RICHTHOFEN: (*By the motorcycle.*)
EVERYONE'S FACELESS, THE WHOLE HUMAN RACE,
BUT THERE'S NO CHOICE. HERE WE ARE ON THE GROUND.

WE MAY WISH FOR TRIPS ON THE FLYING SHIPS,
BUT WHERE ARE WE? HERE WE ARE ON THE GROUND.

IS EVERY MOVE I MAKE ACCIDENTAL?
IS EVERY WORD I SAY PRECONDITIONED AND ORNAMENTAL?

YOU TURN TO A PAGE FROM AN EARLIER PAGE,
BUT THERE'S NO CLUE. HERE WE ARE. NOW IS HERE.

WE SEE WHAT WE CHOOSE BUT THE SIGHT WE REFUSE
TO REALLY SEE IS THAT WE'RE HERE. HERE WE ARE.

BUIE & EVANS: (*Under Richthofen's last two stanzas.*)
ARE WE HERE NOW? HERE WE ARE. ONE CONDITION.
WHERE ARE WE NOW? ON THE GROUND. HERE WE ARE NOW.
ON THE GROUND. SAFE AND SOUND DOWN ON THE GROUND.

RICHTHOFEN:
AND THERE'S NO TIME TO WEIGH EACH CONDITION.
THERE'S COUNTLESS PROBLEMS WITH EACH NEW VISION
BUT THERE'S ONE DECISION.

WE'RE LOCKED INTO FATE AND IT MAY BE TOO LATE,
BUT THERE'S ONE CHANCE. HERE WE ARE.
ON THE GROUND.

(*The motorcycle suddenly rises from the ground and Richthofen flies off and disappears in the East. The Lance Corporal appears on the roadway, wearing the scarf and follows Richthofen off to the East on foot. Secull appears at the piano.*)

BUIE: (*Still digging.*)
MY MIND KEEPS SLIPPING AND SHIPPING ME OFF

ON FISHING TRIPS. BUT HERE WE ARE ON DRY LAND.

EVANS:
I FEEL LIKE SHIT AND THE WORLD'S GONE MAD
AND IT SEEMS A DREAM. WAKE AND SEE.
ARE WE HERE . . .

SECULL: (*Under Buie and Evans's stanzas.*)
WHERE ARE WE NOW? HERE WE ARE. ONE DIMENSION.
HERE WE ARE NOW. IN THE GROUND. HERE . . .

BUIE, EVANS & SECULL:
. . . WE ARE NOW. ON THE GROUND.
HERE WE ARE. WE'RE HERE. WE'RE HERE. WE'RE HERE.

(*Buie and Evans have finished filling in the grave.*)

EVANS: (*Grins.*) There we are, Buie. (*A flash of lightning and a crack of thunder. Evans dashes for the bunker, diving over the sand bags and ducking into the dugout like a jack rabbit. The music resumes. Buie looks down at the bottle of wine the Lance Corporal has left behind, snatches up the bottle and runs after Evans.*)

BUIE: (*In amazement.*) Inch! Inch!

SCENE 20

(*The East. 10:40 p.m., April 20th. Richthofen's room is barely illuminated. Richthofen enters the room in the dim. Pause.*)

RICHTHOFEN: Karl! (*Light. Bodenshatz pops out of the laundry basket like a jack-in-the-box and Goering leaps up from the bath tub where he's been hiding with his ukelele. The three louvered doors burst open revealing the Three Women. They've bathed, dressed up and painted themselves. Everyone wears a party hat.*)

ALL: Surprise! (*They blow little party horns and throw confetti and streamers. Awkward silence.*)

RICHTHOFEN: (*Icily.*) It was in fact a Sopwith Camel. The eightieth kill is official. (*Richthofen throws the insignia at their feet. Goering encourages the Women to play their instruments. The song is obviously rehearsed. Bodenshatz seems slightly embarrassed. Richthofen watches them and listens sternly.*)

CONGRATULATIONS

GOERING, BODENSHATZ & THE WOMEN:
CONGRATULATIONS! ON YOUR EIGHTIETH KILL.
YOU'VE ALWAYS DONE IT. YOU ALWAYS WILL.
AT LEAST WE HOPE YOU'LL STILL BE HERE, DEAR,
RAT-TAT-TATTLE AND HE SCREAMS IN PAIN.
HAVE ANOTHER GLASS OF CHAMPAGNE.

CONGRATULATIONS! WE'VE BEEN WAITING THE WORD.

AND NOW WE'VE GOT IT, NOW THAT WE'VE HEARD.
WE SURELY KNOW YOU WERE SINCERE, DEAR.
RAT-TAT-TATTLE AS YOU BAG A GOOSE.
HAVE ANOTHER GLASS OF CHARTREUSE.

WE HEAR THAT RAT-TAT-TATTLE AND WE KNOW IT'S OUR
  MAN.
RAT-TAT-TATTLE WITH A SHIFT OF THE HAND.
RAT-TAT-TATTLE YES HE'S UP AND AWAY.
RAT-TAT-TATTLE NUMBER EIGHTY TODAY.

IT'S QUITE UNIQUE, YOU CAN'T COMPARE IT.
HAVE ANOTHER GLASS OF – HAVE ANOTHER GLASS OF –
HAVE ANOTHER GLASS OF CLARET.
CONGRATULATIONS! AS YOU MASTER THE SKY
MAY YOU LIVE FOREVER! MAY YOU NEVER DIE.
YOUR EYES ARE CLEAR SO NEVER FEAR, DEAR
RAT-TAT-TATTLE AND IT'S THERE YOU GO.
HAVE ANOTHER GLASS OF PERNOD.
HAVE ANOTHER GLASS OF CHAMPAGNE.
TRY THE CHERRY BRANDY AS THE AFTERTASTE IS DANDY.
HAVE ANOTHER TANK FULL OF GAS.

(*Silence. Richthofen claps very slowly.*)

GOERING: (*Nervously.*) Do you like it? Really?
BODENSHATZ: (*Nervously.*) Hermann composed it.
GOERING: For the occasion.
BODENSHATZ: I think he's at least as good as the Americans.
GOERING: I would like to be an American song writer, Rittmeister.
BODENSHATZ: General Ludendorff sent the women.
GOERING: Musicians for the party along with three cases of champagne.
BODENSHATZ: The women don't speak a word of German.
GOERING: We think they're refugees.
BODENSHATZ: Hermann taught them the words to the song, how would you say. . . ?
GOERING: Syllabically.
BODENSHATZ: It's marvelous. They imitate the sounds like apes.
GOERING: I've named them the Western European Miniature Peasant Orchestra.
BODENSHATZ: I think they're French, Rittmeister. They're not very good musicians.
GOERING: But they've all got marvelous teeth. You might have noticed when they were singing; not many bad teeth. (*Goering smiles nervously. The Women smile back. A pause.*)

RICHTHOFEN: So tell me, gentlemen. What's the occasion?

GOERING: Yes. It's obvious, isn't it? To celebrate the death of another English flyer. ((*Richthofen puts his arm around Bodenshatz.*)

RICHTHOFEN: Karl, I'm afraid I remain slightly confused. Why should this kill warrant a party? You see my point. I've shot down many others. Why all of this sudden fuss?

BODENSHATZ: Yes. Well.

GOERING: Why not? What's wrong with a little sudden fuss? (*He laughs. The Women laugh.*)

BODENSHATZ: Tell him, Hermann.

GOERING: Yes, I will tell you then. I will risk my reputation and my future to tell you. Will we not, Oberleutnant?

BODENSHATZ: We will, Oberleutnant.

GOERING: We intend this to be your retirement party.

BODENSHATZ: Retirement party, yes.

GOERING: It is a time for moral courage.

BODENSHATZ: Germany has been battered and beaten.

GOERING: You will be badly needed in the aftermath. Where does he belong, Karl?

BODENSHATZ: Your place is in the political arena.

GOERING: You should be in Hamburg or Munich.

BODENSHATZ: They'd love you in Munich.

GOERING: And if you can win Bavarians you can—

BODENSHATZ: The time has come for unity.

GOERING: Our spokesman must be ruthless. Our spokesman must be a man of high birth.

BODENSHATZ: Our spokesman must be a man with a good military record.

GOERING: This severely limits the field.

BODENSHATZ: You, Rittmeister, will be our spokesman.

GOERING: And on behalf of the Fatherland we celebrate your retirement from the circus tonight. (*Silence. Richthofen smiles.*)

BODENSHATZ: In all humility, Rittmeister—

GOERING: We take a great risk.

BODENSHATZ: You must realize how we love you.

GOERING: For this outburst, for this liberty we've taken—

BODENSHATZ: You could have us demoted.

GOERING: Disgraced.

RICHTHOFEN: Even shot.

GOERING: Well, yes, I suppose you could.

BODENSHATZ: Pardon.

RICHTHOFEN: I'll have you shot for treason.

BODENSHATZ: I don't understand, Rittmeister.

RICHTHOFEN: It's clear that execution is the only honorable course.

GOERING: (*Laughing.*) Good joke. I beg to ask, Rittmeister, where are your witnesses?

RICHTHOFEN: The women are my witnesses.

BODENSHATZ: Rittmeister, perhaps you misunderstand.

RICHTHOFEN: (*Producing his pistol.*) Why not do it now? Just shake your heads if there's any disagreement, ladies.

GOERING: They don't understand.

RICHTHOFEN: The ladies aren't shaking their heads.

BODENSHATZ: You're joking.

RICHTHOFEN: Kneel, gentlemen. Side by side. Now. I don't believe I've ever shot anyone on solid ground. (*They kneel.*)

GOERING: I sincerely apologize. I am sorry. You've heard me say it now.

BODENSHATZ: Rittmeister, perhaps we could talk about—(*Goering begins to stand.*)

GOERING: This is insane. I won't grovel even for—(*Richtnofen places the pistol to Goering's temple forcing him to return to his knees.*)

RICHTHOFEN: We'll only waste one bullet, gentlemen. As you know the Fatherland is running shy of ammunition. Don't worry, Karl. The bullet will reach your brain almost instantly. I'm sure it will pass through Hermann's skull like so much porridge.

GOERING: I'm going to be sick.

RICHTHOFEN: Heads together! (*Bodenshatz and Goering press temples and cheeks together while kneeling on the floor.*)

GOERING: I don't know anything. Karl said that—

RICHTHOFEN: (*Holding the barrel to Bodenshatz's head.*) Gentlemen, good night.

BODENSHATZ: No, please.

GOERING: I love you. (*Richthofen squeezes the trigger. The pistol clicks harmlessly. Bodenshatz and Goering remain frozen.*)

RICHTHOFEN: Oblivion. What do you think, gentlemen? Will I slay them in the political arena? (*The Women laugh and applaud.*)

GOERING: My God.

BODENSHATZ: (*Laughing with fright.*) Yes, you're certainly good at it.

GOERING: I'm sorry. I don't understand the joke. It amuses you maybe—

BODENSHATZ: Hermann, it doesn't matter.

GOERING: It isn't funny.

BODENSHATZ: Hermann, he's agreed.

GOERING: He's agreed? You've agreed.

RICHTHOFEN: (*Quietly.*) I have taken my last flight into combat. I'll go to Berlin tomorrow and begin to speak to the politicians about peace and the new age.

GOERING: We've done it. He's agreed.

BODENSHATZ: Champagne!

GOERING: And food. Bring out the food.

BODENSHATZ: Bravo. We've done it.

GOERING: We'll be going down in history.

RICHTHOFEN: Don't flatter yourselves, gentlemen. Someone else showed me the way. I met my messenger from Providence in the field tonight.

BODENSHATZ: Oh, a messenger from Providence. Well, Hermann and I will share the political credit if you don't mind. What was the archangel's name? (*Goering opens a bottle of champagne.*)

GOERING: I love you all.

BODENSHATZ: My poor friend Hermann. The Rittmeister gave you quite a little chill. He has such an acidic sense of humor.

GOERING: I knew all along.

BODENSHATZ: Did you? I'd never have guessed, Hermann.

GOERING: I'm a master at learning new games. We should get the women to paint our portraits. Did you see their work outside, Rittmeister?

BODENSHATZ: We have no canvasses for them to paint, Hermann.

GOERING: We'll find something. I'll go first. I love the arts.

BODENSHATZ: Perhaps we've changed the course of the century tonight. I find that frightening.

RICHTHOFEN: Three little men in some back room?

GOERING: (*Quietly.*) Yes, I think that's exactly how things begin, Rittmeister.

BODENSHATZ: Long live von Richthofen.

GOERING: Our fuhrer.

BODENSHATZ: Our fuhrer.

ALL: Our fuhrer. (*They group together around Moritz the stuffed dog. Goering is drinking champagne. The Women play their instruments. Wolfram joins them at the doors to the bunkroom. What begins as a solemn occasion builds into a celebration.*)

STAND UP FOR THE FATHERLAND

BODENSHATZ:
GIVE US YOUR DIVINE HAND.
PEACE ACROSS THE RHINELAND.
PEACE TO YOU, PEACE TO ME.
WE REGRET WE WON'T FORGET IT.
SING ME AN OLD WORKING MAN'S SONG
AND WAIT UNTIL OUR CHILDREN GROW STRONG.

(*The song becomes an anthem.*)

AND WE MARCHED INTO BATTLE TO THE CRY OF VICTORY
SPILLING BLOOD ON THE SACRED BORDERLAND OF GERMANY
BUT OUR MASTERS WERE FAITHLESS AND OUR GENERALS
COWARDLY.

IN THE END WE WILL TRIUMPH FOR OUR NOBLE ANCESTRY.

BODENSHATZ, GOERING AND WOLFRAM:
> STAND UP. THE FATHERLAND WILL COUNT ON YOU MY SON.
> STAND UP FOR THE FATHERLAND AND NEVER REST
> UNTIL THE WAR IS WON. EVERY SON FOLLOWS ONE. SHALL BE DONE.

ALL:
> AND WE FELL BACK TO MUNICH THEY WERE SLEEPING IN THE STREET.
> AND WE WEPT WITH OUR MOTHERS FELT THE SHAME OF OUR DEFEAT.
> EVERY STEP GATHERS ANGER EVERY STEP THAT WE RETREAT.
> WHEN YOU TURN GRANT NO MERCY TO RESISTANCE THAT YOU MEET.
> STAND UP. THE FATHERLAND WILL COUNT ON YOU MY SON.
> STAND UP FOR THE FATHERLAND AND NEVER REST
> UNTIL THE WAR IS WON. EVERY SON FOLLOWS ONE.
> THEY'RE UPON US. BUT WE PROMISE – SHALL BE DONE.

(*Outside, during the song the Lance Corporal walks up to the window and stands in the rain looking into the room with the silk scarf around his neck. He watches the party through the window. No one sees him watching. Darkness.*)

ACT TWO

SCENE 1

(*The West. 11:49 p.m., April 20th. Above the machine gun nest of Buie and Evans, by the tree floats the late N.C.O. Secull at the piano. Music. From out of the bog in No Man's Land a muddy hand emerges and stretches its fingers. The hand grows into an arm which is joined by another arm, tossing up handfuls of dirt. A head is soon followed by the top of a torso. R. Raymond-Barker is digging himself out of the grave. He climbs up from out of the earth and lies, unburied, in the muck.*)

SITTING IN THE GARDEN

SECULL:
 BEFORE I LEFT SYDNEY I TURNED TO ME DADDY
 AND THIS IS WHAT ME DADDY HE SAID.
 IT'S REALLY VERY SIMPLE,
 YOU COME OUT LIVING OR YOU COME OUT DEAD.

(*Buie and Evans are having a quiet party in the machine gun nest. They sit on the sandbags elegantly caked in mud, bathing in the moonlight. Evans drinks wine from the bottle.*)

BUIE AND EVANS:
 IF I WAS A GIRL I'D BE SURE TO MARRY YOU
 SITTING IN THE GARDEN.
 FOR THREE LONG YEARS JUST WHAT'S A BOY TO DO.
 SITTING IN THE GARDEN.
 I SPEND MY NIGHTS THINKING ONLY OF MEN.
 REAL MEN, FRENCH MEN, DEAD MEN.
 I'M LOVING YOU AGAIN MY FRIEND,
 THERE'S NO ONE WATCHING,
 SITTING IN THE GARDEN.

 WHEN WE GO HOME SWEET HOME THEY'RE BOUND TO ASK US

WAS PARIS SO THRILLING?
WAS THE WOMEN WILD AND WILLING?
WAS IT YOU WHO DID THE KILLING?

WE'LL START TO TELL TALL TALES SO CONFIDENTIAL
'BOUT LADIES THAT WE'VE KNOWN HERE.
WASHING WHISKEY DOWN WITH WARM BEER.
MY, IT'S NICE TO HAVE YOU HOME DEAR

WE'LL RECOLLECT, SELECT THE PERFECT STORIES
FOR MOTHER, DAD AND PREACHER
AND YOU'LL COURT THE HISTORY TEACHER
'CAUSE SHE RESEMBLES ME IN FEATURE.

AND WHEN THAT SON OF MINE HE JOINS THE ARMY,
HE'LL ASK ME WHAT HE'S HEADED FOR.
I'LL KICK HIM SMARTLY OUT THE DOOR
AND NEVER EVEN MENTION YOUR NAME.
IT'S SO GODDAMN SHAMEFUL, THE MEMORY SO PAINFUL,
IT MAKES YOU WANNA RAPE, KILL AND MAIM.
I'LL NEVER LET YOU SEE ME AGAIN.

(Buie snatches the bottle from Evans's hand. He drinks and grimaces. Evans looks pleased. In No Man's Land R. Raymond-Barker is looking at his pocket watch.)

SCENE 2

(The East. 11:59 p.m., April 20th. Richthofen's room. Richthofen now wears a party hat. Gift wrapping is spread all over the floor. Empty bottles, soiled napkins, chicken bones, and dirty plates are strewn about. Bodenshatz swings gently in the hammock. Goering kneels on the floor surrounded by a ring of silver loving cups. He is pouring champagne into them and guzzling it down. Behind Goering two of the Women are holding a large mirror on its side. The Cellist is painting Goering's portrait on the surface of the mirror. Shells are exploding nearby.)

RICHTHOFEN: And I followed her all that summer, a member of her entourage of young and handsome European noblemen. We were the toast of the continent.

BODENSHATZ: (Looking at his watch.) It's midnight!

GOERING: (Looking at Moritz, the stuffed hound.) Your dog has been acting strangely depressed, Rittmeister.

RICHTHOFEN: She was already quite old. But she was exquisite.

BODENSHATZ: It's good to hear you talking about women. It's even better to see them in your company, Manfred. Perhaps later you would like to, I'm not sure of the polite term— (*Goering laughs.*)

RICHTHOFEN: I followed her to Brussels and Amsterdam, from Stockholm to Berlin, Vienna, Paris.

GOERING: A toast. To Sarah Bernhardt.

RICHTHOFEN: (*To the Women who watch him.*) She never said a word to me the entire time. When I finally left her in Munich, I felt elated, with my sights trained on the new age, free of the old era at last. It was a feeling of power, victory over the addiction, a feeling of peace. The feeling that comes only from giving up the thing that you love the most. I only wish you could understand me.

GOERING: Manfred, your dog's tail seems to be tied to the sink. I hate to be the one to tell you.

BODENSHATZ: Someone is playing a bad joke.

GOERING: Well, it looks stupid.

BODENSHATZ: Then simply untie the dog's tail.

GOERING: A toast. A toast. I've run out of toasts.

BODENSHATZ: Good. We've had enough toasts.

GOERING: Another toast to Sarah Bernhardt. How generous I am. Benevolence to the enemy even when faced with certain defeat. This is my eightieth drink, Rittmeister. Eighty cups full. Champagne! The veritable cup of blissful French mindlessness. Single handed, I fought and defeated eighty vicious loving cups. "Congratulations on you eightieth cup." Where's my ukelele? (*He drinks from a loving cup.*)

BODENSHATZ: (*Embarrassed.*) I'm sorry, Rittmeister, but there's a fool in every court.

RICHTHOFEN: We have to give Hermann his head tonight, don't we Hermann? It's a very special night to a flyer. It might be his last. After I've gone, Karl, see that the new leader turns his back on the flyers occasionally so that they can run wild. I should have done that.

BODENSHATZ: You surprise me, Rittmeister.

RICHTHOFEN: Go on, Hermann. Entertain us. Make it eighty-one. (*Goering drinks.*)

BODENSHATZ: I suppose I would learn to forgive Hermann his pretensions.

GOERING: (*Turning to the Women.*) I want to see the portrait, now. Turn the mirror around. Pretentious? Moi?

BODENSHATZ: Let them finish. It will be a surprise.

GOERING: (*Talking to the Women as if they are foreigners.*) I can't wait. Let me see the painting. I am your patron. I have my rights, after all, you were commissioned with a sumptuous pair of chicken wings. I want to look at the painting immediately. (*The Three Women slowly turn the mirror around.*)

RICHTHOFEN: It's bad luck to see the portrait before it's finished.

GOERING: I only want to peek. I've never had a portrait painted. I take beautiful

(*Buie puts on his gas mask. Evans searches for his, can't find it, goes madly looking about. He finally runs frantically into the hole to look for it. Raymond-Barker rises in No Man's Land.*)

RAYMOND-BARKER AND SECULL:
WHEN THE GAS BEGINS TO RISE
YELLOW CLOUD GETS IN MY EYES.
THE BOY THAT JUMPS IN THE TRENCH HE DIES
THE GAS IS LYING LOW.

PUT YOUR MASK ON IF YOU PLEASE
BUT THERE'S HE THAT'S ON HIS KNEES
THE GAS GOES PAST REVEALING
YELLOW SOLDIERS IN A ROW.
FLY . . . FLY.

BUIE:
WHEN THE GAS BEGINS TO BLOW
I WISH WINGS WOULD GROW ON ME.

(*Buie stands at the Lewis gun wearing his gas mask, looking up. Having found his mask, Evans joins Buie and clings to his arm.*)

SCENE 4

(*The East. 12:45 a.m., April 21st. Richthofen's room. Richthofen and Goering are standing together by the window. Goering is wobbling slightly.*)

RICHTHOFEN: Where is Karl? He must have found him. He was standing right there.
GOERING: Perhaps he was a ghost. I'm seeing ghosts. At least, I think they're ghosts. Whatever they are, they're peacock blue.
RICHTHOFEN: Help yourself to another chicken neck, Hermann. You must be hungry.
GOERING: I'd better sit down.
RICHTHOFEN: Take some coffee.
GOERING: Or I could lean. (*Goering is quite drunk.*)
RICHTHOFEN: Please don't be sick in here.
GOERING: Manfred. Are you going to bring us a lasting peace? (*A pause.*)
RICHTHOFEN: We're all fighting for peace, aren't we, Hermann? We just end to forget for very long periods of time.
GOERING: Peace. Bravo. And that's the end of me. I've thought about it, I promise you. Hermann is not a politician, he's a soldier. I don't have the

lungs for politics. I've decided to kill myself in the morning.

RICHTHOFEN: You're drunk, Hermann, and as is usual with cheap champagne you are being morbid.

GOERING: I will be taken seriously. This war is ridiculous, stupid . . . lost. I can be of no further use to the Fatherland alive.

RICHTHOFEN: Ah, but we will find a use for you after the war, Hermann; even if it's only to wave your bloody hands in the air like a clown for all the children to see.

GOERING: Now, that's a disgusting thought. Who's being morbid now?

RICHTHOFEN: There will be desperation in this defeat. And where will the public look for confidence? They'll look to the war heroes, Hermann, to the killers, to you and to me. They'll comb the decimated ranks of the military searching for leaders and new maniacs will emerge to join with the theorists, enlightened men like those that led us here—some general who has developed a strong taste for killing, a politician who has never even been in a fist fight; one lusting to return to war, the other ready to stumble into it. But we will remember. We will remind them when they try to forget the horror.

GOERING: I am dying and you're becoming sentimental.

RICHTHOFEN: There is nothing sentimental about trying to keep people alive. We have an obligation to stop these maniacs. It's ludicrous, I know, that this responsibility should fall to glorified assassins, but we will carry it for as long as the people are asleep.

GOERING: Meanwhile, I will be safe in the grave. The German people will need martyrs and fondly I leave my image to them. They can do with it what they please.

RICHTHOFEN: The new masters will find their most faithful servants in dead heroes. The masters control the images.

GOERING: (*Apparently not listening.*) I will make a splendid martyr.

RICHTHOFEN: (*Gently.*) Martyrs aren't normally made out of suicides, Hermann.

GOERING: I'll be shot down in action. No one will ever know that I'm my own victim.

RICHTHOFEN: Losing your life so easily to an Englishman, Hermann? disgraceful talk.

GOERING: (*Whispers.*) I have it planned, I promise you, better than that. I'll find some virgin and chase him low over enemy lines, flying like a madman directly over ground fire pretending not to notice where I'm being led and all the time making certain that my aim is slightly off. I will follow my virgin for miles, skimming the tree tops with English guns blazing below, a long and courageous flight. And it is inevitable that one single bullet from the thousands of anti-aircraft guns will lodge deep in the heart of "Roaring Hermann." I will be dead. Immortalized. And all before noon tomorrow.

photographs they tell me and if so . . . (*Goering stares into the mirror. The face that looks back is hideous, bulbous, mad. The image is superimposed over Goering's face. He looks into his own eyes.*) Bless me. (*Goering shatters the glass with a silver loving cup. He snatches the mirror. Silence.*)

RICHTHOFEN: I hope you're not superstitious, Hermann.

GOERING: (*Screams.*) Witches! I don't see the likeness at all. Get out. Get out, you witches. Get out of my sight. (*The Women quickly leave the room*)

RICHTHOFEN: Witches? You don't believe in magic do you, Hermann? We have to rise above superstition. (*A pause.*)

GOERING: Magic? Oh no. Not for a second. Not at all. Certainly not black magic. But white magic, my friends, is another matter. How I love these parties. (*Goering produces a vial filled with cocaine.*)

BODENSHATZ: Our friend Hermann is excess personified.

RICHTHOFEN: Let him go, Karl.

GOERING: Maps. Maps. We must peruse the maps. The master plan is conceived. (*Goering turns the mirror on its side. He opens the vial and pours the powder onto the shattered surface. He produces a silver, bejewelled straw and a silver straight edge.*) Gentlemen, I give you Europe. According to our trusted observers the Polish line is located here. (*He forms a line of cocaine with the straight edge.*)

BODENSHATZ: Make a very thin line then.

GOERING: The sudden unexpected offensive is the great and timeless German weapon. Our unshakeable human will.

RICHTHOFEN: Hermann hasn't finished losing this war and already he's winning the next one.

BODENSHATZ: Take charge, Hermann. (*Richthofen walks to the window and looks out.*)

GOERING: Suddenly, under cover of darkness, our troops swoop down on the Poles. (*He snorts up the line into one nostril through the straw.*)

BODENSHATZ: And remove them from the face of the earth.

GOERING: (*Dividing another line.*) Germany rules from Pole to Pole. On to France. Now the French line is much more formidable . . . but all of Germany takes a deep breath and . . . (*He snorts the line.*) France is absorbed. Victory. On to battle Britain and to penetrate the most resistant and respected line of all. The line of lines. Straight up the old English Channel. Rittmeister, please, your leadership is needed. (*Goering prepares a huge line of cocaine.*)

BODENSHATZ: (*Seeing that Richthofen isn't listening.*) He doesn't hear you.

GOERING: Rittmeister. Please allow me to represent you myself in this hour of your destiny. (*The shelling outside becomes very heavy. Goering waits for Richthofen to acknowledge him.*)

BODENSHATZ: It's obvious that you, Hermann, are a man of great capacity. The eyes of the world are upon you.

GOERING: With no hesitation I face the enemy and . . . (*He snorts the line. Richthofen is looking out the window. The Lance Corporal is suddenly standing outside, wearing the scarf. Richthofen stares him in the eye through the glass and freezes.*)

BODENSHATZ: You've missed quite a bit, haven't you. I'm afraid we'll have to call that one a failure.

GOERING: No.

BODENSHATZ: You've left quite a bit.

RICHTHOFEN: Karl.

GOERING: I can't take it all by myself. (*The Lance Corporal disappears.*)

RICHTHOFEN: (*Urgently.*) Karl, see that soldier who's looking in the window, see, he's gone now, around the side of the building. Follow him, find him, bring him to me. Invite him in.

GOERING: I need help.

RICHTHOFEN: Hurry, Karl. (*Bodendshatz goes out through the louvered doors. Richthofen stands waiting at the window.*)

SCENE 3

(*The West. 12:15 a.m., April 21st. The machine gun nest of Buie and Evans. They sit together without noticing the late N.C.O. Secull floating behind them playing piano. Music. They perform.*)

IT'S ALL RIGHT, GOD

BUIE:
IT'S ALL RIGHT GOD, HE'S REALLY QUITE RESPECTABLE
SITTING HERE WITH ME; QUITE PROTECTABLE.
IT'S JUST FINE GOD, THE FOOD IS QUITE DELECTABLE.
I DON'T MIND THAT I'M SUSCEPTIBLE
TO PLAGUE, DISEASE, AND GERMS UNDETECTABLE.
THE TERMS ARE QUITE ACCEPTABLE
BUT GOD, THE ONE THING THAT I ASK IS
SAVE US FROM THE GAS.

BUIE AND EVANS:
IT'S ALL RIGHT GOD, WE KNOW YOU GOT YOUR PRINCIPLE.
GOD KNOWS WE'RE NOT INCINCIBLE.
IT'S JUST FINE GOD, WE'RE REALLY QUITE CONVINCIBLE.
YES, WE'LL FIGHT THE DIABOLICAL.
BUT MUSTARD GAS TURNS THE WHOLE WORLD INVISIBLE.
BLINDS, BURNS, IS QUITE UNCOMFORTABLE
SO GOD PLEASE GET OFF YOUR ASS AND
SAVE US FROM THE GAS.

RICHTHOFEN: You're an ass, Hermann.

GOERING: I'll miss you.

RICHTHOFEN: You don't even have a machine.

GOERING: Perhaps I'll be flying your machine in the morning, Rittmeister, since you will no longer have any use for it. (*Bodenshatz returns.*)

RICHTHOFEN: Where is he, Karl?

GOERING: With all due respect I've always looked grand in red.

BODENSHATZ: (*Shaken.*) No one was there. At least I couldn't find anyone.

GOERING: Ghosts.

RICHTHOFEN: No one?

BODENSHATZ: I thought I saw someone going into one of the barracks but when I got there, there wasn't a soul.

GOERING: Ghosts. And tomorrow I'll be among them, haunting all of you. (*Wolfram enters. He is just finishing dressing hurriedly.*)

WOLFRAM: You wanted to see me, Rittmeister?

RICHTHOFEN: No. I didn't want to see you at all.

WOLFRAM: I'm sorry. There's been a mistake. I was told that you wanted to see me. You didn't leave me the gift? (*The Women appear suddenly through the louvered doors. Wolfram becomes uncomfortable.*)

GOERING: Excuses, excuses. News of these whores is obviously travelling. What gift? I didn't get a gift?

WOLFRAM: A soldier woke me and told me to come to you. He gave me this. He left before I could thank him. (*Wolfram produces a white silk scarf.*)

GOERING: Oh, it's real silk, young man. Your admirers are so bashful. But so generous.

WOLFRAM: It has the letter "R" embroidered on it. "R" for Richthofen.

RICHTHOFEN: Which soldier?

WOLFRAM: I didn't see his face. I was half asleep. He said he was a messenger.

RICHTHOFEN: (*Urgently.*) Where is he now?

WOLFRAM: I don't know. Gone.

RICHTHOFEN: Give the scarf to me.

WOLFRAM: No, I'm quite sure it was meant for me, Rittmeister.

GOERING: I'll settle this. Let me try it on.

RICHTHOFEN: (*Snatching the scarf from Wolfram.*) Give it to me. "R" for Richthofen. I am still Richthofen.

BODENSHATZ: Rittmeister. (*A pause.*)

GOERING: Naturally, I have to pay out of my own pocket to own a silk scarf.

RICHTHOFEN: Lieutenant Richthofen, do you remember the unwritten law? (*The women are staring at Wolfram who blushes.*)

WOLFRAM: (*Snapping to attention.*) Yes, Rittmeister.

RICHTHOFEN: And who are they, Wolfram?

WOLFRAM: They are women, Rittmeister.

RICHTHOFEN: And where should you be?

WOLFRAM: Alone in my bed.

RICHTHOFEN: Then go there. (*Wolfram brushes past the women and scurries out. Richthofen walks to the window, one hand to his wound, the other clutching the scarf.*)

GOERING: (*Taking off his belt.*) Women. See the trouble you've caused. Prepare yourselves for a whipping in the next room where we can avoid polluting the Rittmeister's view. You with the paints. Into the other room. Strip. Lower your knickers. Bend over the mattress. Stop looking so noble. I'm the one that's dying tomorrow; you will feel sorry for me. This is not lust. It's military discipline. Strip. Instantly. As I once did for my strong, young mother. (*Goering leads the women into the bunkroom. The Cellist hesitates, staring at Richthofen. Goering pushes her and they are gone.*)

RICHTHOFEN: Stop him, Karl!

BODENSHATZ: I don't know if I can now, Rittmeister. I don't outrank him and he seems to be feeling rather randy. Perhaps if you had let me stop him before—

RICHTHOFEN: Bodenshatz, close the door. (*Bodenshatz steps into the bunkroom and closes the door behind him. Richthofen is left holding the scarf and looking out the window.*)

SCENE 5

(*The West. 2:00 a.m., April 21st. The machine gun nest of Buie and Evans. Buie and Evans sit up on the sandbags, with their arms around each other and their gas masks on, waiting for the mustard gas attack. They resemble two rather large, wingless dragonflies in mating season. The late N.C.O. Secull floats above them, undetected at the piano. Raymond-Barker stands by him with a cup of tea.*)

1918

SECULL AND RAYMOND-BARKER:
GOT NO NEED FOR PERSONALITY.
I'VE GOT NO MORE JOKES IN STORE FOR NEW PLATOON BOYS,
SING MY TUNE BOYS. IT DON'T TAKE LONG. THAT OLD CAMP
SONG.

BUIE AND EVANS: (*Muffled through their gas masks.*)
1914 TO 1918 AND NOT A CLEAN SHEET IN BETWEEN.
WE'RE ON THE TAIL, THE DONKEY'S ASS OF HISTORY.

SECULL AND RAYMOND-BARKER:
AND ME I'VE GOT NO TIME
FOR SENTIMENTAL STORY WARS FOR THE SOFT AND GENTLE.
FIGHT LIKE BULLFROGS, SING LIKE BULLDOGS
THAT OLD CAMP SONG. AND SAY SO LONG. SO SAY SO LONG.

1918. 1918. 1918.

SECULL AND RAYMOND-BARKER:
AND ME I'VE GOT NO TIME
FOR SENTIMENTAL STORY WARS FOR THE SOFT AND GENTLE.
FIGHT LIKE BULLFROGS, SING LIKE BULLDOGS
THAT OLD CAMP SONG. AND SAY SO LONG. SO SAY SO LONG.
1918. 1918. 1918.

(*No Man's Land. The image of Buie and Evans remains in the West. Secull vanishes. Moonlight. A thick yellow cloud of mustard gas clings to the surface of No Man's Land. Buie and Evans watch the sheet of gas envelop No Man's Land as it approaches from out of the East. They stand on the sandbags in amazement. Out of the East walk two of the Women in the half light. They seem to glide a foot or two above the earth, supported by the gas in their long nightgowns. They wear party masks, no gas masks. Their skin is bright yellow but they show no other sign of ill effect from the gas. Evans rushes to them, urging Buie to follow. Buie joins them reluctantly. The women take them by the hand. They form two couples and waltz in the mud. Simultaneously across the line . . .*

The East. Richthofen's room is dim. Richthofen is sitting in a silk chair by the window wearing the silk scarf. He has fallen asleep. The Cellist stands with her back to him at an easel, painting with furious brush strokes. She wears two goggles. She sings with the two Women who dance with Buie and Evans in No Man's Land. As the Women sing the chair on which Richthofen sleeps floats up into the air and hovers fifteen feet above the floor.)

DEAR ICARUS

THE WOMEN:
THREE TIMES THREE TIMES THREE TIMES THREE
IS EIGHTY-ONE.
I SEND YOU ONE LAST LETTER AS YOU FLY INTO THE SUN.

THE YEARS IN THE VALLEY SINCE YOU LEFT, DEAR ICARUS
PASS JUST THE SAME IF YOU'RE WONDERING OF US
WE'RE HERE BY THE STEEPLE WHERE HANDKERCHIEFS
   FLUTTER,
WHERE STILL THE OLD PEOPLE BELIEVE IN THE GODS.

IF YOU LOOK DOWN YOU CAN SEE THE OLD TOWN
WHERE THE ELDERLY MEN WEAR THEIR PRIESTLY WHITE
   DRESSES.

LIKE MOTHS ROUND A CANDLE, ARRANGE ON THE MANTLE
YOUR GOGGLES AND LEATHERS AND FEATHERS AND WAX.

YOUR SISTERS AND I FOUND YOUR NAME GOLDEN ICARUS.
NUMBERED AND BRONZED ON A PLAQUE AT THE LIBRARY.
WOMEN TAKE TEA THERE, TAKE BOOKS FOR THEIR
    DAUGHTERS
TO KEEP THEM FROM WITNESSING FLIGHTS OF THEIR SONS.

IF YOU LOOK DOWN TO THE TOYS ON THE GROUND,
WHERE THE DOLLS BECOME SPIDERS AND MOTOR CAR RIDERS,
WE'LL ALL FROWN, THE WHOLE TOWN,
WHEN THE SUN MELTS YOUR WINGS DOWN
TO GOGGLES AND LEATHERS AND FEATHERS AND WAX.
IN A HEAP FROM THE HEAT OF A SUN BEAM'S ATTACKS.

(No Man's Land. The Two Women wave goodbye to Buie and Evans. Evans dances
Buie back to their machine gun nest where they sit straining to watch the women
disappear in the East.
    The East. Richthofen's chair drifts back down to rest on the floor.)

THE CELLIST:
    THE TOWN WILL FORGET YOU
    AND PRESENTLY ICARUS, EVEN YOUR SISTERS
    WILL NAME YOU RIDICULOUS.
    THEY'LL WRITE THE BOOKS AND THEY'LL TEACH ALL THE
        LESSONS
    ON GOGGLES AND LEATHERS AND FEATHERS AND WAX.
    WHAT WILL IT TAKE TO MAKE YOUNG MEN RELAX?

SCENE 6

(The East. 2:55 a.m., April 21st. Richthofen's room. Richthofen opens his eyes and
stands. He seems to be fully awake but behaves irrationally. The Cellist watches him.)

RICHTHOFEN: Karl! Is that you? Bodenshatz. Where is Karl! Asleep, Yes, let him
    sleep. (Richthofen realizes the Cellist is watching him.) What did you say?
    Didn't you ask me something just now? Ah. You don't understand a single
    word, I forgot. Not that Karl really understands. He just keeps records.
    That's all. He records my dreams. I've been learning to control the images
    that appear in them. It's an exercise. I dream in aerial photographs. I project
    my imagination into the sky and magnify whatever I see below me. In these
    latest dreams I've been trying to force myself to action. But my eyes are lock-

ed to the earth. I have no control. Everything is automatic. The range of my view begins by covering miles but my eyes unwillingly become telescopes and my view narrows until I'm finally forced to examine the range of climbing insects on a single blade of grass. For the longest time I watched two tiny creatures with four bulbous eyes, hanging from a metal twig. (*Pause.*) At any rate, I won't need the exercises any more. No more ice baths . . . foot races . . . flight reports. (*Richthofen turns and begins to wash his hands in the basin.*)

THE CELLIST: I've climbed trees.

RICHTHOFEN: (*Whirling around.*) Pardon.

THE CELLIST: I've never been flying. I've only climbed trees, that's all I meant to say and I shouldn't have said that and now I'll say nothing at all. I'll be quiet.

RICHTHOFEN: You didn't tell us that you spoke German.

THE CELLIST: You didn't ask. No one ever asks. A German man could never admit that a German woman is reduced to rags.

RICHTHOFEN: You've been spying on us.

THE CELLIST: I have far too much to say to be a spy.

RICHTHOFEN: Do your friends speak German?

THE CELLIST: They never speak. My sisters keep very quiet. Confidentially, it it makes them rather dull.

RICHTHOFEN: Where do you live?

THE CELLIST: Last night we slept in a tree.

RICHTHOFEN: What do you do?

THE CELLIST: Do?

RICHTHOFEN: How do you manage?

THE CELLIST: We're portrait painters and beggars and teachers and thieves, sisters, mothers, daughters, gypsies, whores, witches . . . and half-serious musicians.

RICHTHOFEN: In a rather small orchestra.

THE CELLIST: (*Approaching him.*) We used to be much larger. There were some pretty young men at the beginning of the war in the brass section. (*A pause.*)

RICHTHOFEN: I'm sorry if I seem awkward. It's been a very long time since I've discussed music with a—

THE CELLIST: (*Covering his mouth.*) If the others hear me talking to you they'll die of fright. Please don't ask me any more about the orchestra because I like talking about the orchestra best of all.

RICHTHOFEN: (*Frightened by her closeness.*) I can arrange for an automobile.

THE CELLIST: Where would we go?

RICHTHOFEN: Where are your parents?

THE CELLIST: Where do you suppose?

RICHTHOFEN: We must seem idiotic from your point of view, with our schoolboy politics, talking of peace.

THE CELLIST: I hope you're better at preventing wars than you are at preventing beatings.

RICHTHOFEN: (*Awkwardly.*) I can't seem to cope with Hermann tonight. I'm sorry. But he's promised to kill himself in the morning so we should be rid of him by midday.

THE CELLIST: He didn't beat me.

RICHTHOFEN: I'm glad.

THE CELLIST: He begged and pleaded for me to beat him.

RICHTHOFEN: I trust you gave him a good one.

THE CELLIST: I refused. He was too drunk to protest. He wept himself to sleep. (*Richthofen smiles.*)

RICHTHOFEN: And what did you see from the top of the tree?

THE CELLIST: You're laughing at me.

RICHTHOFEN: I'm smiling. This must be smiling. I don't think I ever laugh.

THE CELLIST: I could see into the sky and across the earth from the top of the tree. I could calculate when carriages would meet at the intersections of distant roadways. I could predict collisions between flocks of birds in the air. It was almost like seeing into the future. My sisters finally had to order me to climb down from the branches. They said it was all dangerous. I envy you. I would love to fly. I'm sure it all seem silly to you now.

RICHTHOFEN: (*Becoming warmer.*) No, I understand. I do. I remember. When I was eleven I decided to climb the famous steeple at Wahlstatt where I was schooling. It began to rain, the gutters became slippery and so there I was, teetering in the storm one hundred feet in the air, tying my handkerchief to the top of the lightning conductor. I found my terror absolutely exhilarating. Ten years later, when I returned to visit my yonger brother, a boy's handkerchief was still flying from the top of that steeple. I've never managed to recapture that first thrill in the air. Not even once in two and a half years in a flying machine.

THE CELLIST: I would like to be as famous as you are.

RICHTHOFEN: Anyone can become famous today. You only have to kill a large enough number of human beings.

THE CELLIST: I want to be a member of a famous orchestra. We've played in Paris once already, before the war. Lately there's just been too much noise. You see how I love to talk about the orchestra? It comes up from nowhere right in the middle of a conversation.

RICHTHOFEN: You speak French.

THE CELLIST: Yes, a little. Are you going to ask me to make love in French? You have very strange ideas it seems to me.

RICHTHOFEN: (*Eagerly.*) No. I have some discs for the phonograph, poetry recitals in French. Perhaps you can translate for me. (*Richthofen winds the phonograph and plays a disc of Sarah Bernhardt reciting excerpts from Shakespeare in French.*)

THE CELLIST: You can't very well dance to that, can you? (*They almost kiss. Richthofen looks up. The Lance Corporal is looking in through the window.*

Richthofen stares at him. The Cellist turns to see him. The Lance Corporal slowly turns and goes.)
RICHTHOFEN: *(Taking his coat.)* I have to talk to him. *(She pulls Richthofen's pistol from under her skirts and gives it to him.)*
RICHTOFEN: *(Putting the pistol in his pocket.)* I have to go.
THE CELLIST: Mazeltov. Mazeltov. *(Richtofen climbs out through the window and steps onto the edge of No Man's Land. Sarah Brenhardt speaks from the phonograph. The Cellist stands at the window inside the room looking out.)*

SCENE 7

(No Man's Land. 3:45 a.m., April 21st. Sarah's voice carries on. Richthofen doesn't look back. He opens the umbrella and searches for the Lance Corporal in the rain and the darkness. Music.)

SARAH

RICHTHOFEN:
WHEN I FIRST HEARD SARAH BERNHARDT IN NINETEEN
    HUNDRED AND THREE
DRINKING CHAMPAGNE AND TEA, MOTHER AND ME
WELCOMING THE TWENTIETH CENTURY.

THE FIRST NIGHT I HEARD SARAH BERNHARDT RECITE
IN BRUSSELS IN 1903 IF THE CROWD HAD WATCHED ME
THEY'D HAVE WITNESSED MAN'S FEARLESS FIRST LIGHT.
IN THE EYES OF A BOY IN THE FOURTH BALCONY.
"SARAH OUR SUNRISE, OUR LADY OF LIGHT,"
CRIED THE CROWD AS THE WORDS POURED LIKE SILK
FROM THEIR SARAH,
BUT SADLY THEY LISTENED WHEN SHE THREW BACK HER
    HEAD,
AS SHE TURNED FROM THOSE VERSES SHE READ
AND SHE SAID,

"I DON'T WANT TO BE THE ONE TO HOLD THE LIGHT,
CHOOSE A NEW SUN FROM THE STARSCAPE TONIGHT.
I NEED TIME TO CATCH MY BREATH HEAL MY SCARS,
TELL THEM IN PARIS THAT I'VE LEFT THEM FOR MARS,
TELL THEM THAT I LEAVE MY PAPA, SWEET MY MAMA,
OULALA, LEAVE THEM ALL GLADLY,
I TREAT THEM SO BADLY."
CRIED THE WHOLE CROWD, "PLEASE SARAH, PLAY ON."

"I DON'T WANT TO BE THE STATUE AT THE GATE.
HERE IN THE FUTURE I FEEL QUITE OUT OF DATE.
I'M SO AFRAID TO TURN TO STONE UPON THE STAGE.
BURBAGE AND BOOTH STAYED IN BED AT MY AGE"
CRIED THE CROWD, "AGAIN SWEET SARAH, BIEN SWEET
  SARAH
OULALALA, SOMETIMES ROMANTIC."
THE YOUNG MEN WERE FRANTIC.
CRIED THE WHOLE CROWD, "PLEASE SARAH PLAY ON."

THE FIRST NIGHT I HEARD SARAH BERNHARDT
SING-SONGING SHAKESPEARE IN FRENCH.
THAT EVENING OF MAGIC WITH FARCICAL, TRAGICAL
SARAH WENT ON AND ON AND ON.

"I DON'T WANT TO STAND ALONE BEFORE THE CROWD.
THE LAUGHTER IS FRIGHTENING AND THE BAND'S MUCH TOO
  LOUD.
IT'S QUITE UNFAIR, I GIVE YOU BLOOD, YOU THROW ME
  FLOWERS.
SHE THREATENED TO LEAVE US BUT SHE TALKED ON FOR
  HOURS.
CRIED THE CROWD, "ENCORE, SWEET SARAH, MORE, SWEET
  SARAH.
OULALALA YOUR VERSES ARE TIMELESS.
THEY HELP TO REMIND US."

CRIED THE PEOPLE, "PLEASE DON'T GO, CONTINUE WITH THE
  SHOW.
WE LOVE OUR SARAH SO, OH SARAH PLAY ON."

THE FIRST NIGHT I HEARD SARAH BERNHARDT,
PUTTING HER PUBLIC TO SLEEP,
SHE SAID SHE WAS LEAVING BUT HER WORDS WERE
  DECEIVING
FOR SARAH PLAYED ON AND ON AND ON.

"I DON'T WANT TO BE THE ONE TO HOLD THE LIGHT."
THE PEOPLE WERE SILENT AND SHE TALKED ON ALL NIGHT.
"I NEED TIME AND TIME AND I ARE GETTING ON."
THE PEOPLE WERE SNORING BUT SHE TALKED ON TIL DAWN.
"WAKE THE PEOPLE NOW," SAID SARAH. "NOW," CALLED
  SARAH,

OULALALA SARAH WAS WEEPING.
THE PEOPLE WERE SLEEPING.
CRIED A YOUNG BOY, "PLEASE DON'T GO, CONTINUE WITH
THE SHOW.
I LOVE YOU SARAH SO, OH SARAH PLAY ON."

I DON'T WANT TO BE THE KEEPER OF YOUR DREAM.
I DON'T WANT TO BE THE SAVIOR OF YOUR SOUL.
I DON'T WANT TO BE THE ONE TO HOLD THE LIGHT.
OULALALALA, OULALA, OULALALA,
I DON'T WANT TO BE THE ONE TO HOLD THE LIGHT.
OULALALALA, OULALA, OULALALA.
"WAKE THE PEOPLE NOW," SAID SARAH.
"NOW," CALLED SARAH.
OULALALA, SARAH WAS SCREAMING,
THE PEOPLE WERE DREAMING.

CRIED A YOUNG BOY, "PLEASE SARAH PLAY ON."
AND SARAH PLAYED ON, AND SARAH PLAYED ON AND ON
AND ON.

SCENE 8

(*The West and No Man's Land. 4:40 a.m., April 21st. A beam from a search hits Richthofen. He has wandered across the entirety of No Man's Land. He stands by the machine gun nest of Buie and Evans. Evans points the searchlight over the sandbag wall. Richthofen holds his umbrella up to the rain. Buie and Evans squint through the raindrops.*)

EVANS: Here come the cigarettes.
RICHTOFEN: Switch off the light. Don't touch your gun. I won't touch mine.
BUIE: I don't think he smokes.
EVANS: Is this the new N.C.O. ?
BUIE: I doubt it.
RICHTOFEN: I'm not sure exactly where I am.
EVANS: What the fuck is he saying?
RICHTOFEN: (*Uncomfortable in the light.*) Do you speak French?
EVANS: He's got a nice umbrella. What language is he talking?
BUIE: French.
EVANS: How do you know?
BUIE: This is France, isn't it?
EVANS: Well, we're in France and we're not talking French are we?
RICHTOFEN: I've been following a man. He's dressed . . . a lot like you, in fact,

he's filthy. You can't see his uniform for the mud. I'm sure he's harmless. He's around here somewhere.

EVANS: I wonder if he's got any cigarettes. How do you say "I'd kill for a cigarette" in French?

BUIE: Give him one.

EVANS: Don't be cheeky. We've only got one.

BUIE: Put out the lamp and give it to him.

EVANS: (*Switching off the search light.*) Oh. I understand. It's a trick. You've got a plan. Got it. There you are, sir. Have the last one. (*Evans gives Richthofen their last cigarette. Richthofen hesitates.*)

RICHTHOFEN: (*Accepting the cigarette.*) Thank you, but I don't use tobacco.

EVANS: (*Very disappointed.*) I told you he smoked. He's probably got lots, the greedy thing. Now what?

RICHTHOFEN: (*Producing a full packet.*) I always carry cigarettes though, for the others. You can have them if you like. (*Richthofen tosses Evans the cigarettes. Evans furiously opens the packet, takes one for himself and gives one to Buie.*)

EVANS: I don't believe it. Nobody gives cigarettes away like that. It's not natural, Buie.

BUIE: Nothing wrong with a friendly smoke, Mister Inch.

RICHTHOFEN: I've never acquired the habit, never smoked. (*Buie lights a match. The three of them light the cigarettes under the umbrella. They smoke. Evans reads the packet.*)

EVANS: Buie. These are Fritz cigarettes.

RICHTHOFEN: It seems like the rain will never stop.

EVANS: Look. Look at the picture. Definitely Fritz. That's Fritz he's been talking in. Perfect opportunity. I'll get your rifle. Act normal.

BUIE: Inch.

EVANS: Keep conversing with him. (*Evans runs to the hole.*)

BUIE: Inch. Forget it.

RICHTHOFEN: (*To Buie.*) I'm afraid you haven't coverted me. I still don't like the taste of tobacco but the gesture was appreciated. (*Richthofen puts out the cigarette. The click of a rifle comes from the hole.*) I must go. Enjoy the rest of the cigarettes.)

BUIE: (*Quietly.*) And here's to you, Captain. (*Richthofen begins to fade into the early morning darkness. Evans returns with Buie's rifle.*)

EVANS: Buie. He's getting away. Here. Take it. Shoot him, Buie. Shoot him.

BUIE: He's our ally.

EVANS: He's not. Shoot him.

BUIE: You cannot shoot a man that you do not know in the back.

EVANS: You haven't got it in you, Buie, do you? Why not admit it? You're never going to get us a Fritz. We're doomed to obscurity. We'll never play the Music Hall at this rate.

BUIE: We'll never play the Music Hall anyway.

SCENE 9

(No Man's Land. 5:30 a.m., April 21st. Music. Dawn. The Lance Corporal is kneeling and watching, waiting for something to appear on the eastern horizon. His body sways and he swings his arms spasmodically in the mist. Richthofen approaches from the West during the Lance Corporal's song and stands quietly behind him.)

I DON'T ASK ABOUT TOMORROW

THE LANCE CORPORAL:
I DON'T ASK ABOUT TOMORROW,
TOMORROW I DON'T CARE FOR,
BREATHING OUT, BREATHING IN,
ONE DAY BY ONE DAY BY ONE DAY,
MY EYES TO THE BIRDS IN THE MORNING.
I COUNT THEM ONE BY ONE BY ONE.

(The sun begins to rise. The faint voices of children join in with the Lance Corporal's singing. Birds begin to whistle.)

BUT SOMEDAY SURVIVORS IN WHISPERS
MUST DANCE OUT OF MOURNING
AND WAKE THEM ONE BY ONE BY ONE.

BUT DON'T ASK ABOUT TOMORROW.
TOMORROW WON'T BELIEVE YOU.
RIDE ON TODAY AND TOMORROW IGNORE
FOR TO REACH THE UNBORN
YOU MUST SAVE THEM YOUR WARNING
BECAUSE THEY SLEEP, BUT WAIT, THEY'LL WAKE,
THEY'LL COME BY ONE BY ONE BY ONE.

(Richthofen and the Lance Corporal face each other.)

RICHTHOFEN: You've been expecting me, Corporal.
LANCE CORPORAL: Not expecting you. Not exactly. I don't make predictions.
RICHTOFEN: I predicted that you would be waiting here for me.
LANCE CORPORAL: Perhaps you are in a better position to see into the future.
RICHTOFEN: I've been hunting you. You want to be hunted.
LANCE CORPORAL: It's admirable that you're so quick to deal with the opposition; but first you must learn to determine who the opposition is. I've just eaten the uncooked flesh of a rodent. I don't have the strength to oppose anyone. A filthy, emaciated, little fellow like me is hardly worth the hunt-

ing.

RICHTHOFEN: Why did you give the scarf to my cousin, Corporal?

LANCE CORPORAL: Why did you follow me?

RICHTHOFEN: There are vampires in this world. I discovered them the first time my photograph appeared in the newspapers. Bloodsuckers who are anxious to ride with the ascendant, eager to drool over his descent. These ghouls can be dangerous, Corporal, as you obviously know. Why did you give the scarf to my cousin?

LANCE CORPORAL: It was a test.

RICHTHOFEN: Who are you to test my cousin?

LANCE CORPORAL: (*Angered.*) The test was for you and you failed. Ghosts, ghouls, vampires, you have the future of our people at your fingertips. The rest of us grovel in the mud. There is no room in this century for superstition. There is only the will of the human spirit. If you think clearly the people will believe what you think. And you're busy thinking of black magic and silk scarves that bring bad luck.

RICHTHOFEN: Where is the body of the dead flyer?

LANCE CORPORAL: I buried him. I'm standing on his grave. Shall I dig him up so you can return the bad luck? Is that why you came here? (*He digs with his hands.*)

RICHTHOFEN: You are trying to manipulate me. You're interfering with my family, my decisions. (*Richthofen pulls out his pistol, cocks the trigger and points it at the Lance Corporal.*)

LANCE CORPORAL: Do you expect me to be afraid?

RICHTHOFEN: Yes. If you have any sense.

LANCE CORPORAL: There is little left that frightens me. I don't pay much attention to guns. This particular situation doesn't call for a decision from me. Even without our decisions events will continue to occur. Lessons will be taught.

RICHTHOFEN: And which lesson is being taught now?

LANCE CORPORAL: You think that I'm your enemy and you're learning what you must do with your enemies. Nothing else matters. It will hopefully be easy for you to order others to kill when you kill so easily yourself. And you will have to continue to kill after the war. You will have to kill Germans in order to gain control. I understand now.

RICHTHOFEN: What do you understand?

LANCE CORPORAL: I followed you because I sensed it was my duty. I knew i had some role to play but I didn't know what it was to be. I see it now.

RICHTHOFEN: Do you presume that your role is to teach me a lesson, Corporal?

LANCE CORPORAL: There will be a great slaughter in Germany after the war. Political groups will murder each other off for control. Only the strongest will survive. The great cities will be in chaos, terror will be the only effective tool. You will have to murder your own people to bring in the new age. You are learning that lesson tonight. Look into the future. Take no chances.

RICHTHOFEN: Germans will never kill Germans.

LANCE CORPORAL: Germans are already killing Germans. It will get much worse. I understand now.

RICHTHOFEN: There is nothing to understand.

LANCE CORPORAL: (*Screaming.*) My blood is to be the first German blood that our new leader spills. I am to be your first sacrifice. I understand. The machines advance and when you master the machines you must dispose of the beasts. You've made the decision. You can pull the trigger now. Don't apologize. Don't explain. After the trigger is pulled the reason for your decision won't matter. Germans will demand revenge. You must lead them to it. You've shown that you have no mercy for your enemies. That's why you've been chosen. And although the world spins on the edge of a coin I believe that Germany is destined to teach a great lesson here tonight . . . please, take my hand, squeeze it and I'll close my eyes and I'll begin to count so that I can forget about what you're about to do and now back away from me and whenever you're ready, aim carefully please and do it. Do it. I understand. (*Silence. Richthofen slowly backs away with the outstretched pistol pointing at the Lance Corporal's head. He aims.*)

RICHTHOFEN: You think that your death has a cosmic purpose, that you're on some great mission.

LANCE CORPORAL: Do it. I understand. You must learn to do it. You have a responsibility.

RICHTHOFEN: But you're just another suicide with lofty illusions. You brought me here to be the agent of your death so that you could escape the gas attacks, the starvation, the disease and so that you could escape doing it yourself. You have no real courage.

LANCE CORPORAL: If you are truly the leader that the Fatherland is waiting for, you have to do it. Do it. (*Richthofen fires three times at the Lance Corporal. Each time that he fires he pulls the pistol into the air at the last moment so that all three shots miss. A long pause.*)

RICHTHOFEN: (*Shaken.*) You're a pathetic creature. You won't last forty-eight hours. I'll still consider you my eighty-first kill, but you're lost on all other counts. Good morning, Corporal. (*Richthofen throws the scarf over his shoulder and walks quickly off into the East. The Lance Corporal opens his eyes, rises calmly and turns to look in Richthofen's direction. Richthofen has left his umbrella behind. The Lance Corporal picks it up.*)

SCENE 10

(*The West. 8:00 a.m., April 21st. The machine gun nest of Buie and Evans. The sun has risen. The rain has stopped. Buie and Evans have just awakened. Buie fiddles with the machine gun. Evans looks for something to eat. They perform.*)

APRIL TWENTY-ONE

BUIE & EVANS: (*With Raymond-Barker and Secull.*)
APRIL TWENTY-ONE, BARELY BUT BEGUN.
HOPE TODAY IS OUR DAY.
WE THINK IT'S SUNDAY AND WE LIKE SUNDAY
AND SURELY ONE GOOD DAY WILL COME OUR WAY
BUT APRIL TWENTY-FIRST, WE EXPECT THE WORST,
HOPE TODAY IS MY DAY.
TWENTY-ONE, TWENTY-ONE, SEE THEM RUN, TWENTY-ONE.
KISS GOOD MORNING APRIL TWENTY-ONE.

SCENE 11

(*The East. 9:25 a.m., April 21st. Richthofen's room. Sunlight. Richthofen still wears his rain cape. He is peering into the empty room from outside through the window. Silence. Everyone seems to be asleep. The room contains the aftermath of the party. Richthofen puts a foot on the sill and quietly enters. Bodenshatz enters from the bunkroom simultaneously.*)

BODENSHATZ: Is there something wrong with the lock? Or do you simply prefer windows to doors?
RICHTHOFEN: (*Quietly.*) Where's Hermann?
BODENSHATZ: In the other room under the blankets.
RICHTHOFEN: Good morning, Karl.
BODENSHATZ: You've been out walking.
RICHTHOFEN: Yes.
BODENSHATZ: How was that?
RICHTHOFEN: The rain has stopped.
BODENSHATZ: Yes.
RICHTHOFEN: What is Hermann doing under the blankets, Karl?
BODENSHATZ: I don't know. He hasn't moved for hours.
RICHTHOFEN: Then he's either sleeping or he's dead. Either way he'll need his rest.
BODENSHATZ: You should be sleeping too, Manfred.
RICHTHOFEN: With Hermann? Certainly not. I looked in on the others. They were eating a good breakfast.
BODENSHATZ: They're very wise.
RICHTHOFEN: I feel better.
BODENSHATZ: Good.
RICHTHOFEN: Yes.
BODENSHATZ: And you spoke with your chaser pilots? You said goodbye. (*A pause.*)

RICHTHOFEN: No. As a matter of fact. They're all waiting for me. My cousin is very excited. They're all waiting. (*A pause.*) Berlin will still be in Germany next week, Karl. Will it or won't it?

BODENSHATZ: Who can say? (*A pause.*)

RICHTHOFEN: Will you get me ready to fly, Oberleutnant? (*Bodenshatz picks up Richthofen's goggles. Richthofen strips off his cape. Bodenshatz prepares the leather flying jacket and head gear. Richthofen doesn't bother to put on a shirt. Bodenshatz holds out a pair of leather gloves as if he is preparing a surgeon to perform.*)

BODENSHATZ: I know Hermann would want me to wake him.

RICHTHOFEN: We'll let Hermann sleep, Karl. Jacket!

BODENSHATZ: Your cousin will be flying the new machine that was meant for Lothar.

RICHTHOFEN: I'll watch for Wolfram. I wish I had time to shave. Helmet.

BODENSHATZ: (*Going.*) I'll heat the water.

RICHTHOFEN: No. Gloves. We don't want to disturb anyone, do we? I'll shave after the first kettle. Walking stick. And I have my pistol.

BODENSHATZ: Heavy cloud coverage. Ceiling at fifteen hundred meters.

RICHTHOFEN: We'll bump our heads. (*Bodenshatz staps a bulky pack to Richthofen's back.*)

BODENSHATZ: Visibility—fair. Arm, please.

RICHTHOFEN: (*Referring to the parachute.*) I can't wear the stupid thing, Karl. The English aren't wearing them.

BODENSHATZ: They're not allowed to wear them.

RICHTHOFEN: I have no patience for all the buckles and straps.

BODENSHATZ: But you'll wear it because you don't want mother to worry, Manfred. (*They begin to hurry the procedure.*)

RICHTHOFEN: How do I look?

BODENSHATZ: You should have shaved.

RICHTHOFEN: (*Looking in a mirror.*) Conservatively flamboyant. Mustn't forget the scarf. I remember after having seen my handkerchief flying from the steeple at Wahlstatt how I wished that I'd left my silk scarf instead. (*Richthofen puts on the scarf.*)

BODENSHATZ: (*With a clipboard.*) Wind out of the East at nine knots. Remember you haven't had any sleep.

RICHTHOFEN: Good morning, Moritz, you noble beast. Karl, will you please have someone untie the dog's tail.

BODENSHATZ: (*Heading for the door.*) The wind is gusting.

RICHTHOFEN: (*Standing by the window.*) Oberleutnant. This way out.

BODENSHATZ: This is a rather unorthodox way to enter the field, Rittmeister.

RICHTHOFEN: Step up, I'll follow you.

BODENSHATZ: We look foolish, Rittmeister. (*They climb onto the sill and out.*)

RICHTHOFEN: No one will see.

BODENSHATZ: Everyone is looking. They all see.

RICHTHOFEN: Then we'd better smile, Karl.

BODENSHATZ: Yes, Rittmeister. (*Obviously they're being watched. Music. The members of a military marching band are parading out from behind Richthofen's room playing their instruments. They wear full German military dress uniforms. Richthofen doesn't notice that the band is comprised of the Three Women. Wolfram is waiting in his flight gear on the airfield.*)

WOLFRAM: Rittmeister.

RICHTHOFEN: The English are coming, Wolfram. We're going up to court them. Climb into your machine. Stay a thousand feet above the fighting and watch.

WOLFRAM: Yes, Rittmeister. Good hunting, cousin. (*Wolfram heads off for his machine. Richthofen looks at the musicians.*)

RICHTHOFEN: Who ordered the music?

BODENSHATZ: Von Ludendorff wanted a marching band to send you off to Berlin.

RICHTHOFEN: Good. They no longer have a reason to play.

BODENSHATZ: Leave them. It's your celebration.

RICHTHOFEN: The only way to celebrate concentration is with silence.

BODENSHATZ: Ignore them. Keep smiling. What's your favorite number today? (*Richthofen gives Bodenshatz his walking stick.*)

RICHTHOFEN: Eighty-one.

BODENSHATZ: And counting, Rittmeister.

RICHTHOFEN: Have some eggs waiting, will you please, Karl? (*Richthofen walks out into the field. The band continues to play The red Fokker triplane floats down and lands on the earth. Richthofen climbs into the cockpit, buckles his chin strap and safety belt, tucks in his scarf and pulls the goggles down over his eyes. The sound of an engine. Thumbs up. The aeroplane automatically lifts into the air and Richthofen's final flight begins. The Women continue to perform as the Marching Band. Bodenshatz turns and walks away.*)

SCENE 12

(*The West. 10:10 a.m., April 21st. The machine gun nest of Buie and Evans. They sit at the machine gun.*)

EVANS: Well, I was just trying to be friendly.

BUIE: So you eat our breakfast, sneaking off by yourself, you piggish gob, William Evans. "Merry Morning," yourself.

EVANS: I got hungry.

BUIE: And what about your starving colleague here?

EVANS: I'll give you the dry pair of underpants. I've been saving these.

BUIE: Are they clean?

EVANS: They're dry.

BUIE: You sweating swine. (*Buie is loading the Lewis gun.*)

EVANS: Now you put those down, they're very dangerous. What do you want with live bullets?

BUIE: We may be having wieners. I'm loading up the wiener machine.

EVANS: This futile pursuit will not impress anybody here, Buie.

BUIE: We'll just see then, won't we, Inch?

EVANS: See what?

BUIE: Action, Mr. Inch, if my little theory proves correct.

EVANS: You fixed Lewis?

BUIE: We'll see.

EVANS: What then could Lewis's trouble have been?

BUIE: What has been surmised here has been surmised here. The technical complexities would be too much for your pimply little brain to digest.

EVANS: You're too embarrassed to admit that it was something glaringly obvious.

BUIE: Lewis here is a delicate and sophisticated instrument which by nature is destined to remain a mystery to certain individuals. You need the mathematics.

EVANS: It's amazing how close we're getting, Buie, my love. I eat breakfast and you fill up with gas.

BUIE: I think the safety catch might have been on.

SCENE 13

(*The East, the West and No Man's Land. 10:30 a.m., April 21st. In the East Boden-shatz stands inside of the room looking up out of the window and waiting. The Women outside continue to play. In the West Buie and Evans sit waiting. Richthofen is flying. Music. Raymond-Barker stands looking up in No Man's Land.*)

RAYMOND-BARKER: Yesterday afternoon I became von Richthofen's eightieth and final kill. It is now 10:40 Allied time on the morning of April twenty-one. Richthofen leads a precision kette comprised of his cousin Wolfram, Reinhardt, Karjus and Wolfe into the West. They are joined by a larger formation of German aircraft and move on in a flock. (*The West. Buie and Evans sit in their machine gun nest without seeing Raymond-Barker.*)

BUIE: Do you hear rumbling?

EVANS: It's your stomach, cobber.

BUIE: Not surprising. I'm half starved, Inch, you pig.

EVANS: Well, you'll just appreciate your dinner all the more. (*No Man's Land.*)

RAYMOND-BARKER: A formation of fifteen R.A.F. Sopwith Camels appear from behind a cloud, two thousand feet below the kette that Richthofen leads. He signals to Wolfram to stay above the fighting and dives with the others. (*The West.*)

BUIE: (*Climbing the tree.*) You hear the buzzing?

EVANS: Your problem Buie is you don't know how to take your relaxation.

BUIE: (*Looking to the East.*) I can hear something. (*No Man's Land.*)

RAYMOND-BARKER: It's 10:43. Richthofen is flying in loops around the core of the air battle, firing at enemy machines at random. In several weeks Hermann Goering will become Rittmeister of the Richthofen Squadron and Karl Bodenshatz will become his adjutant. The appointment will later contribute to Goering's great popularity as a leading member of the party. Bodenshatz will become General of the Luftwaffe in 1940. On July 20th, 1944, he will be representing Goering at a meeting at the Wolf's Lair. An assassin's bomb intended for the Fuhrer will explode under a table where Bodenshatz will be standing. His hands will be badly burned. His eardrums will burst. (*The West.*)

BUIE: (*Up in the tree looking back to the West.*) They're signalling us, Inch. We're being signalled to keep a watch out.

EVANS: Ignore the bastards.

BUIE: I can hear the buzzing. Look up, Inch. Best be ready. (*No Man's Land.*)

RAYMOND-BARKER: It's 10:45. Wolfram stays a thousand feet above the air battle which is drifting in an east wind over enemy lines. Lieutenant Wilfred R. May is an Allied pilot who is on his maiden mission. He has been instructed by Flight Leader A. R. Brown to stay a thousand feet above the air battle to watch. Wilfred May and Wolfram almost fly into each other. They become engaged. Richthofen sees that Wolfram is in trouble and chases May off his tail. Lieutenant May jams his Lewis gun and flees toward his own line with Richthofen in pursuit. (*The West.*)

BUIE: (*At the machine gun.*) Get set up, Evans, we're being watched.

EVANS: Are you sure Lewis is fixed?

BUIE: We've been told to get set.

EVANS: I don't see what for. (*No Man's Land.*)

RAYMOND-BARKER: It's 10:47. Richthofen has broken from the pack and is chasing Wilfred May low over enemy lines. He follows on May's tail firing virtually point blank, eighty feet above the tree tops. On and on they fly with May an easy target and Richthofen firing and missing and firing again and again. R.A.F. Flight Leader Roy Brown makes a pass at Richthofen, fires a round and banks off leaving Richthofen following right behind Wilfred May and firing. (*The West.*)

BUIE: There they are.

EVANS: How many? Three?

BUIE: Two. Feed Lewis, Inch, come on.

EVANS: Here they come. Behind the trees. Jesus. Get 'em both, Buie.

BUIE: Just the one. Just the second one. (*No Man's Land.*)

RAYMOND-BARKER: Wolfram von Richthofen will become a fanatical member of the party and kill himself in May of 1945. Hermann Goering will become a leading member of the party and kill himself in October of 1946.

The Lance Corporal will become the Fuhrer of the party and kill himself in April of 1945. (*The West.*)

BUIE: Stay set. Don't panic. Get ready to feed me.

EVANS: Ready, steady, stupid bastards are asking for some. (*No Man's Land.*)

RAYMOND-BARKER: William Evans will drink himself to death in Sydney in April of 1925. Robert Buie will die alone in his fishing dinghy in Mooney Mooney Creek in April of 1964, forty-six years after the death of von Richthofen. (*The West. The engine sounds become louder.*)

EVANS: There they come, Buie.

BUIE: Feed me now, Mister Inch.

EVANS: Hit 'em, Buie. Come on. Hit 'em.

BUIE: No. Wait. Don't want to hit the wrong one.

EVANS: Hit 'em, Buie. Hurry.

BUIE: Wait.

EVANS: Come on, Buie. Fire. Fire for Christ's sake. (*The engine sound becomes deafening.*)

BUIE: I can see him.

EVANS: Lewis doesn't work, does it? It doesn't fucking work, does it, Buie? I knew it all along. (*Buie fires the machine gun up at Richthofen's Fokker triplane. Flames shoot out from the end of the barrel of the gun. The aeroplane dips immediately, falls to earth and rests on its nose in No Man's Land. Richthofen slumps forward in the cockpit. A silence.*) Jesus!

BUIE: I think we did all right.

EVANS: Buie, Jesus, you've hit something. Souvies. Come on, Buie. We got one. Jesus. (*Evans jumps over the sandbags and walks cautiously to the fallen aircraft. Buie follows.*)

BUIE: I think we did all right.

EVANS: (*Looking in the cockpit.*) He's gone. Dance with me, you bastard. Congratulations. You got one for us. Congratulations. (*They jump up and down and embrace.*)

BUIE: We got a red one.

EVANS: Let's rat him. Free souvies. Think of the future. Think of the grandkids.

BUIE: You're a festering sore, Mr. Inch. (*Evans takes the scarf from around Richthofen's neck.*)

EVANS: Got a nice scarf for you here, Buie. Congratulations. We'll be famous at this rate. (*Buie puts on the scarf. They pull Richthofen's body out of the cockpit and drop it like a sack on the ground. Evans accidentally activates Richthofen's parachute. They take his fur-lined boots, his leather jacket, his wallet, his pistol, his goggles, his head gear. Richthofen bleeds profusely from the fatal wounds. The East. In Richthofen's room, Hermann Goering and Karl Bodenshatz sit by themselves. Goering holds Richthofen's walking stick. Wolfram looks in from the bunkroom. A painting of Von Richthofen's sitting in a chair is hanging on the wall.*)

THE SKIES HAVE GONE DRY

GOERING, BODENSHATZ & WOLFRAM:
THE SKIES HAVE GONE DRY
AND THE GRASS TURNS BROWN
AND WE'LL TORCH OUR MACHINES
WHEN THE SUN GOES DOWN.
HEAR THEM CLIMBING, STALLING, FALLING,
WATCH THEM REACH THEIR SPEED,
KEEP ME THINKING OF YOU.

(No Man's Land. Buie and Evans disappear into the West, leaving Richthofen's motionless, half-naked body behind. The East. The Lance Corporal is standing outside the window again, looking in, unnoticed by Goering, Bodenshatz, and Wolfram. The Lance Corporal is now recognizable as Adolf Hitler.)

SARAH (Reprise)

THE WOMEN:
I DON'T WANT TO BE THE ONE TO HOLD THE LIGHT.
OULALALALA, OULALA, OULALALA.
I DON'T WANT TO BE THE ONE TO HOLD THE LIGHT.
OULALALALA, OULALA, OULALALA.
"WAKE THE PEOPLE NOW," SAID SARAH.
"NOW," CALLED SARAH, OULALALA,
SARAH WAS SCREAMING,
THE PEOPLE WERE DREAMING,
CRIED A YOUNG BOY, "PLEASE SARAH PLAY ON."
AND SARAH PLAYED ON.
AND SARAH PLAYED ON AND ON AND ON.

(Richthofen sits up and looks out. Darkness.)

END

Deep Sleep

John Jesurun

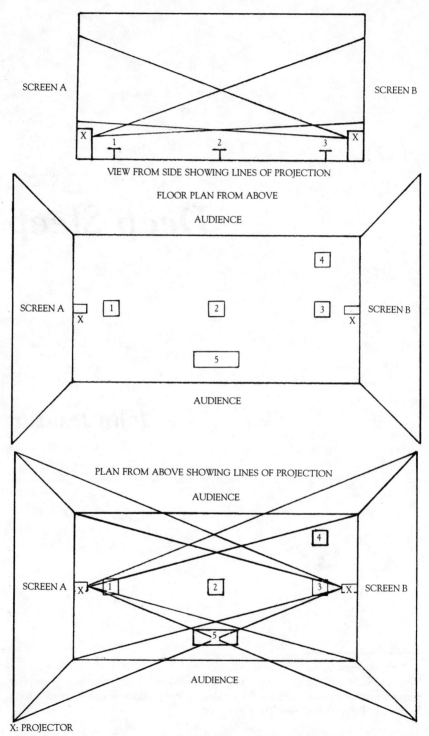

VIEW FROM SIDE SHOWING LINES OF PROJECTION

FLOOR PLAN FROM ABOVE

AUDIENCE

SCREEN A

SCREEN B

AUDIENCE

PLAN FROM ABOVE SHOWING LINES OF PROJECTION

AUDIENCE

SCREEN A

SCREEN B

AUDIENCE

X: PROJECTOR

TABLE 1: MANITAS; TABLE 2: BRONSKI; TABLE 3: EMILY; TABLE 4: SPARKY; TABLE 5: WHITEY.

Massimo Agus

Deep Sleep was first performed at La Mama ETC in New York City on February 1, 1986 with the following cast:

Whitey	*Steve Buscemi*
Emily	*Valerie Charles*
Bronski	*Larry Tighe*
Manitas	*Sanghi Wagner*
Sparky	*Michael Tighe*
Bodine	*Black-Eyed Susan*
Smith	*John Hagan*
Miranda	*Annie Labois*
Lee	*Robyn Hatcher*

Director: John Jesurun
Technical Director: Jim Coleman
Camera/Film Coordinator: Richard Connor

(At the center of each end of the playing floor is a large clear plexiglass box, five feet high. Each box contains a projector. Both projectors remain on throughout the performance. Behind each projector, six feet of the ground is a large screen. twenty-one feet high by twenty-eight feet wide. Images from the projectors will be received by these two screens. Four identical three by three wooded top tables. One at the center of the space, another in one corner. Each of the remaining two is positioned in front of a projector. There is a large three by six mirror-topped table opposite the center table. Each of these tables is accompanied by one or two wooden office chairs. On each table: A plate and eating utensils. On table four [Sparky's table]: A turntable, a record album, a bread roll. On one of the chairs at the center table is a clothed wooden puppet. On center table: A bread roll..)

STAGE

(Sparky, nine years old in leather knickers, sits at the corner table. Emily sits at the table nearest him, her chair is blue, her dress is blue, she wears a long black leather coat. Bronski sits at the center table in a dark business suit. Manitas sits in front of the other projector in pants and a denim jacket. Except for Sparky, the live performers smoke almost continuously throughout the performance.)

SCREEN

(Projectors on. Screen A: Extreme closeup of Whitey's face moving slowly across the screen [thirteen seconds].

Screen B: [Simultaneously.] Extreme closeup of Whitey's eye which zooms out to his full face [thirty seconds].)

CUT

(Screen A: Wide shot—seated around a blue tabletop, Whitey, Lee, Bodine, Miranda. Smith stands in the center, wearing a black suit. Miranda a red silk dress. Lee a blue dress, Bodine a black dress. Whitey, a young man with a red shirt and white hair. The scene is viewed from a very high angle. When the actors on the screen address those on the stage, they look up.

Screen B: A large window, through which is seen a blue sky. A translucent curtain is blowing in the wind. The window is full screen.)

LEE: Good morning.
BODINE: Sorry I'm late, I couldn't find a place to park my car.

SMITH: That's alright.

MIRANDA: I didn't know you had a car.

BODINE: I just bought one.

SMITH: How's your daughter?

BODINE: She's fine. How are you Whitey?

SMITH: Whitey.

MIRANDA: Sit down.

LEE: This is . . . who is this?

WHITEY: Oh.

MIRANDA: Who is this, you know who it is.

SMITH: This is our friend Miranda.

WHITEY: Miranda.

LEE: Now let's see if you can close your eyes.

SMITH: Close your eyes.

MIRANDA: That's right close them.

BODINE: What color do you see?

WHITEY: I don't.

LEE: What color do you see?

WHITEY: Blue.

BODINE: What kind of blue?

LEE: What kind?

SMITH: Sky blue, sea blue, cirulean blue, cobalt blue?

WHITEY: Prussian blue.

SMITH: Prussian blue.

LEE: Is it nice?

WHITEY: Yeah.

BODINE: Take this hand. (*Offers her hand to Whitey.*)

WHITEY: Who's hand is it? (*Takes Bodine's hand.*)

BODINE: It's Bodine's hand.

SMITH: Right, and who is Bodine?

WHITEY: Bodine is my friend.

MIRANDA: What color do you see?

WHITEY: Blue, light blue.

MIRANDA: That's right.

LEE: Now is that the color you want to see or the color we want to see.

SPARKY: Whitey.

SPARKY: Whitey.

SPARKY: It's me Sparky.

SPARKY: Whitey, it's me.

SPARKY: It's me Sparky.

WHITEY: It's the color I want to see.

BODINE: What else do you see?

WHITEY: I see an angel face. It's on top of an angel food cake and it is my own face and my own cake and Pinry is there too.

SMITH: Who's that?

LEE: Who's that?

WHITEY: Sparky?

BODINE: You know Sparky, your friend Sparky. He was on the roller coaster ride when you fell off.

WHITEY: I flew off. Is my doll there?

LEE: Pinry?

MIRANDA: Pinry.

WHITEY: Yes.

WHITEY: Who's that?

WHITEY: Hi Sparky.

BODINE: Where's Sparky?

SMITH: He's here in this room.

BODINE: And what is your name?

WHITEY: What is my name? Sparky.

SMITH: Your name is not Sparky.

WHITEY: What is my name?

BODINE: You know your name. What is your name?

WHITEY: I don't have a name.

LEE: You have a name.

WHITEY: I don't know my name. What is my name?

SMITH: You know you have a name.

WHITEY: I know I have a name.

MIRANDA: And what is that name?

WHITEY: That name is Sparky.

MIRANDA: No, Sparky is over there.

WHITEY: What is my name?

SMITH: You know your name.

LEE: Sparky is over there.

WHITEY: My name is Sparky.

LEE: Sparky is not your name, Sparky is over there.

MIRANDA: Do you see Sparky?

WHITEY: I see Sparky.

SMITH: Do you see Sparky?

WHITEY: I see Sparky.

BODINE: Then what is your name?

WHITEY: My name is Sparky.

BODINE: Your name is not Sparky.

WHITEY: My name is not Sparky.

LEE: What is your name.

WHITEY: Then what is your name? I don't know.

BODINE: What is my name? My name is Bodine.

WHITEY: Your name is Bodine.

BODINE: Right. My name is Bodine.

MIRANDA: And my name is . . . ?

WHITEY: Sparky.

MIRANDA: My name is not Sparky.

SPARKY: I'm Sparky.

WHITEY: You are Sparky.

SMITH: And who is that?

WHITEY: That is Lee.

BODINE: That is Lee.

LEE: And who is that?

WHITEY: That is Smith.

LEE: Right, that is Smith.

WHITEY: And that is Whitey.

LEE: No, you are Whitey.

WHITEY: I am Whitey.

SMITH: Your name is Whitey.

WHITEY: My name is Sparky.

BODINE: That is Sparky, you just said that your name is Whitey.

WHITEY: My name is Whitey Sparky.

EMILY: Your name is Whitey.

WHITEY: My name is Whitey.

LEE: Your name is Whitey.

WHITEY: My name is Whitey?

MIRANDA: There you are. What is

your name?

WHITEY: My name is Sparky.

MIRANDA: Your name is not Sparky, your name is Whitey.

SPARKY: Why don't we just switch names?

SMITH: Because he must learn his name.

EMILY: Not with his brain in that condition.

SPARKY: What condition?

BODINE: You know what condition it is.

WHITEY: I don't want to talk about that now.

SPARKY: Whitey.

WHITEY: Sparky.

EMILY: Whitey.

BODINE: Let's not talk about it now.

WHITEY: And don't think I don't remember what happened.

MANITAS: We know you remember what happened.

WHITEY: And don't try and hide it from me.

SMITH: No one is trying to hide anything.

WHITEY: Yes you are, yes you are.

LEE: We are not Whitey.

WHITEY: My name is Sparky.

BRONSKI: That is Sparky.

EMILY: Not with his brain in that condition.

BODINE: And you know what condition. You can't expect someone's brain to be okay if they've just fallen out of a roller coaster.

BRONSKI: It happened several years ago.

WHITEY: I fell out of a roller coaster and so what? I don't even know my own name.

MANITAS: Who's that?

EMILY: It's the people who have been sent for to fix him up.
BRONSKI: Give up.

WHITEY: Not give up.

BRONSKI: He's witless.
SPARKY: And stop that laughing.

WHITEY: What is your name and what can you do? Who are you?
BODINE: Antonia. Let me put my hands on his head, it will help me tell. (*Rises and stands behind Whitey.*)

SPARKY: Tell what?

BODINE: Tell what is wrong and then I can cure him. (*Puts her hands on Whitey's head.*)

EMILY: Go ahead.

BODINE: Alright, I can tell.

SPARKY: You can't tell anything, don't believe her. It's only a trick, tricksters.
BRONSKI: Goathead.

BODINE: Silence, a moment of silence.
LEE: You are very tired and sleepy.
WHITEY: Don't try and hypnotize me.

SPARKY: Tricksters, hucksters.
MANITAS: Shut up.
BRONSKI: Shut up.

WHITEY: Heads will roll.
MIRANDA: Are you sure you remember? First you . . .
BODINE: Don't tell me, I know what I'm doing. Would you like a book?
WHITEY: Yes.

SPARKY: Don't touch it, it's the book of the dead.

SMITH: Exactly.
BODINE: Osiris awakes, the wary god wakens, the god stands up, stand up, thou shalt not end, thou shalt not perish, the world is losing its grip. A moment of silence, a moment of silence. What's your name?

WHITEY: You remember my name.

BODINE: What is your name Sparky?

WHITEY: I told you it doesn't work.

LEE: A moment of silence.

BODINE: A moment of silence.

LEE: A dark period.

MIRANDA: A moment of silence.

WHITEY: Though I walk through the valley of shadows I feel no evil.

BODINE: It's just a shadow.

LEE: Pay no attention to the man behind the curtain.

SMITH: Whitey.

WHITEY: Sparky.

BODINE: Are you seen from way below? Are you?

WHITEY: Believe me I am. I was crumpled out of it.

BODINE: And then?

WHITEY: I don't know why I'm so uncomfortable here.

BODINE: And then.

SPARKY: (*Stands.*) It's worse than the movies or the Catholic church, all tricks done with mirrors and strings. And the bullfights, the bullfights, everyone knows that bull gets up again, they dust it off and send it back into the ring for the next fight. Everyone knows that. (*Sits.*)

WHITEY: Bagpipes.

LEE: Off with his head.

BODINE: You are rampant, delirious, dehydrated, bald of all thought and action.

SMITH: Say it again.

BODINE: You are rampant, delirious, dehydrated, bald of all thought.

WHITEY: And I will always be with you until you run out.

BODINE: Sing it again, say it again.

LEE: Remove the doubt.

WHITEY: Wait a minute.

BODINE: No. (*Sits.*)

MIRANDA: Remove the doubt.

WHITEY: Wait a minute.

BODINE: No. (*Sits.*)

MIRANDA: Remove the doubt.

WHITEY: I will always be with you until my bulb burns out. I am an act of love.

SMITH: Remove the doubt.

SPARKY: It's all tricks.

BODINE: The shred, once upon a time there was a shred.

WHITEY: Get me out of here, get me out of here I said.

BODINE: Numbness, getting numb. One of you is totally deluded, angrily so, oh so angrily so.

WHITEY: It's yelling at itself.

SMITH: The poor exhausted flies, the maggots died of hunger, the deer flesh was all eaten up, they broke their teeth on the bones, they tried but they died of hunger and fantasia.

WHITEY: That would be nice and then the light came into the room and destroyed everything.

BODINE: Blew it away. Tell me what you are seeing.

WHITEY: I'm seeing the light come into room and blow everything away, one of you is accused of murder and the other, you have the right to remain silent.

SPARKY: I will.

BODINE: Order in the court, monkey wants to speak.

WHITEY: I don't want to set the world on fire. Got a match?

EMILY: He's delirious. Whitey.

LEE: Delirioso.

EMILY: Whitey.

WHITEY: Tell it to the judge.

SPARKY: This is ridiculous, I won't have it.

MANITAS: You will have it.

SPARKY: One is stupid, one doesn't know what to think.

WHITEY: But you're wrong. I do want to set the world on fire. I want to burn it all down to shreds. (*Laughs.*)

EMILY: Whitey!

WHITEY: Sparky!

BODINE: A spark is a shred of light.

WHITEY: You have to do it or you won't win.

BODINE: Do you want to win?

WHITEY: I want to win.

MIRANDA: Do you want to win over god and the devil?

BODINE: And the deep blue sea?

WHITEY: Yes I do.

BODINE: Do you have a burning desire to fail and burn with god in heaven?

WHITEY: Yes, yes, yes.

SPARKY: This isn't funny, he's retarded.

MANITAS: I wish you'd be a little nicer to them after all they've done.

SPARKY: Oh, alright, sorry.

MIRANDA: You see, we all have to adapt to each other.

BODINE: I want to make it clear and precise.

LEE: Lights, shadows, reflection, translucence, do you understand?

BODINE: The Milky Way is your face.

LEE: That's right dear.

MIRANDA: That's right dear.

SMITH: Try and get a little rest.

WHITEY: I don't want a little rest.

BODINE: That's right dear, try and get some rest.

WHITEY: I don't want some rest, where are my pants?

CUT

(*Stage is dark.*)

(*Window and table switch screens. The table image is slightly closer now and viewed from a slightly lower angle than before. The figures on the screen continue to look upward [toward the camera] when speaking to stage players. The size of the window remains the same, filling the screen. Whitey, Smith, Lee sit around table. Bodine stands.*)

MIRANDA: How do you feel?

WHITEY: What do you care?

LEE: We really do care, we want to help you.

WHITEY: Help me what? Why don't you help them?

BODINE: They don't need any help right now.

SMITH: When the time comes.

WHITEY: And when will the time come?

MIRANDA: Why do you ask so many questions?

SMITH: Let him ask, that's good.

WHITEY: Why is it good?

BODINE: Because it is good.

LEE: If you ask questions, you get answers.

WHITEY: I'm not getting any answers.

SMITH: Yes you are.

MIRANDA: Every time we ask you something, you get an answer.

BODINE: Do you see?

WHITEY: Yes, I see.

LEE: He understands.

WHITEY: No, I don't see or understand.

MIRANDA: Yes you do.

WHITEY: I don't.

LEE: You do.

WHITEY: I do. I'll understand anything you want me to.

BODINE: It's difficult.

WHITEY: When will I be able to see?

LEE: Close your eyes.

MIRANDA: What do you see?

WHITEY: Blue.

BODINE: There, you're beginning to see.

WHITEY: I am.

SMITH: Do you see me?

WHITEY: I don't know.

SMITH: What do I look like?

WHITEY: You are tall and you have red hair.

SMITH: Yes. And what does she look like?

WHITEY: Short with blue hair.

MIRANDA: Right.

BODINE: You can see.

LEE: How many windows does this room have?

WHITEY: Five on one side and six on the other.

LEE: Correct.

SMITH: How many fingers am I holding up? (*His hands remain down.*)

WHITEY: Six on one and five on the other.

SMITH: Right.

LEE: And what is your name?

WHITEY: My name is Whitey.

LEE: Right.

BODINE: And what do you look like?

WHITEY: I am tall with black hair.

SMITH: Right.

MIRANDA: You see? That's all.

BODINE: And now you can go.

WHITEY: I'll go. How did you do it?

LEE: Just by suggesting.

BODINE: And you believed us and so you can see.

SMITH: Come back some time.

BODINE: Come back some time, do you hear me?

WHITEY: Yes.

MIRANDA: Come back some time.

BODINE: Alright?

WHITEY: How did you do it?

LEE: You did it.

SMITH: Come back some time.

BODINE: I'll be back.

LEE: Do you understand?

WHITEY: Yes, I understand the problem.

LEE: The problem is to bring rationality to bear in an inherently irrational situation.

SMITH: Exactly.

MIRANDA: You seem tired.

WHITEY: I am.

BODINE: What was that dream you had?

WHITEY: Oh, there was this strange orange frog lizard iguana with red orange eyes and green whites. It was trying to stare the other smaller lizards down, trying to convince them, but they wouldn't pay any attention to him so the dream ended.

LEE: That was some kind of a bad snooze.

WHITEY: If you have to kill for breakfast then you shouldn't get up.

BODINE: Try not to think about it.

SMITH: Try not to think about it.

WHITEY: I want to think about it.

MIRANDA: But don't, you'll confuse yourself.

SMITH: Come over here to this window.

(*Whitey follows Smith as he walks out of frame and into the frame of the opposite screen. They stand on either side of the window and look out.*)

LEE: Look out it.
BODINE: Do you see out?
MIRANDA: What do you see?
BODINE: Tell me what you see.
WHITEY: Water, trees, wind.
LEE: Is it nice?
WHITEY: Yes.
MIRANDA: Think about what you see.

(*Table and window switch screens.*)

BODINE: And don't think about any-
    thing else.
SMITH: When you go back, have rest.
WHITEY: Are you trying to trick me?
BODINE: No, not at all.

(*Table and window switch screens.*)

WHITEY: Alright.
LEE: What is the sky like?
WHITEY: Pearly irridescent.
BODINE: It's okay, you're alright, the
    ace of spades is dead.
WHITEY: Is that true?

(*Table and window switch screens.*)

SMITH: The answer is absolutely yes.
BODINE: When you came here, you
    were seventy pounds, voiceless,
    sightless, mindless, heartless, in-
    criminated, a drop of water in a
    cracked glass.
WHITEY: Nothing, I fell out of a roller
    coaster.

(*Table and window switch screens.*)

MIRANDA: That's all?

SMITH: That's all.

WHITEY: That's true.

BODINE: And now?

LEE: And now the high altar was made low, the low sky was made high, the blue sky was made red and god was satisfied.

BODINE: And now it's clear, he's fixed in hindsight.

SMITH: And now you can return.

MIRANDA: Do you want to go back?

(*Table and window switch screens.*)

WHITEY: Yes, thank you.

SMITH: Come and visit.

WHITEY: Thanks for helping me.

BODINE: You're welcome.

SMITH: Thank you.

MIRANDA: What is my name?

WHITEY: You are Miranda, and you are Smith, and you are Lee and you are Bodine.

MIRANDA: Right.

WHITEY: Thank you.

BODINE: Come and visit any time.

WHITEY: And I am Whitey.

MIRANDA: Whitey.

LEE: Yes.

WHITEY: I'm fixed.

CUT

(*Whitey is now seated at the mirror-topped table. Sparky, Bronski, Manitas and Emily each sitting at a table. They eat off the empty plates in front of them.*)

(*Screen A: The four figures of Smith, Bodine, Miranda, and Lee are seated at the blue table and are seen from the waist up. The table is viewed from a slightly lower angle than the last scene. Each figure eats from an empty plate. Bodine smokes.*

Screen B: The large window seen previously. The window and the table will alternate screens several times during the scene.)

SPARKY: Because of that and so thank you for repairing his eyes.

BODINE: You're welcome. If there's anything else we can do.

BRONSKI: Bodine, how did you discover the treatment?

BODINE: Oh it wasn't me.

SMITH: It was Lee, she's been working on it for years.

BODINE: I couldn't have done it without my colleagues.

LEE: And collaborators.

MIRANDA: And such a gentle way to approach things.

SMITH: We believe that is the best way.

MIRANDA: A more sensual approach to the senses.

BODINE: How old is the boy?

WHITEY: Nine years old.

MIRANDA: How old are you?

SPARKY: Nine years old.

BRONSKI: But it was his eyes.

LEE: Oh yes it was his eyes. He was totally sightless.

BODINE: It's as if they had been melted out in some kind of shock.

SPARKY: We were doing a test on the roller coaster. He was sitting in the front and flew out.

EMILY: He told us.

BRONSKI: You still look a little pale Whitey.

SMITH: You think so?

MIRANDA: He'll be alright.

LEE: He'll be alright.

BODINE: When will the park be operational?

SPARKY: Not for several months.

BRONSKI: The accident was widely

publicized even though we tried to keep it quiet.

EMILY: Whitey was our best technician, he conceived the entire course. He decided to ride it alone that day.

WHITEY: Of course.

SPARKY: I work on the spark plugs, the spark elements, do a lot of soldering.

MANITAS: I build a lot of the engines.

MANITAS: Thank you.

EMILY: A lot of it is computerized.
SPARKY: Except for the sparks.

EMILY: I handle the business end and sometimes I play records during the rides.

BRONSKI: I'm not involved, I'm just a friend, an advisor.

SPARKY: I'm chewing, I'm chewing.
EMILY: That needle on the turntable is screwy.
SPARKY: I know. I'll fix it. (*Roams about the space lipsynching a man's Spanish recitation of poetry by Pablo Neruda. He punctuates various phrases by raising his arms and gesturing with his hands towards the screen or to the stage actors.*)
Eres la boina gris y el corazón en calma.

BODINE: More broccoli?

MIRANDA: And Sparky, what do you do?

LEE: And Manitas?

LEE: Of course, I can tell. Your hands, such beautiful hands.

SMITH: Is most of it computerized?

MIRANDA: Emily, what do you do?

LEE: And I'm sorry, I've forgotten your name.
BODINE: Bronski.

MIRANDA: Chew that well Sparky.

En tus ojos peleaban las llamas de crespúculo
y las hojas caían del agua de tu alma.
Apegada a mis brazos como una enredadera,
Las hojas recogían tu voz lenta y en calma.
Hoguera de estupor, que mi sed ardía,
dulce jacinto azul, torzido sobre mi alma.
Siento viajar tus hojos y es distante el otoño.
Boina gris, voz de pajaro y corazón de caza,
hacia donde me gravan mis profundos anhelos y
caían mis besos allegres como brazas.
Cielo desde en navío,
campo desde los cerros, tus recuerdos de luz,
de humo, de estarte en calma.

SPARKY: I made it up.

SPARKY: Oh no thanks.

SPARKY: I'll be busy in the shop. (*Fiddles with needle on record player.*) The needle's fixed. (*Sits.*)
EMILY: And what do you do?

BRONSKI: No.

MANITAS: Yes it is.
WHITEY: How far to the other side?

LEE: Where did you learn that?

BODINE: It's quite beautiful.
SMITH: You must come and recite it.

MIRANDA: Oh you must.

MIRANDA: I don't do anything, but I don't have to.
SMITH: Did we show you?

LEE: Look.
BODINE: It's quite beautiful, isn't it?

SMITH: About twenty miles.

MIRANDA: In the winter it's covered with ice.

BODINE: In the summer it's broiling. (*Lights cigarette.*)

LEE: What color is it?

WHITEY: Blue.

MANITAS: It's so blue.

WHITEY: Today it's sky blue.

SPARKY: Why is it so blue?

BODINE: It's the translucence of the air, the moisture in the air, even our breath makes it blue, the thousands and millions of panting birds in the atmosphere combine with it all, all the smoke from anything that ever burned anywhere and the wind blows it all around and mixes it up and then the vibration from every sound that's ever made heats it with the sunlight.

SMITH: And makes it blue.

EMILY: But why does it end up blue and not red?

LEE: Because all these things harmonize to make it blue.

MIRANDA: And if they don't then the sky will get to be red or purple or green.

LEE: But mostly red.

MANITAS: Have you ever seen it red?

SMITH: Once or twice.

LEE: Even the rain was red.

MIRANDA: I hate it when it's red.

BODINE: But it's mostly always blue, always blue, one blue or the other. But it almost always stays blue.

SMITH: Always blue.

BODINE: Blue always.

LEE: Except when something goes wrong.

SMITH: But that's very seldom.

MIRANDA: And thank god for that.

BODINE: But if something goes off and it goes red, the blue usually swallows it up.

LEE: And it's purple around the edges for a few minutes or days.

SMITH: When will the park become operational?

WHITEY: In one or two months if we work hard.

MANITAS: And do you have many patients?

SMITH: Oh, a lot.

LEE: We see them day to day.

BRONSKI: Do they all get fixed?

BODINE: Oh almost all.

EMILY: And the ones that don't?

LEE: They go away.

MIRANDA: It's very sad, when there's nothing to be done.

BODINE: What color do you see?

WHITEY: Blue.

MIRANDA: It's very sad but there's nothing to be done.

SMITH: Where is Pinry?

EMILY: Over there?

BODINE: Hello Pinry.

SMITH: Why do you talk to that puppet?

WHITEY: It's a doll puppet.

SPARKY: Sometimes it talks back.

BRONSKI: And it's quite wonderful.

BODINE: But why do you talk to it?

SPARKY: Probably not.

EMILY: It's very shy. (*Picks up puppet and pets it. She passes it to the others.*)

SMITH: I see.

LEE: Will it talk tonight?

BRONSKI: Not always, but one day it just spoke.

MIRANDA: Did it always talk?

BRONSKI: It said ojo caliente.

WHITEY: It means hot eye in Spanish.

LEE: And what did it say?

MIRANDA: Ojo caliente.
LEE: That suggests red.

EMILY: Oh, no.
SPARKY: It suggests a very strong iron
blue.
BRONSKI: But not red.

BODINE: Will it talk tonight?

EMILY: I don't think so. It only talks to
us but it hears everything, it always
hears everything and stores it up in
his brain. He's quite friendly when
he gets the chance.
MANITAS: But he gets sad sometimes.
WHITEY: We put him in front of the
window and he gets better.

SMITH: Maybe we can help him.

BRONSKI: Oh no, he doesn't need any
help.

LEE: Are you sure?

SPARKY: We're sure.

MIRANDA: Are you sure Pinry?

WHITEY: He says he's sure, he's O.K.

LEE: Where did he come from?

SPARKY: We found him in the street.
EMILY: He didn't talk for months and
then he said it, ojo caliente.

BODINE: But what does that mean?

WHITEY: Hot eye, the eye that sees it
all.
BRONSKI: It sees everything every
way.

SMITH: But where did he come from?
LEE: How can he be alive?

BRONSKI: He just is.

BODINE: Maybe he was a dead man
once and it was inhaled into the
doll and made it alive.

EMILY: I don't think so.
BRONSKI: The doll has always been
alive. Right Pinry?
MANITAS: That's right.
BRONSKI: So he'll stay here with us.

MIRANDA: Can he come and visit us

MANITAS: I don't think so. He likes it here.

EMILY: We'll ask him and he'll tell us eventually.

WHITEY: Oh yes.

SPARKY: Oh, sometimes at night when I play records.
EMILY: He can jump very high.
BRONSKI: But no strings.

BRONSKI: He doesn't belong to anyone.
SPARKY: I found him on the street one day . . .
EMILY: And it was Whitey's birthday.
WHITEY: And I went home one day and I opened that present and it was the puppet, but he doesn't really belong to anyone.
SPARKY: He likes to sing.

WHITEY: All kinds of songs.
EMILY: A lot of blues.
MANITAS: Crazy blues.

EMILY: We'll ask, but I think he'll say no. (Puts puppet down on Manitas's table.)

BRONSKI: Both, because he is wood, but he loves electric too.

MANITAS: Pinry, do you want to sing?

sometime?

SMITH: But maybe he'd like it here.

LEE: But he looks like he'd like to stay here.
BODINE: He's quite nice.
MIRANDA: Is his head wooden?

LEE: Does he dance?

BODINE: Oh, no strings?
SMITH: Who does he belong to?

MIRANDA: What does he sing?

MIRANDA: He must come and visit.

BODINE: Does he like electronic music or wooden music?

SMITH: I see.
MIRANDA: I wish he would sing now.

WHITEY: I don't think so.

EMILY: Maybe if we play, he'll sing. (*Stage players gather around Manitas's table.*)

LEE: Let's try it.

SPARKY: We'll sing and you play.

BODINE: We'll get our instruments.

SMITH: What shall we play?

SPARKY: Oh, anything.

(*Live actors lip synch "All In the Game" by the Four Tops.*)

(*Screen A cuts to Bodine, Miranda, Smith and Lee playing instruments: french horn, violin, piano, banjo.*)

CHORUS: Many a tear has to fall.

BRONSKI: But it's all in the game

CHORUS: All in the wonderful game

MANITAS: That we know, that we know is love

WHITEY: You had words, with him

SPARKY: And your future's looking kind of dim

EMILY: But these things, your heart will rise above

WHITEY: Ohohohohoh

CHORUS: Once in a while, he won't call

SPARKY: Mmhmm (*Music out.*)

(*Screen: Instrument playing stops.*)

WHITEY: Did you sing? (*Picks up puppet and holds close to him.*)

EMILY: I don't think so.

MANITAS: No, he didn't.

MIRANDA: And what do you advise them on?

BRONSKI: Oh, on lots of things, this and that.

LEE: What kind of things?

BODINE: How long have you known the puppet?

BRONSKI: I've known the puppet longer than they have.

SPARKY: You didn't tell us that.

BRONSKI: Yes I did.

SMITH: How long have you known

him?

BRONSKI: A few years, five or ten.

WHITEY: You never told us that.

BRONSKI: He belonged to some friends of mine but it was so insulting that they threw it out. So I picked it up out of the garbage. Then I came home one night and he was disappeared. Then these guys found him on the street.

EMILY: You never told us that.

BRONSKI: It never occurred to me that it was the same puppet 'til right now. He's changed a lot, his face used to be quite sour, he's not insulting anymore. He used to be a strange hideous little puppet child but he's changed.

MIRANDA: The poor thing.

LEE: Well, what do you have to say for yourself?

BODINE: Say something.

WHITEY: You are not to be trusted.

EMILY: How could you deceive us?

SMITH: Leave him alone, I'm sure he's had a hard time.

WHITEY: Pinry, how could you deceive us?

EMILY: He's just a puppet for god's sake.

BRONSKI: What do you have to say for yourself?

EMILY: I don't think he will for a long time now.

SPARKY: We've upset him and now he's upset.

MANITAS: How can you tell?

SPARKY: His face has absolutely no expression.

EMILY: Absolutely expressionless.

BRONSKI: Mindless.

WHITEY: He's thinking in there some-

MIRANDA: He's not talking.

where in that wooden head.

SPARKY: It's no big deal really.

EMILY: Maybe if we play catch with him, he'll speak.

SPARKY: Don't.

EMILY: He loves it. (*They play catch with the puppet.*)

LEE: Any expression?

EMILY: No.

SPARKY: Not a thing.

MIRANDA: The poor thing.

LEE: Let us see him.

MANITAS: I think he wants to stay down here.

BODINE: Let him think for himself.

SMITH: Pinry, do you want to stay here?

WHITEY: No answer.

SPARKY: Let's just leave him.

WHITEY: Put him to sleep.

EMILY: Let him have some nice puppet dreams.

BODINE: Goodnight Pinry.

SPARKY: You little wooden pygmy.

MANITAS: Sweet dreams, my dear little woodenhead.

CUT

(*Manitas, Bronsky and Sparky asleep at their tables. Emily and Whitey begin to investigate projector boxes.*)

(*Miranda appears on Screen A, Lee on Screen B. Each is seated at a blue table, viewed head on, eye level, medium close up. Miranda and Lee will alternate screens several times during the scene.*)

LEE: Don't touch that.

WHITEY: Why?

MIRANDA: Don't touch that I said. (*Sips a glass of wine.*)

LEE: Just don't touch it.

EMILY: What is it?

WHITEY: But what is it?

MIRANDA: It's a machine.

EMILY: What does it do?

LEE: Nothing much.

MIRANDA: It makes light.

WHITEY: Why?

LEE: No reason in particular.

EMILY: But, why? (*Emily and Whitey put their fingers in front of projector lights and make shadows.*)

MIRANDA: It's a lamp, it's not going to be touched.

LEE: It could hurt you.

WHITEY: What's it connected to?

LEE: Nothing.

MIRANDA: Don't get too near it.

LEE: Don't do that.

EMILY: What?

MIRANDA: Don't do that, don't put your hands there.

LEE: You're making shadows.

MIRANDA: Don't do that, don't ever do that.

WHITEY: It's fun.

LEE: Please stop.

MIRANDA: Do you want us to lose our patience?

EMILY: We're curious.

LEE: Curiosity killed that cat.

WHITEY: Is that what killed it.

MIRANDA: Yes the cat made too much of a shadow.

EMILY: How can you be such an authority on this?

LEE: We've been around.

WHITEY: How can you continue to believe that theory?

MIRANDA: Don't touch that.

LEE: It may cause a massive problem for which we may have to create a massive solution.

MIRANDA: Have some wine.

WHITEY: No thank you.

LEE: Oh, please do.

EMILY: Why are you always offering us wine?

EMILY: Why?

MIRANDA: I love wine.

WHITEY: I didn't know that.

EMILY: No thanks.

WHITEY: Nothin, I didn't say nothin.

EMILY: I live right here.
WHITEY: I think you'd better stop drinking that.
EMILY: You're starting to get tipsy.

WHITEY: Well, you're going to tip over.

EMILY: He's around.
WHITEY: What do you want with that puppet?

EMILY: Everyone likes it.

WHITEY: Sure.

EMILY: You're getting too drunk now.

WHITEY: Why do you always stay up there? Why don't you come down here?

EMILY: Why not? You keep asking us to go up there and you never come down here.

EMILY: Why is that?

EMILY: Sparky, wake up and do the poem.

MIRANDA: It's a wonderful drink, it's wonderful, it's sensual and as you know, I'm a sensualist.

LEE: Have some.

MIRANDA: And what is your problem?

LEE: Where do you live?

MIRANDA: I know.

MIRANDA: So what if I do? (*Drunk.*)
LEE: So what if she does?
MIRANDA: Where's the puppet?

LEE: We just like it.

LEE: Does it really talk?

MIRANDA: When can we see it talk?

MIRANDA: I am not.

MIRANDA: We don't want to.

LEE: Up is better than down.

MIRANDA: Just is.
LEE: I just wish that kid would do his poem again. He's so good at it.

SPARKY: What for?
WHITEY: Just do it. She wants you to.
SPARKY: (*Lip synchs poem.*)
    Eres la boina gris y el corazón en
    calma.
    En tus ojos peleaban la llamas de
    crepúsculo
    y las hojas caían del agua de tu
    alma.
    Apegada a mis brazos como una
    enredadera,
    las hojas recogían tu voz lenta y en
    calma.

LEE: That's wonderful. (*Falls asleep.*)

EMILY: Why don't you come down
    here?

MIRANDA: I told you.

WHITEY: Hey, she fell asleep.

MIRANDA: She always does.

EMILY: So come down here.

MIRANDA: Oh no, I can't.

WHITEY: Come on, why not?

MIRANDA: I can't, I'm a coward.

EMILY: What's to be scared of?

MIRANDA: A lot. I'm sorry, I can't
    because if I do you see, I won't be
    able to come back and . . . (*Falls
    asleep.*)

WHITEY: She's lost consciousness.
EMILY: They both have.
WHITEY: Hello.
EMILY: Hello.
WHITEY: Bodine.
EMILY: Miranda.
WHITEY: What the hell were their
    names again?

LEE: Don't touch that.

EMILY: I thought you were alseep.

LEE: We never sleep.

CUT

(*Bodine and Smith on Screen A, Miran-da and Lee on Screen B. Waist up behind blue tables, eye level.*)

LEE: We want the puppet.

EMILY: What for?

MIRANDA: Because we do. We want to talk to it.
SMITH: We're losing our patience.

WHITEY: Patience for what?
BRONSKI: We are losing our patience.
MANITAS: Well, you can have it.

SMITH: What's the matter with you?

SPARKY: Nothing at all.

BODINE: Whitey, come here.
LEE: Tell them we want the puppet.

WHITEY: Why do you want the pup-pet?

SMITH: Maybe we can help it talk.

SPARKY: It's fine the way it is.
BRONSKI: So leave it.
EMILY: Where is it?

EMILY: No.

MIRANDA: Something wrong?

SPARKY: Blue.

BODINE: What color do you see?

MANITAS: No.

LEE: Something wrong?

MIRANDA: You're going through with-drawl.
SMITH: Screensick. You're being un-poisoned, that's all.

WHITEY: There's nothing wrong with me.

LEE: Screensick.

MANITAS: Is that like seasick or home-sick?
WHITEY: Or maybe you can shut up.

BODINE: Whitey.
LEE: See what you have become. What's happened to you?

MANITAS: Maybe you can just shut up for a minute and let me think.

SMITH: Alright.

BODINE: Emily, why don't you leave the room?

LEE: Give me your undivided attention.

SMITH: Look at my face.

EMILY: I will not leave this room.

MIRANDA: What's happened to you?

EMILY: No thanks.

LEE: We don't need any of your advice.

EMILY: No thanks, I don't like your face.

BODINE: You're becoming deluded. We've helped you and now you are . . .

BRONSKI: Excuse me, do we have any privacy?

MIRANDA: So ungrateful. You act like we're not even here.

SMITH: You're turning a deaf eye to us.

MANITAS: Leave us alone, will you?

LEE: What color do you see?

BODINE: What color do you see?

WHITEY: Would you please leave?

BRONSKI: I'm starting to see red.

MANITAS: You're wrapped around their fingers.

MIRANDA: You're seasick, you're tired.

EMILY: You're being intercepted.

BRONSKI: Anticipated.

EMILY: Don't you see that?

MANITAS: Would you please leave?

LEE: What for?

MANITAS: We'll have to disrupt you then.

BODINE: And how will you do that?

SMITH: We'll wrap you around our fingers.

MANITAS: We'll cut them off.

WHITEY: I will disrupt you.

MANITAS: I can figure it out. There's a way.

MANITAS: I will disrupt you. Interrupt you.

LEE: I doubt it.

SMITH: Momentarily perhaps.

MIRANDA: Look at this blue. Feast your eyes on it.

EMILY: Don't look.

BODINE: That's O.K., you will be correctible, erasable.

BRONSKI: And so will you.

LEE: We are indelible.

BODINE: You will be correctible.

WHITEY: I will be incorrigable.

WHITEY: So O.K., fine.
SPARKY: Incorrigible.

SMITH: We will remedy that.

SMITH: The world is so small, we must all be civil to each other.

SPARKY: Get out of here.

MIRANDA: You will finally come to understand the way things are done.

EMILY: I have come to understand.

LEE: Relax.

WHITEY: I don't want to relax.

MIRANDA: But you've got to.
BODINE: We'll leave now.
SMITH: We'll be back.

BRONSKI: Please don't come back for a while.
MANITAS: Wait 'til the sky is more blue than it is.
BRONSKI: As you can see, it's become quite red.

SMITH: I like red sometimes.

BRONSKI: I don't.

SMITH: Things can't always be all blue.

SPARKY: That's not what you said before.

LEE: Things can't always be all blue.

WHITEY: That's not what you said before.

WHITEY: The hell it is.

WHITEY: I don't want to.

BRONSKI: Don't do what they say.

MANITAS: Come on, we'll calm them
down.

EMILY: They're always calm.

BRONSKI: They're trying to trick us.

SPARKY: You're trying to convince us
into something.

SPARKY: I think they should leave.

SPARKY: My hands hurt.

SPARKY: What?

BODINE: We changed our minds.

LEE: It's okay when things get red.

SMITH: It is.

MIRANDA: Shall we play a song?

LEE: Of course, that will ease things.

BODINE: Things can become bluer
then.

LEE: The blues then.

SMITH: The blues.

MIRANDA: Come on.

.BODINE: We are not.

LEE: Try not to think about it.

SMITH: Come on, let's play.

BODINE: Come on.

SMITH: Of course they do, you little
junkie.

CUT

(*Stage players lip synch "Master of Eyes"
by Aretha Franklin.*)

EMILY: One look in your eyes, baby
turns me on.
So inviting to me, you know
I feel that they're my own.

CHORUS: Darling reach out just
for me.

EMILY: And I, I had to surrender

(*Screen A: Bodine, Miranda, Lee, Smith
play instruments.*
  Screen B: Window.)

my sense of pride
Your touch from behind on my
shoulder
on my shoulder so tender.
CHORUS: The deepness of your eyes
EMILY: I can't stop lovin' you baby
CHORUS: The deepness of your eyes
EMILY: I can't stop lovin' you . . .
(*Music cut.*)

EMILY: Of course you can't you little
junkie.
SPARKY: Of course I'm a little junkie,
so what I can work like that, it
helps me, I can pay for it, I make
enough. (*Picks up puppet.*)
WHITEY: And you don't spend money
on anything else.
MANITAS: What else is there to spend
money on, vitamins, movies?
SPARKY: It helps me to be graceful.
BRONSKI: Graceful.
EMILY: You're ruining your angel face.
WHITEY: And you're ruining your angel face. You're in love with that
scavenger, that vulture.
BRONSKI: The others are vultures, she
is not.
MANITAS: They're all vultures and
they'll have us all up there if they
get their way.
BRONSKI: And that will be the end of
the Milky Way.
SPARKY: They'll suck us out of our
space. They'll rot our space up.
How can you let them do that?
Don't you see what they're doing?
BRONSKI: You're a deluded little
junkie.
SPARKY: Even the puppet can see
what's happening.
WHITEY: They're convincing you,
they're tricking you but they won't
get me.

(*Both screens go blank.*)

BRONSKI: How can you talk that way about them after all they've done for you?

SPARKY: They're watching us, listening to us.

MANITAS: They can't hear us.

EMILY: God forbid if they do.

WHITEY: You're so ungrateful.

SPARKY: Just shut up.

BRONSKI: Don't tell him to shut up.

EMILY: He can say what he wants.

BRONSKI: And turn us against them after they fixed Whitey?

SPARKY: Whitey fixed himself. Manitas, you're so silly, you'll be the first to go.

WHITEY: There's nothing wrong with them. I've been up there and come back. Nothing happened. It's no big deal. We should send you up there.

SPARKY: What could they do to me?

BRONSKI: Unjunk you.

SPARKY: Nothing could convince me to go up there.

WHITEY: And stop playing with that doll.

SPARKY: It's my friend. It's our friend. It's not like them, right Pinry? Hush little baby, don't you cry. (Hugs puppet.)

EMILY: Stop it you lunatic.

BRONSKI: When are they coming again?

MANITAS: Whenever they want.

EMILY: What's that noise?

SPARKY: There's no noise.

(Screen A: Blank.
   Screen B: Miranda walks into a dingy room through a dark doorway and walks forward until half her body fills the screen. She is holding a glass of wine from

MANITAS: Of course we're here.

BRONSKI: Of course.

SPARKY: Don't go.

MANITAS: Sure, no problem.
BRONSKI: Don't go.

EMILY: No thanks, we're busy.
WHITEY: I'm not.
SPARKY: Whitey, don't.
WHITEY: What's the big deal?
SPARKY: If you go, be careful.
WHITEY: What do you mean Sparky?
SPARKY: Nothing.
BRONSKI: Too many needles. Don't listen to him.

BRONSKI: I'm sure she would.
MANITAS: Cut it out.
SPARKY: The smell of veins exploding.

EMILY: (*Rises and walks to Miranda on screen.*) No thank you, I don't eat sugar. But did I ever tell you about when I was a little girl in Montana I used to ride the six o'clock train that left with the coffins in the morning. I'd sit and do my homework on top of the coffins. It was me and the train master alone

which she occasionally takes a sip. She is seen from slightly below eye level.)

MIRANDA: Hello. Is anyone there?

MIRANDA: Can I come in?

MIRANDA: Manitas, I want to know if you could come and fix my car engine, we don't know what's wrong with it. Maybe you could tell us, advise us.

MIRANDA: What?

MIRANDA: Maybe you'd all like to come.

MIRANDA: Maybe Bronski would like to come. I'm sure Bodine would like to see you.

MIRANDA: Have some candy.

(*Screen: Slow zoom to extreme close up of Miranda's face.*)

with the dead people in the coffins. When the coffins would be moved off the train, my cousin would meet us. She'd throw her voice because she was a ventriloquist. She'd have the coffin say "Let me down easy boys."

EMILY: I think it's fascinating.

EMILY: And so I accepted death at a very early age.

EMILY: Thank you.

WHITEY: Don't mind them.
BRONSKI: Spark plug blew.
SPARKY: I'm inside a chestnut rotten from the inside out.

MANITAS: Oh please, don't be so negativistic.
SPARKY: Go fix that car, will ya?

SPARKY: Oh no I won't because . . .
   (Gets up and walks away.)
WHITEY: Where are you going?

(During this speech, "Heroin" by Lou Reed, Sparky wanders around the entire playing space in large circles. The others sit watching and smoking.)

SPARKY: I don't know just where I'm going but I'm gonna try for the kingdom if I can because it makes me feel like I'm a man. When I put a spike into my vein and I tell you

MIRANDA: What a stupid story.

MIRANDA: I don't.

MIRANDA: Your sentiments are ugly.

MIRANDA: What is this change of heart.

MIRANDA: You are.

MIRANDA: Listen little boy, morning will come and you'll still be dead and the day will go on into the night and the year will keep going and that's how I ended up.

things aren't quite the same. When
I'm rushing on my run and I feel
like Jesus's son and I guess but I just
don't know and I guess but I just
don't know. I have made a big decision, I'm gonna try to nullify my
life 'cause when the blood begins to
flow and it shoots up the dropper's
neck when I'm closing in on death.
You can help me now, you guys
and all you sweet girls with all your
sweet talk, you can all go take a
walk and I guess I just don't know
and I guess that I just don't know. I
wish that I was born a thousand
years ago. I wish that I sail the
darkened seas on a great big clipper
ship goin' from this land here to
that on a sailor's suit and cap,
away from the big city where a
man cannot be free of all the evils
of this town and of himself and
what's around. Oh and I guess but
I just don't know, oh I guess but I
just don't know. Heroin, be the
death of me heroin. It's my wife
and it's my life because a mainer to
my vein leads to a center in my
head and then I'm better off than
dead. Because when the smack
begins to flow I really don't care
anymore about all the jimjims in
this town and all the politicians
making crazy sounds and everybody putting everyone else down
and all the dead bodies piled up in
mounds. 'Cause when the smack
begins to flow, then I really don't
know anymore and when the heroin is in my blood and the blood is
in my head then thank god that I'm
as good as dead and thank your god
that I'm not aware, and thank god
that I just don't care and I guess I

just don't know, oh and I guess I
just don't know. See how the needle goes down so gently and softly?
(*Places needle on record.*)

MANITAS: Stop talking about that record player.

WHITEY: I'll break those turntables.

SPARKY: Don't make me live without
them.

WHITEY: You'll live without them.

SPARKY: Oh no I won't.

WHITEY: Oh yes you will.

SPARKY: Oh no I won't. Just shut up.

BRONSKI: Don't tell him to shut up.

EMILY: He can say what he wants.
I'll break those turntables.

(*Screen: Miranda in close up switches
screens.*)

EMILY: From what to what?

BRONSKI: First they say that if we go
up there, we can come back. Then
Manitas wants to go up there and
we know she won't want to come
back. (*Sparky picks up puppet.*)

MIRANDA: Well now they've changed
their story.

MANITAS: They said that we wouldn't
have to stay up there.

EMILY: And we don't.

SPARKY: It's your only way out.

MIRANDA: I never said that.

BRONSKI: Why?

MIRANDA: Your future's looking dim.

SPARKY: Why?

MIRANDA: It just is from here, from
what I can see.

MANITAS: I don't like this game.

MIRANDA: You're almost in tears.

BRONSKI: But I don't want to, you
play it.

SPARKY: I already did and I'm out.

EMILY: You can't be out.

MIRANDA: You have to play it.

BRONSKI: Don't blame him because

MIRANDA: That's because he's stupid.

he's stupid.

WHITEY: It is not.

SPARKY: They're standing in there waiting with sharp knives.

SPARKY: I am. (*Throws puppet to floor.*)

MIRANDA: It's his own fault that he's stupid.

MIRANDA: You seem to be in a mild state of hysteria.

CUT

(*Screens go blank.*)

EMILY: I get these headaches.

BRONSKI: From thinking.

MANITAS: Think harder.

BRONSKI: I'm trying.

MANITAS: If we agree to go up there.

BRONSKI: If we do, we'll all be stuck.

MANITAS: Well, we all don't have to go.

EMILY: Just one first.

WHITEY: Then another.

BRONSKI: One by one and take them over.

EMILY: Won't work.

MANITAS: I'm going to try to do something. Let me go up there first.

EMILY: They'll keep you up there.

MANITAS: Who cares? We can't stay trapped in here like this.

WHITEY: Don't do it.

MANITAS: Watch something. Watch this. See what happens when I do this? (*Puts hands in front of projector head.*)

EMILY: It makes a shadow.

BRONSKI: To us it does.

MANITAS: But to them? Didn't you notice that when we did that they told us to stop? It bothers them somehow.

EMILY: If we do everything they tell us

not to.

WHITEY: Then what?

MANITAS: Then maybe we can break something down.

BRONSKI: And the projectors?

EMILY: If we touch them.

BRONSKI: Break them, knock them over.

WHITEY: That won't work.

EMILY: How do we do it?

MANITAS: Pull the plug.

EMILY: No don't, not yet. Pinry's stuck up there.

CUT

(Sparky runs behind screen into a large storeroom and begins climbing a ladder as if searching for something.)

EMILY: I can feel them resonating, radiating everywhere around us. They can see us, they can hear us, everything.

WHITEY: They cannot. They left the room.

BRONSKI: Just because they left the room it doesn't mean they're not here.

WHITEY: Where do they go when they go away?

MANITAS: Into the wires, just like electricity.

EMILY: How shall we do this?

BRONSKI: We have to anticipate them.

MANITAS: Intercept them.

BRONSKI: But now they come and go whenever they want.

SPARKY: Pinry's gone.

EMILY: Where?

SPARKY: He's gone, they took him.

MANITAS: How do we know that?

SPARKY: He's not here.

WHITEY: Maybe he went out.

EMILY: He never goes out.

MANITAS: Then, where is he?

SPARKY: I don't know. I've looked all over. He's nowhere.

WHITEY: He has to be here somewhere.

SPARKY: He isn't. I looked everywhere.

BRONSKI: What did you do with him?

SPARKY: Nothing. He was listening to a record and I fell asleep and he was gone.

WHITEY: Pinry.

BRONSKI: Pinry.

MANITAS: They've got him.

SPARKY: Then we have to get him.

WHITEY: What do we need him for. He's just a puppet.

EMILY: How do we go up there?

WHITEY: The same way I came off, through a wire.

MANITAS: I just agree to go up there the next time they ask.

BRONSKI: Here comes someone.

(Screen A: Bodine, medium closeup, blue background.

Screen B: Smith, medium close up, sobbing, blue background. Screens switch every few lines. These faces will from now on be seen from progressively lower angles. When they speak to stage players, their focus is downward.)

SMITH: Hello.

EMILY: Good morning.

SMITH: I'd like to talk to you.

BRONSKI: Fine. Come in. Where's the puppet? Where's Pinry?

SMITH: The puppet is dead. He hung himself.

SPARKY: Impossible.

SMITH: Possible. Probable. A fact. The

fact is that he is dead.

SMITH: Why would we do that?

SMITH: That's impossible.

SMITH: But you did.

SMITH: The fact is that someone killed him and someone has to pay.

SMITH: My advice is to . . .

SMITH: You need my advice.

SMITH: Hung up somewhere, wherever one of you hung him.

SMITH: But how can we be? We have always been very clear.

SMITH: I am trying to clarify.

BODINE: I want to make something very clear.
SMITH: I want you to understand something.

BODINE: Do you realize that . . . ? I've got to figure out a way to tell you this, to make it make sense to you. I want to explain it to you so that it makes sense to you. I know it will sound ridiculous. Do you see the machines? They're the projectors. They are projecting you.

BRONSKI: The probability or the possibility is that one of you hung him up.

EMILY: I'm sure you have your reasons.

BRONSKI: You can't kill a puppet.

EMILY: Shut up. You're trying to confuse me.

MANITAS: Get off it.

EMILY: We don't want your advice.

SPARKY: Where is Pinry?

SPARKY: You're confusing us, deliberately confusing us.

SPARKY: Deliberately confusing us.

MANITAS: What? Is something wrong?

MANITAS: (Pause four seconds.) Well, what is it?

EMILY: You must be kidding.

BRONSKI: You are the ones that are being projected.

BODINE: You're silly.

MANITAS: We are here. You're up there.

EMILY: You are the projection.

BRONSKI: Once upon a time someone put you on emulsion and projected you. You're all wound up on the film and I can prove it to you . . .

MANITAS: By turning off the projector.

BRONSKI: I'll show you.

BODINE: Because you'll turn yourselves off and then what?

SMITH: Stop and think. You'll shut yourselves off and then what?

MANITAS: Idiotic.

BRONSKI: Sooner or later the film will run out and we'll see who ends up on a roll.

BODINE: You're headed for the brink.

EMILY: And it won't be us.

BODINE: It will be you.

WHITEY: This is impossible.

SMITH: You'll see.

BODINE: What we're trying to make you realize is that you must get off that roll of film so that when the film runs out you'll be safe.

WHITEY: We are safe.

BODINE: But believe me.

WHITEY: It's not true.

BRONSKI: I'll turn off the projector and then we'll see.

SMITH: You have to realize that you're chained into that machine and if you don't get out of it, you'll be stuck in there forever. Can you understand that?

BODINE: Is that clear?

SMITH: Don't you feel yourselves slipping away?

BODINE: You're just shadow and light and sound.

SMITH: Pieces of things.

EMILY: No.

BODINE: Believe us.

EMILY: Can't believe that.

SMITH: I hope you understand that we are running out of time and that we'll have to try every way we can to help you. You may not understand but you'll thank us in the end.

WHITEY: Thanks, but no thanks.

BRONSKI: What are they talking about?

WHITEY: I don't know really. I don't remember.

MANITAS: You're really nice but I don't think you know what you're talking about.

(Screen: An extreme close up of Whitey's eye replacing Bodine for fifteen seconds.)

BODINE: If there was only some way we could convince you before it's too late.

MANITAS: Listen, you people are nut brains.

SMITH: Think, think hard. Somewhere deep down in your thought machines it must make sense to you.

SPARKY: It doesn't make any sense.

BODINE: It's unchangeable. We're trying to help you figure it out.

SMITH: Why are you letting yourselves run out?

EMILY: I don't want to figure it out.

MANITAS: Thanks for your concern but as you can see we're just not concerned. How can you ask us to believe something so illogical?

WHITEY: I don't like thinking so hard.

EMILY: There's nothing to figure out.

WHITEY: No.

BRONSKI: I guess. It's got to be some kind of story.

EMILY: It's got to be some kind of story.

BRONSKI: But let me tell you the story. One day we lived on the bottom of the world. We'd like to tell you a story about how we live. You might be surprised. On my father's funeral the dogs cried and vomited. We were so sad and one fine day the swans on the lake died. There was such a weird sound early in the morning he died. The dog chewed the chain 'til all his teeth fell out. The shepherd had not gone far when he heard a tiny voice. The mouse and the ant lived happily . . . la ormigita y el raton. And the bread was moving in there all by itself.

EMILY: What a stupid, stupid story.

BODINE: We're not asking you. We're telling you.

SMITH: You're so unwise. Think, think harder.

SMITH: Think about it. Figure it out. It makes sense.

SMITH: You'll die in the darkness.

BODINE: You're so unwise.

SMITH: What are we telling you, some kind of story?

BODINE: Do you think we're lying to you?

SMITH: I'll tell you a story.

BODINE: Where is your sympathy for yourselves?

(Screens A & B: An extreme close up of Whitey's eye appears on both screens simultaneously for fifteen seconds. Bodine and Smith return.)

SMITH: Now that is a story. It's a story that's not particularly true and these are the facts. Those are the machines and you are coming out of the machines.

EMILY: No more stories.

WHITEY: Prove it then.

MANITAS: How can we prove it? There's no way to prove it, except by turning off the projectors and we know you won't do that.

SMITH: Go ahead and see what happens.

BODINE: There's no way to prove it except by turning off the projectors and you know we won't do that.

EMILY: Scare us.

BRONSKI: Let's see what happens.

BODINE: Or what unhappens.

WHITEY: They picked my brain apart and put me back together again. Convinced me.

EMILY: I know it without a doubt.

BRONSKI: I appreciate you're trying to be our guiding light but I don't believe you.

SMITH: Without a doubt.

BODINE: I know it without a doubt. And you know what certain words mean.

EMILY: One at a time.

(Bodine and Smith speak simultaneously.)

SMITH: Without a doubt.

BODINE: You have a beginning and an end and now you must find the middle.

WHITEY: Okay, no more stories. I don't believe them. Now one at a time.

BODINE: No one asked you to believe.

WHITEY: So why tell it?

(Screens go blank.)

CUT

MANITAS: Do you believe it?

EMILY: Of course I don't.

BRONSKI: I don't either.

WHITEY: It might be true.

SPARKY: Nothing can convince me that I'm a projection.

MANITAS: So.

BRONSKI: Where do they go when they go away.

EMILY: Out away.

BRONSKI: What do you think I'm some kind of idiot that I'm going to believe some people on a screen telling me that I'm the one on the screen. You've got a hitch in your giddyap.

WHITEY: Why else would they tell it to us?

MANITAS: I don't know.

BRONSKI: You're acting like this is some twilight zone show.

EMILY: Tales from the great beyond.

MANITAS: Some junkie story.

BRONSKI: The fact is that they are on the projector and we know it so the case is closed. Just wait for them to run out of sprocket holes and put them in a can.

SPARKY: Right.

MANITAS: Then, we'll be done with it.

WHITEY: If they're right then we're digging our graves with our own sprockets.

EMILY: Don't start trying to believe all this.

WHITEY: Look if the film runs out, then they can just put us back into the projector again, rewind us and we'll be back again.

MANITAS: Who's going to do that? We'll all be on the reel.

BRONSKI: See how stupid this all is?

EMILY: Well, they can put us back on the projector.

BRONSKI: What are you talking about? They're the ones on film. We'll put them back on the projector if we want to, but at this point, I'm not so sure I want to be around them.

EMILY: I think they're out of their minds.

WHITEY: They're very nice, but come on . . . Then if we run out, they can put us on again.

BRONSKI: We're not going to run out. They are. Get that through your head. We are not going anywhere.

EMILY: I'm going to pull the plug and we'll see who goes where. (*Emily goes to pull the plug, Whitey pulls her back by the coat.*)

WHITEY: No don't.

SPARKY: Come on.

MANITAS: Take a chance in killing ourselves?

BRONSKI: You're turning into an idiot. We are not on a projector.

WHITEY: We might be.

EMILY: You might be but I'm not.

MANITAS: Either we are or we aren't.

SPARKY: We aren't.

EMILY: I'm going to pull the plug and we'll see who goes where. (*Emily runs to pull plug, Whitey pulls her back by her coat.*)

SPARKY: Come on.

MANITAS: Take a chance in killing ourselves?

BRONSKI: You're turning into an idiot. We are not on a projector.

WHITEY: We might be.

EMILY: You might be but I'm not.
MANITAS: Either we are or we aren't.
SPARKY: We aren't.

CUT

(Screens A & B: Four heads in close up alternate rapidly according to who is speaking.)

LEE: I want to make it clearer again.

BRONSKI: I don't want to hear anymore.
MANITAS: Bite the dust will you?

MIRANDA: I hate dust.

EMILY: Okay, so you hate dust, now get lost.

SMITH: Listen to me.

EMILY: I don't want to listen to you.
SPARKY: You're all weird.

LEE: You are going to end up in a can.

MANITAS: You are going to end up in a can.

BODINE: Your lamb is in a puddle. You're a brahma bull in Chicago. Don't you understand what I'm trying to tell you?

SPARKY: Cut the hoi polloi.
BRONSKI: The hui hui.
MANITAS: Fade away.

LEE: Not fade away.
MIRANDA: We're losing our patience.

EMILY: I've heard that.

BODINE: We're trying to bring ration-ality to bear in an inherently irra-tional situation.

(Bodine's voice falls out of sync.)

BRONSKI: I've heard that before too.

BODINE: Just beware that when the rules of your irrational, illogical behavior become in excess, our policy will be one of swift and effec-

EMILY: Pull it.

WHITEY: No more stories.

BRONSKI: I know what you mean chili bean.

EMILY: It's over, it's finished. It's not important.

SPARKY: You're trying to convince us to trick us.

EMILY: Get us out of here.

SPARKY: You people make me sick. (*Spits food.*)

BRONSKI: You're an idiot, a ticket taker, a shadow, an administrator, a slam dancer, a projectionist, a dramaturg, so get lost.

tive retribution. In other words we're going to pull the plug.

BODINE: But we live in an area of limits to our powers.

LEE: Let it also be understood that there are limits to our patience. You're becoming rabid, bleeding, flagrant.

SMITH: What color do you see?

(*Bodine's voice returns to synch.*)

BODINE: You're digging your own grave with your own . . .

LEE: Sprockets.

SMITH: I'm not leaving 'til you listen to me.

BODINE: The world is so small we must learn to be civil to one another.

SMITH: You're going through withdrawl.

LEE: We're trying to intercept you.

BODINE: Anticipate, contracept, intercept.

BODINE: I am all those things and I can inhale you and burn you up. We can inhale the smoke and make fuel out of you. We can make fuel out of anything. Does that shock you?

EMILY: Yes, it shocks me.

SMITH: It should and when you're through with your inky little plot to pull the plug, I will disrupt you.

EMILY: Momentarily perhaps.

BODINE: You will be correctible.
LEE: Erasable.
MIRANDA: Incorrigible.
SMITH: Simpleton, use your mind.
LEE: You will finally come to understand.
BODINE: That you are our own projection, our own creation, our postcard if you will.

EMILY: I won't.

BODINE: Yes you will and it has been recorded.

BRONSKI: The hell we are.

LEE: We?

EMILY: You.

MIRANDA: You forget that you're about as brainless as that puppet.

SPARKY: I hate the way you smell.

BODINE: Your angel face is only a shadow.
MIRANDA: Do we smell?

EMILY: Stop trying to edit me you bureaucrat, social climber, user, flatterer, crystal blue persuader, pigfucker, pancake. (*Throws bread rolls at screen.*)

LEE: You're out of control.

BRONSKI: What did you say?

BODINE: Pancake.
SMITH: And so we administrate.

EMILY: Flapjack.

BODINE: You should be thankful. It is our pleasure, our inspiration, our duty, our dedication, our configuration. You are arrogant, ungrateful.

LEE: I'm sorry, there's nothing more we can do for you. I'm sorry, I really am.

EMILY: I'm horrified.

BRONSKI: I thought you said you were sorry.

BRONSKI: I know what you mean chili bean. I know exactly what you mean.

BODINE: I never said that.

MANITAS: The sun comes through the window. I can help myself.

SPARKY: What color do you see?

SMITH: Help comes from above, trouble from below.

MANITAS: I don't know nothin'.

SMITH: No color. Look at your friend, you know what happened to her.

SMITH: You don't know nothin'.

LEE: Bury the hatchet.

BODINE: Why is he shaking?

SMITH: He's afraid.

MANITAS: Get lost.

BODINE: I will for a while.

(*Screens go blank.*)

BRONSKI: Why are you shaking?

SPARKY: I'm afraid. I'm not brave, I never was.

EMILY: You're out of control. Relax.

SPARKY: I can't, I'm only nine years old. I get these headaches.

MANITAS: Well, stop getting them.

SPARKY: I'm going to keep getting them because I'm out of junk. (*Runs to Manitas.*) Can I ask a dumb question?

EMILY: What?

SPARKY: Is the Milky Way still in my face?

MANITAS: Yes.

SPARKY: No it isn't. You know it isn't,
tell me the truth.

EMILY: Alright, it isn't.

SPARKY: I get these headaches and
shaking. They told me if I go up
there I'll stop.

BRONSKI: Hold on a little while.

SPARKY: I can't, I'm only nine years
old. They can help if I go up there.

WHITEY: They say they can.

SPARKY: They can. I know they can.

EMILY: They can't.

SPARKY: Well then, who is going to
help me?

EMILY: I don't know.

MANITAS: We're out of food too.

SPARKY: Then we have to go up there.

BRONSKI: Hell no, I'm not going up
there with those putrid face, puke
mouths.

SPARKY: Well I'm going to eventually.
I can just tell. I can't hold on any
longer.

EMILY: I'm going to give them the puppet.

BRONSKI: They have the puppet.

EMILY: They have a fake puppet and
they know it and they know we
know it.

BRONSKI: And we know they know
we know they know it.

EMILY: And the puppet knows it.

BRONSKI: And the puppet is very sad.

MANITAS: Then give them the puppet.

EMILY: I will. I want to see what's
going on up there.

SPARKY: There's nothing going on up
there. It's just shadows and light.

BRONSKI: Haven't you seen enough?

EMILY: I have and I don't want to see
anymore. I'm giving them the puppet and if I don't get out then I
don't get out. Look at me when I

talk to you. Everything has been educated against itself, every proportion in this room is conspired against itself. Everything is contradicted. I'm finally convinced that I want to see what it is because I can't understand this anymore.

MANITAS: You are so graceful, so silent. Don't make your face angry. It is so ugly.

EMILY: It is ugly. It will be ugly.

BRONSKI: Please don't show me that face.

EMILY: I will show you that face. I will show you that face. I will always show you that face forever. It is ugly, it will be ugly because of them.

BRONSKI: Don't show me that ugly face, don't make it ugly and angry.

EMILY: It will be ugly and angry and mad and terrible and brutal. Brutal brutality. You'll get no love from my face ever again. You'll never see me again. The film will run out and you'll never see me again, so remember my ugly, brutal and angry face that they have created. This is no angel face no more, sweet and innocent and graceful no more. It has another meaning now.

SPARKY: Where is your diginity?

EMILY: I have no dignity. I can spit on you from up there. No more, Sparky, no more. No more Milky Way. This is the end of the Milky Way. Welcome to the end of the film. Welcome to the end.

BRONSKI: This is an act of hate.

EMILY: It's an act of love.

BRONSKI: Where is your dignity?

EMILY: That's my dignity up there.

SPARKY: What does that word mean?

EMILY: It doesn't mean anything. It's an act of dignity and hate. The two are tied together. Stop the projector, don't make me do this.

BRONSKI: I'm not. Don't make me do this. Don't make me.

EMILY: The poor exhausted flies, the maggots died of hunger, the deer flesh was all eaten up, they broke their teeth on the bones, they tried but they died of hunger and fantasia.

MANITAS: Where will you go?

EMILY: Somewhere out into outer space. Hopelessly out into outer space, alone. Want this coat?

SPARKY: Sure. (*Emily throws coat to Sparky.*)

CUT

(*Sparky, wearing Emily's coat, stands alone at center table. The rest of the stage is dark.*)

SPARKY: What? Where are you?

SPARKY: Where is Manitas?

SPARKY: Why?

SPARKY: What is it?

SPARKY: What do you mean, they

(*Bronski on Screen A: close up of face. Screen B: close up of burning candle.*)

BRONSKI: Sparky.

BRONSKI: Over here.

MANITAS: Here it's me. I'm a candle now.

BRONSKI: She thought she had the jump on it but she didn't and now she's a candle.

MANITAS: Wax.

BRONSKI: They were right.

were right?

SPARKY: Why?

SPARKY: How could they be right? Manitas told me that they were wrong and that we should stay here.

SPARKY: I don't believe you.

SPARKY: You are not. You're lying.

SPARKY: How could they turn her into a candle?

SPARKY: I don't believe you.

SPARKY: I'm going to pull the plug on you. I don't believe you.

SPARKY: I can't.

SPARKY: It's not true.

SPARKY: They changed you.

SPARKY: You're a coward and they changed you. You're not brave, you never were. You're not loyal,

BRONSKI: You've got to get up here quick.

BRONSKI: They were right.

BRONSKI: You can't stay there. You'll run out and that'll be it. They were trying to save us. Get Whitey and get up here before it runs out. It's running out. Save yourselves.

BRONSKI: Believe me, I'm telling the truth.

BRONSKI: Look at Manitas. She didn't believe them and now she's a candle.

BRONSKI: It was the light. She screwed up. Believe me, save yourselves. Wake up Whitey.

BRONSKI: Don't pull the plug.

BRONSKI: You've got to.

BRONSKI: Please, you're shaking, you're out of junk I can tell. They can help you up here if you come right now they can fix you up.

BRONSKI: It has to be true.

BRONSKI: No one changed me.

you never were.

SPARKY: I can't believe you. I can't believe you. I know you can't help yourself.

SPARKY: You can't help us because you're stuck up there. If you can help us then come down here and help us pull that plug.

SPARKY: So then we will.

SPARKY: We have to. I'm not going to be convinced or persuaded.

SPARKY: I can see what's going on. I believe my own eyes.

SPARKY: I don't want to think anymore.

SPARKY: No.

SPARKY: You touch my skin. Then we'll know what's what.

SPARKY: I'm sorry. I don't believe you.

SPARKY: You're trying to trick me.

SPARKY: Bronski. Come back.

BRONSKI: I am loyal. That's why I'm trying to help you. Believe me.

BRONSKI: I can help myself and I can help the two of you.

BRONSKI: If you pull the plug you'll kill yourselves.

BRONSKI: Don't do it.

BRONSKI: Can't you see what's going on?

BRONSKI: Think, think.

BRONSKI: Touch your skin.

BRONSKI: Touch your skin.

BRONSKI: You know what.

BRONSKI: Alright, be clever and don't believe me but you'll be sorry.

BRONSKI: I'm not. Please believe me. I'm your friend. If you don't believe me I don't know what else I can do if . . .

(*Screens go blank.*)

CUT

(*Sparky is visible behind Screen A standing behind a large tilted white tabletop. Whitey is alone on stage at center table.*)

(*Screen B: Emily, extreme close up of face.*

Screen A: Emily's eyes, extreme close up.)

SPARKY: Where are you?

EMILY: Whitey, Sparky.

SPARKY: What happened?

EMILY: Over here.

WHITEY: Can they hear?

EMILY: Listen to me.

SPARKY: What shall we do?

EMILY: I think so.

WHITEY: Where?

EMILY: Hide yourselves.

SPARKY: What's going on?

EMILY: Anywhere.

EMILY: Don't let them find you.

WHITEY: They've found us anyway. They'll find us again.

EMILY: They'll see whatever we do.

SPARKY: I've got to get some stuff. I can't, I'm hungry, I'm starving.

EMILY: Don't let them see you.

WHITEY: What shall we do?
SPARKY: Don't believe him.
WHITEY: Why?
SPARKY: They're all lying up there.

EMILY: Believe me.

WHITEY: Shall we smash the projector?

EMILY: No don't.

SPARKY: What do we do?

EMILY: If you can somehow make everything black.

EMILY: Black everything out.

WHITEY: What for?

EMILY: Paint it so they can't see you and turn the projector backwards, rewind it.

SPARKY: How?

SPARKY: It won't go.

EMILY: Yes it will. If you can rewind it

WHITEY: Impossible.

SPARKY: We can't rewind it. There's no button.

WHITEY: We checked and checked and checked.

SPARKY: How do you know?
WHITEY: Do you believe him?

SPARKY: Bronski.

WHITEY: How did you do it?

SPARKY: We'll think about it.

WHITEY: But we don't know how.

SPARKY: I don't believe you.
WHITEY: You're trying to make us wreck it all.
SPARKY: I can't stay here much longer. I'm cold, I'm freezing.

SPARKY: No don't. Don't believe him.
WHITEY: What about Bronski and back to the beginning.

EMILY: It works. They were talking about it, I heard them.

EMILY: Yes there is somewhere.

EMILY: Keep looking. There is a button. There's a way to do it.

EMILY: Listen to me. Watch this, watch what I did. I got a knife and I went in there and look.

(Screens A & B: Jumbled pieces of film rush by, jump cuts. Screen A returns to Emily, Screen B is blank.)

EMILY: Did you see what I did?

EMILY: The razor's edge. But that's no remedy, you've got to turn it back. Backwards until the beginning, that's the only way.

EMILY: Don't think too long. If they find out and see what you're doing. You have turn turn it back and cut them up.

EMILY: You can just cut them out of it.

EMILY: Turn it back.

Manitas?

EMILY: Do you believe them? Everyone has their own configuration about this and now you've got to think and figure it out. But don't just sit there. If you can somehow make it all black first, then they can't see you. Believe me, it's the only way to do it. There is only one way.

WHITEY: There's no way.

SPARKY: I'm cold. (*Lies on table.*)

EMILY: There's only one way to do it. There is only way way because I heard them saying that . . .

CUT

(*Screens go black.*)

(*Screen A: Manitas, medium close up seen from above, sitting at blue table. Screen B: Close up of candle burning.*)

MANITAS: Whitey.

WHITEY: Yes, where are you?

MANITAS: Up here, up here. Where's Sparky?

(*Sparky, asleep on table, is visible through Screen A.*)

WHITEY: He's asleep. He's been up all night trying to find a way out of the projector. What's going on up there? Where is everyone?

MANITAS: Asleep.

WHITEY: Can they hear you?

MANITAS: Probably, I'm sorry.

WHITEY: What is it? What are you now?

MANITAS: I'm just a vagabond, floating around in the emulsion now.

WHITEY: I was right. Where is everyone else?

MANITAS: They're here too but we hardly see each other.

WHITEY: Why?

MANITAS: We just don't. It depends what pieces of film we're on. Sometimes yes, sometimes no.

WHITEY: What can we do?

(*Manitas switches to Screen B, candle to Screen A.*)

MANITAS: Pull the plug.

WHITEY: No, if we pull the plug, then you'll all be gone.

MANITAS: Turn the projector backward.

WHITEY: It doesn't go backwards, no rewind.

MANITAS: It's going to run out. Stay where you are.

WHITEY: You're trying to trick me. You're like them now. You're trying to trick me, convince me.

WHITEY: I can't.

MANITAS: I'm not. Trust me.

WHITEY: I don't believe you.

MANITAS: It's going to run out and us with it. You should be glad.

WHITEY: I don't know.

MANITAS: Believe me.

MANITAS: You know, you have a brain, think, touch your own skin. Feel it?

WHITEY: Yes.

MANITAS: It's going to run out and us with it. Where's the doll?

WHITEY: The doll? It's dead I think. Sparky's shaking, he can't go on much longer.

MANITAS: He has to.

WHITEY: I don't believe you. They've changed you.

MANITAS: They haven't. Think.

WHITEY: I can't think anymore.

WHITEY: We'll see, we'll see.

WHITEY: Touch me.

WHITEY: Are you going to be on again.

(*Sparky leaves table behind screen and walks to stage.*)

WHITEY: Get me out of here.

WHITEY: I don't believe you. I don't believe you.

(*As film ends, Sparky surprises Whitey from behind and pushes him violently at center table.*)

SPARKY: Alright. Tell me everything you know.
WHITEY: I don't know much. All I know is this story.
SPARKY: Then forget the story, forget it. Cut out the lights and forget the story. Have you forgotten it?
WHITEY: Yes.
SPARKY: Tell me what you remember.
WHITEY: The dogs chewing the chains and that's it.
SPARKY: That's it?

MANITAS: Let it run out.

MANITAS: We'll see. I'm going now. I can see myself coming up on the projector again.

(*Screen A: Close up of Manitas's eyes upside down, moving across screen.*)

MANITAS: I can't.

MANITAS: I don't know, I can't tell. I'm not brave, I never was.

MANITAS: No, stay there.

MANITAS: Believe me because if you can ju . . .

CUT

(*Screens go blank.*)

WHITEY: That's all.

SPARKY: Now forget that. Have you forgotten it?

WHITEY: Yes.

SPARKY: Tell me what you remember.

WHITEY: The chewing.

SPARKY: Alright, now forget that.

WHITEY: Alright.

SPARKY: Now what do you remember?

WHITEY: Nothing, nothing at all.

SPARKY: Tell me what you know.

WHITEY: Nothing.

SPARKY: What is your name?

WHITEY: Nothing.

SPARKY: What is your name?

WHITEY: Nothing.

SPARKY: Fine, now we can start again.

WHITEY: With nothing.

SPARKY: (*Puts his hands on Whitey's head.*) We will resurrect you from nothingness. From nothing. Your name is Whitey. Yes.

WHITEY: And the chewing dogs.

SPARKY: I thought you said you forgot that.

WHITEY: I did.

SPARKY: Don't lie. Forget it, forget the chewing dogs.

WHITEY: I have.

SPARKY: What is your name, Whitey? Your memory is in the minority, the inferiority.

WHITEY: Exactly.

SPARKY: You will have no references to anything but what is happening right now and you can speak again.

WHITEY: And my name is Whitey.

SPARKY: Put your ear to the ground and listen. (*Pushes Whitey's head onto table.*) How do you feel?

WHITEY: Mesmerized. My name is Whitey. I smell a rotting banana.

SPARKY: What is a banana?

WHITEY: A banana is a book.

SPARKY: Right. You smell a rotting book.

WHITEY: I'm sad about something but I don't know what it is. Something's walking around up there.

SPARKY: And you don't know what it is. You are inside out.

WHITEY: Inside out.

SPARKY: And don't look back. Don't look back. Remember the pillar of salt, the pillar of salt. Would you like a book or something? Touch me, do you feel my skin? (*Turns his back and holds his hand behind him.*)

WHITEY: Yes. (*Touches Sparky's hand with his index finger.*)

SPARKY: Don't break the rhythm. Don't look back. Touch my skin.

SPARKY: Why?

WHITEY: Why?

SPARKY: Why are you trained to a razor's edge?

WHITEY: You've put yourselves back

(*Screens A & B: Extreme close ups of heads, Bodine, Lee, Miranda, Smith alternate with lines.*)

BODINE: We are losing our patience.

SMITH: You can't escape our influence.

LEE: We're trained to a razor's edge.

SMITH: Why?

MIRANDA: Because we have to be.

SMITH: We can teach you to depend on us.

LEE: On our honest goodwill.

BODINE: We can teach you to pretend and how to deal with this mess you've created for yourselves out of yourselves.

SMITH: We can teach you to tear every moment apart bit by bit, softly and put it back together again properly, the way we have been.

together again?

SPARKY: To a razor's edge?

BODINE: Yes.

CUT

(*Both screens blank.*)

WHITEY: It's all broken. (*Throws chair across room.*)

SPARKY: We'll fix it. (*Sparky appears behind Screen B behind large rectangular white tabletop.*)

WHITEY: I can't believe that.

SPARKY: You'd better believe it.

WHITEY: I'll never believe anything again.

SPARKY: So fake it.

WHITEY: Wait 'til Sunday.

SPARKY: It is Sunday.

WHITEY: I don't care. Stop playing that piano.

SPARKY: No.

WHITEY: Stop it. I'll smash it up.

SPARKY: And then I'll smash you up. Your nose will be a bloody red tomato.

WHITEY: Get that piano out of your brain.

SPARKY: What are we going to do?

WHITEY: Where's that stupid doll puppet?

SPARKY: What for?

WHITEY: Maybe it knows something. (*Picks up puppet from floor.*)

SPARKY: That woodenhead don't know a thing. Leave it alone, it's sad.

WHITEY: Upset?

SPARKY: It can't think anymore than we can.

WHITEY: Say something. Tell us what to do. How can we get them back?

Really?

SPARKY: What's it saying?

WHITEY: It's not saying anything. (*Throws it violently into chair.*)

SPARKY: You must sit and think. Think, think.

WHITEY: I can't think.

SPARKY: Think.

WHITEY: I can't, can't.

SPARKY: Think about it, think about it.

WHITEY: Think about it yourself.

SPARKY: My brain can't.

WHITEY: Your brain.

SPARKY: My brain can't. It can't go anymore. It's stopped up.

WHITEY: Think about it.

SPARKY: I don't want to think about it.

WHITEY: My brain is corroded. It won't go anymore.

SPARKY: What are we going to do?

WHITEY: It's a hopeless case.

SPARKY: What does that word mean?

WHITEY: I don't know what it means goddamnit.

SPARKY: Then, goddamn you.

WHITEY: We can't figure our way out of this.

SPARKY: We're done for.

WHITEY: Done for what, birdbrain?

SPARKY: You're a birdbrain.

WHITEY: An innocent birdbrain.

SPARKY: You're a poor polluted, corrupted little brain.

WHITEY: My brain's out of control, it won't work.

SPARKY: Deorganize it.

WHITEY: I can't, it's organized and wrecked.

SPARKY: Then throw your brain out and use your hands. One by one they turned us around.

WHITEY: They had to testify.

SPARKY: They betrayed us.

WHITEY: My friends will never betray me.

SPARKY: Yes they will, the way you did.

WHITEY: I did not. That wasn't me up there. I don't know who that was.

SPARKY: Why don't you give in. Admit they already did.

WHITEY: They did not.

SPARKY: They don't care about you. If they did, they wouldn't have left you high and dry.

WHITEY: They won't ever do that.

SPARKY: They will because they already did. Why don't you admit it now everything has to change.

WHITEY: No, I'm going to hold out.

SPARKY: You're crazy. High and dry.

WHITEY: What a way to go.

SPARKY: I'm going.

WHITEY: Then go. You're a coward.

SPARKY: I'm not brave, I never was. I'm going. I'm sorry. Goodbye.

WHITEY: See you around.

SPARKY: Maybe we'll end up in the same can.

WHITEY: I doubt it.

SPARKY: Please let me go.

WHITEY: Alright go. Get lost.

CUT

(*Sparky appears on both screens. Screen A: wide shot of long rectangular room. Sparky at far end, face bloody.*
   Screen B: identical empty room.)

SPARKY: Whitey.

WHITEY: Sparky get out of there.

SPARKY: I can't.

WHITEY: Why did you go up there?

SPARKY: I had to. I was hungry and cold and I got to get fixed up. I've got to get fixed up. Whitey, help me.

WHITEY: How. Why did you do it? Where is everyone?

SPARKY: I don't know. I don't see anyone. Get me off of here. Touch my skin, wake me up.

WHITEY: Do you hear anything?

SPARKY: No. It's all blue everywhere. How do I get out of here. Get me out of here, get me out of here. I'm bleeding get me out of here. (*Runs back and forth between walls.*)

WHITEY: Where are they?

SPARKY: Whitey. Whitey.

WHITEY: Who is it?

SPARKY: It's me, Sparky.

WHITEY: Where are they?

SPARKY: They went out.

WHITEY: Don't talk too loud. They might hear you. What shall we do?

(*Sparky runs off Screen A and onto Screen B.*)

SPARKY: I know what to do. I heard them talking.

WHITEY: About what?

SPARKY: Remember when they said something about tearing every moment apart bit by bit?

WHITEY: The razor's edge.

SPARKY: Right, well that's it.

WHITEY: About how they put themselves back together again?

SPARKY: Right. Well if they put themselves back together again, then you can take them apart.

WHITEY: How?

(*Sparky runs from Screen B onto Screen A.*)

SPARKY: In the machine, the projector.

WHITEY: How?

SPARKY: Stop the projector.

WHITEY: I can't. I checked. There's no button, no plug.

WHITEY: If I break it, won't be able to fix it.

SPARKY: Then break it.

SPARKY: So what? Then they'll be gone.

(*Screens A & B: Sparky runs back and forth between walls.*)

WHITEY: And you will too.

SPARKY: I don't care.

WHITEY: You'll all be smashed up inside the machine.

SPARKY: Then that's the way it'll have to be.

WHITEY: Do you want to get out of there?

SPARKY: Yes.

WHITEY: Then come down.

SPARKY: I can't.

WHITEY: Why can't you?

SPARKY: I can't. I don't know how. (*Feels wall.*)

WHITEY: Yes you do.

SPARKY: I don't know how, I can't.

WHITEY: You can.

SPARKY: Show me how. I can't.

WHITEY: I can't show you. You have to know how, you have to know how.

SPARKY: I can't, I can't. There's no way out, there's no way off.

WHITEY: Try.

SPARKY: I have tried.

WHITEY: And what happens?

WHITEY: There's no brick wall here. I don't see one.

WHITEY: Do you want to get out?

WHITEY: Well, why did you go up there?

WHITEY: Do you want to get back?

WHITEY: Do you want to?

WHITEY: Please.

WHITEY: Isn't there a crack or something in the wall?

WHITEY: Try. Push.

WHITEY: Try again.

WHITEY: Goddamn you.

SPARKY: There's a brick wall.

SPARKY: Yes there is. (*Kicks wall.*)

SPARKY: Yes.

SPARKY: I just wanted to see what it was like and now I can't get out.

SPARKY: Yes I do. I want to, I want to, I want to.

SPARKY: Stop asking me that. I want to, I really want to but I can't. There's no way. I don't know how.

SPARKY: How? How do I do it? There's no way.

SPARKY: Yes but it's very small. It's too small to get through.

SPARKY: It's too small. (*Sparky runs frantically between walls, opposite screen shows identical image upside down.*)

SPARKY: I keep trying and I can't. It's just a tiny crack. There's no way.

SPARKY: Oh goddamn you. It was your idea for us to go up there and now I can't get back and it was your idea and now the crack is too small and I can't get back and you keep asking me and now what can I do? I really want to get off and I

WHITEY: You know how to do it and you're just not doing it. You're just like them and you won't do it. You want me to stay up there, you want to, you want to.

WHITEY: I can't help you. I don't know how.

WHITEY: You help me.

WHITEY: Why did you do it? Why did you go there?

WHITEY: I did but I never thought you couldn't get back.

WHITEY: I never tricked you.

WHITEY: Not if you get away first.

WHITEY: Kick the wall.

WHITEY: Do you want to get out of there?

WHITEY: I can't help you.

can't. There's just no way, just ain't no way.

SPARKY: I don't want to. Help me.

SPARKY: Yes you do. You can tell me something to help me. You must know something.

SPARKY: I can't do it. I can't do it. Get me out of here.

SPARKY: I don't know why I did. You wanted to go up here.

SPARKY: You tricked us into getting here and now we can't get back.

SPARKY: And now they're going to come back and take me away.

SPARKY: But I can't, I can't.

SPARKY: I keep kicking and kicking until my feet are bloody and I can't anymore. I can't anymore, I can't, I can't, I can't.

SPARKY: Help me.

(*Sparky falls into corner of room. Zoom from wide shot of room to medium close up. Opposite screen shows identical image upside down.*)

WHITEY: Kick. Push.

WHITEY: Hide where?

WHITEY: Kick.

WHITEY: I don't know how to help you.

WHITEY: I can't do anything.

WHITEY: I can't.

WHITEY: Show me.

WHITEY: Where are you?

WHITEY: Turn on the lights.

WHITEY: Where are you?

(Whitey hides under mirrored table.)

SPARKY: Goddamn you. Help me get out of here, they're coming back.

SPARKY: I can't. They're coming, I have to go and hide.

SPARKY: I don't know, they can see me, they'll find me in here.

SPARKY: I can't, they're coming.

SPARKY: Do something.

SPARKY: You can't do anything.

SPARKY: Help me, they're coming.

SPARKY: There's no way. Whitey, Whitey.

SPARKY: Whitey, where are you?

SPARKY: Whitey!

SPARKY: Whitey, it's me, Sparky. It's me. Say something. No don't, don't say anything, don't say anything. Hide. Don't let them find you.

(Sparky, now extreme, close up remains on Screen A.
    Bodine, Miranda, Lee and Smith appear on Screen B, extreme close up.)
BODINE: Whitey.
SMITH: Answer us. Come on.
MIRANDA: We know you're there.
SPARKY: He's gone. He's not here. He left.
SMITH: He can't leave. There's no way out of this.

SPARKY: He left.

LEE: Shut up Sparky.

SPARKY: No.

SMITH: Shut up.

BODINE: Whitey, don't. Don't be a child.

SMITH: Say something.

MIRANDA: Sooner or later you'll have to.

LEE: (*Sings.*) "I don't want to set the world on fire." Whitey, what are you doing?

SMITH: You are so graceful, so silent. Don't make your face angry. It is so ugly.

SPARKY: It is ugly. It will be ugly.

WHITEY: Please don't show me that face.

(*Screen B: Sparky in corner upside down, medium shot.*)

SPARKY: I will show you the face. I will show you that face. I will always show you that face forever. It is ugly, it will be ugly because of you.

MIRANDA: Don't show me that ugly face, don't make it ugly and angry.

SPARKY: It will be ugly and angry and mad and terrible and brutal. Brutal brutality. You'll get no love from my face ever again. You'll never see me again. The film will run out and you'll never see me again, so remember my ugly, brutal and angry face that they have created. This is no angel face no more, sweet and innocent and graceful no more. It has another meaning now. You've made me a mess.

MIRANDA: Where is your dignity?

WHITEY: Sparky.

SMITH: No more Sparky, no more.

SPARKY: No more Milky Way. This is the end of the Milky Way. Welcome to the end of the film. Welcome to the end monster.

SMITH: This is an act of hate.

SPARKY: It's an act of love.

LEE: Where is your dignity?

(Screen B: *Large window*.)

SMITH: What does that word mean?

SPARKY: It doesn't mean anything. It's an act of dignity and hate. The two are tied together. Stop the projector.

WHITEY: Don't make me do this.

WHITEY: Don't make me do this. Don't make me.

SPARKY: I'm not.

WHITEY: Where will you go? (*Gets out from under table*.)

SPARKY: We'll just live without them. (*Pause*.)

SPARKY: Somewhere out into outer space. Hopelessly out into outer space. Alone. Alone. I will be dreamy and sad, dreamy and sad, always dreamy and sad for a very long time and I will last forever because I am on film and it will be my pleasure to play you over and over and over again for my pleasure and freedom and my inspiration. I will play you over and over and over again until you are shredded year after year, year after year for a thousand years, real soft and real loud whenever I want, however I can, whenever I want because after that that's all I'll be able to do, over and over again for a thousand years because that's all

I'll ever know how to do by then
and I'll just keep doing it and I'll
just keep playing over and over
again for you, over and over again
until I turn to shreds and when I
turn to shreds you'll still hear me in
your brain cavity over and over
again for a thousand years and
you'll always feel free because of
that and even when they say I
don't have a brain I will have a
brain because I will have a brain
because I do have a brain because I
am a brain because the brain is
right there in the plug or in your
hand or in the light bulb or in the
emulsion or the groove or whatever, in the plastic for a thousand
years even without electricity or
whatever, over and over again
because I do have a brain and I can
sing if I want to because I can sing,
because I can. Is that right? Do you
understand me? Right? What is
your name?

WHITEY: Whitey.

WHITEY: What did you say?

WHITEY: That's what I thought.

WHITEY: Whitey.

SPARKY: You'll always remember my
name.

SPARKY: Nothing.

SPARKY: What is your name?

WHITEY: You'll remember my name.

SPARKY: Whitey.

SPARKY: Always, always and forever,
forever and ever. Gloria in excelsis.
Don't let me run off the reel.

WHITEY: I won't.

WHITEY: I can always put you on a-
gain.

SPARKY: Please don't. If I go off then
you won't have anything.

SPARKY: Maybe not.

WHITEY: Maybe yes.

WHITEY: Nothing was shining.

WHITEY: Where is everyone?

WHITEY: Sparky, come down.

WHITEY: I can't. What do I do?

WHITEY: How?

WHITEY: I can't. (*Runs back and forth between projectors.*)

WHITEY: I will.

SPARKY: What was happy about it? What could I celebrate that was shining?

SPARKY: And I will always trust you because you will never disintegrate and I will never disintegrate or grate on my nerves or get on my nerves or make me nervous because I can always shut you up or turn you off.

SPARKY: They're gone but I hear footsteps. Help me, don't let them do this to me.

SPARKY: Help me.

SPARKY: Help me. Don't let them do this to us. They're going to do something to us. Don't let them do this. They're coming. Stop them Whitey, stop them. There's got to be something you can do. Get me out of here. Stop the projector. Stop them. You have to stop the projector.

SPARKY: Help me.

SPARKY: Stop the projector. Stop them. Do something, stop it.
SMITH: Whitey, don't stop it. You can't.

LEE: You can't.
SPARKY: Whitey stop the projector. Help me Whitey, the projector.
BODINE: Don't stop the projector, the film is running out.
SMITH: Let it run out Sparky.

MIRANDA: Don't let it run out Sparky. Listen to me.

SMITH: What color do you see.

SPARKY: Help me. Don't touch the projector. Let it run out. Do something.

BODINE: Whitey, turn the projector back. Turn it backward but don't turn it off.

SPARKY: Turn it off. Break it, smash it, end it. It's running out. I can see it.

SMITH: Whitey don't. Turn it backwards. Don't do this to us.

SPARKY: Whitey, don't do it. Get me out of here.

BODINE: Listen to me Whitey.

SPARKY: Help me. Don't let them do this to me. Get me out of here. If you don't, I'll always hate you.

SMITH: Turn it back.

SPARKY: Let it run out. Stop it.

BODINE: Don't let it run out. Don't.

SPARKY: Whitey.

(*Both projectors run out of film. Screens go white.*)

WHITEY: I will be dreamy and sad, dreamy and sad, always dreamy and sad for a very long time and I will last forever because I am on film and it will be my pleasure to play you over and over and over again for my pleasure and freedom and my inspiration. I will play you over and over, over again until you are shredded year after year, year after year for a thousand years, real soft and real loud whenever I want, however I can, whenever I want because after that that's all I'll be able to do, over and over again for a thousand years because that's all I'll ever know how to do by then and I'll just keep doing it and I'll just keep playing over and over again for you over and over again until I turn to shreds and when I turn to shreds you'll still hear me in your brain cavity over and over again for a thousand years and you'll always feel free because of that and even when they say I don't have a brain I will have a brain because I will have a brain because I do have a brain because I am a brain because the brain is right there in the plug or in your hand or in the light bulb or in the emulsion or the groove or the whatever, in the plastic for a thousand years even without electricity or whatever, over and over again because I do have a brain and I can sing if I want to because I can sing, because I can. Is that right? Do you understand me? Right? What is your name? (*Walks across space and gently tips each table over, 'til he reaches a projector.*)

Whitey

You'll remember my name.

What did you say?

Nothing.

That what I thought.

What is your name?

Whitey.

Whitey.

You remember my name.

Always, always and forever, forever and ever. Gloria in excelsis. Don't let me run off the reel.

I won't.

Please don't. If I go off then you won't have anything.

I can always put you on again.
Maybe not.
Maybe yes.
What was happy about it? What
could I celebrate that was shining?
Nothing was shining.
And I will always trust you because
you will never disintegrate and I
will never disintegrate or grate
on my nevers or get on my
nerves or get on my nerves or
make me nervous because I can
always shut you up or turn you
off.
Do you understand me? Do you
hear me?
Do you hear me?

END

The Birth of the Poet

a play in three acts

Kathy Acker

Beatriz Schiller

The Birth of the Poet was first performed at the Brooklyn Academy of Music Next Wave Festival in New York City on December 3, 1985 with the following cast:

Stabbed Arab Lover	*Frank Dahill*
Ali/Hinkley	*Zach Grenier*
Cynthia	*Jan Leslie Harding*
Maecenas	*Stuart Hodes*
Shadow from San Francisco	*Anne Iobst*
Propertius	*Max Jacobs*
Hassidic Book Delivery Man	*Warren Keith*
Barbarella	*Anne Lange*
Stabbed Arab Wife	*Brooke Myers*
Steet of Dogs Town Crier	*Harsh Nayyar*
Danielle	*Ingrid Reffert*
Lady With the Whip	*Valda Setterfield*

Director: Richard Foreman
Music: Peter Gordon
Scenery and Costume Design: David Salle
Lighting Design: Pat Collins
Sound Design: Otts Munderloh

ACT ONE

(The stage looks exactly what New York City looks outside the theatre. The middle of a huge nuclear power plant. Dark and cavernous.)

WHITE WW 1: *(I.e., World Worker 1; explaining to a potential worker.)* This factory is the newest of the new.

WHITE WW 2: *(To the same girl.)* Yes. We don't even get paid.

WHITE WW 1: *(Before she can open her mouth.)* Everything is provided for us.

WHITE WW 2: We do everything for ourselves because we're modern.

POTENTIAL WORKER: Oh. *(A limbless White Worker enters.)*

WHITE WW 2: We even hire limbless spasmodics. *(The limbless White Worker is carrying ten-foot-long pipes on his head.)*

WHITE WW 1: The only thing we need to keep going is files. Files of the workers' medical insurance, files of the workers' life insurance, files of the workers' car insurance, files of the workers' theft insurance, files of the workers' fire insurance.

WHITE WW 2: This is the only reason we need workers.

POTENTIAL WORKER: *(Enthusiastic.)* Yah!

WHITE WW 2: Products are out-of-date. No one can afford to buy anyway.

POTENTIAL WORKER: *(Or P.O.W.)* What about the Bosses?

WHITE WW 1: They're on salary like the rest of us. The business pays for everything.

WHITE WW 3: *(Talking to a visiting Rich Man who's coked-up.)* We make energy!

WHITE WW 1: Coal is obsolete and dirty. Oil almost brought the world to its knees begging for survival. This new energy will drive millions of new machines forever and ever. We are creating it. Nuclear mixed with solar energy allows the possibility of worldly existence.

WHITE WW 2: We need solid capable workers. We need workers who can understand what we're doing. Who will work harder harder because there is nothing to work for. *(The underground cavern grows darker, areas of shifting hall-light, huge cavernous pillars like the rocks in the ancient Roman days, machines, just huge shapes.)*

WHITE WW 2: Production production continues uninterrupted. We will never again allow a shortage of energy in the modern world.

RICH COKED-UP VISITOR: (*Turning around to White WW 2.*) And what if this place should blow up? (*White WW 2 doesn't answer.*)

WHITE WW 4: (*To White WW 5.*) What d'you want now? We were just betting on the temperature of the air outside.

WHITE WW 5: I got a report from the factory.

WHITE WW 4: Your machine?

WHITE WW 5: Some fission material is missing.

WHITE WW 4: Where?

WHITE WW 5: During the process.

WHITE WW 4: A leak?

WHITE WW 5: Probably a computer mistake.

WHITE WW 4: Has it happened more than once?

WHITE WW 5: I've been watching steadily. For five hours now.

WHITE WW 4: There's nothing wrong with the computer?

WHITE WW 5: (*Slightly panicking.*) I'd better find out.

RICH COKED-UP VISITOR: The world's ending! The world's ending!

(*In a corner of the factory.*)

SHADOW 1: Please love me.

SHADOW 2: I can't love you anymore. I'm pooped.

SHADOW 1: I'm so desperate for you. I've been traveling all over the world. Well, in San Francisco. Being in San Francisco is so boring it's like being everywhere in the world. I've got to have you I'll even brandish a whip to get you.

SHADOW 2: You've never gone that way before.

SHADOW 1: I'm growing up.

RED WW 1: Report from third workshop—production one point below quota.

RED WW 2: Report from fifth workshop—production two points below quota.

RED WW 3: Report from fifth computer—fission leakage up three points.

RED WW 4: Control stations on fourth level register reduced energy production. By performance up to twelve behind target.

RED BOSS: Whose fault is it?

RED WW 1: All computers work perfectly.

RED WW 2: All seismographs work perfectly.

RED WW 3: All cyclotrons work perfectly.

RED WW 4: All Browning effects work perfectly.

(*The Rich Visitor starts taking off his clothes and shits on the floor.*)

BLUE WW 1: Report from first workshop—all alarms sounding.

BLUE WW 2: Report from second workshop—all transport buses racing from their sheds.

BLUE WW 3: All workers while trying to escape under total discipline and time cards.

BLUE WW 4: Steady food supply with generous priorities while collapse of workers at gauge-gear-pedal lever.

BLUE BOSS: Movement becomes autonomous for survival. Excessive duration of the one action stops the body from digesting. Poison piles up.

TRANSLUCENT WW: Power in its essence is in no way material, it has no essence at all in a philosophical sense, and it is an apparently unnameable figment of the imagination.

(*Slowly, the large window glass is cracking. After this cracking sound, all is totally still, suddenly BAM BAM BAM [very rhythmical]. Nuclear-solar leakage looks gray and red. The whole stage blows to bits and the play is over.*)

BLACK WW 1: I'll bet ya' the nuclear leakage factor is up fifteen points.

BLACK WW 2: Twenty.

BLACK WW 1: How much?

BLACK WW 2: Ten.

BLACK WW 1: Fuck you. Look at the weather outside. Nothing's wrong there.

(*They all look through the now totally opaque because so shattered and splintered panes of the huge windows.*)

BLACK WW 3: I'll take both of you on for as much as you want that leakage is up fifty points.

BLACK WW 2: What're ya' doing?

BLACK WW 1: I'm calling WEATHER to find out how much nuclear leakage is in the air.

BLACK WW 4: The phone lines aren't working.

(*The squawkings of peacocks kangaroos ostriches and leopards can be heard slightly. The workers fall down dead.*)

LAST WW: Report from control-room: this is the end of the world.

(*There is just rubble and smoke. Out of this rubble rises,*

ACT TWO

I'M THINKING ABOUT YOU RIGHT NOW AND I'VE BEEN THINKING ABOUT YOU FOR DAYS WHEN I JERK OFF I SEE YOUR FACE AND I'M NOT GOING TO STOP WRITING THIS CAUSE THEN I'LL BE AWAY FROM THIS DIRECTNESS THIS HAPPINESS THIS ISNESS WHICH IS. AT THE SAME TIME I'M NEVER GOING TO HAVE ANYTHING TO DO WITH YOU AGAIN. BECAUSE YOU, EVEN IF IT IS JUST CAUSE OF CIRCUMSTANCES, WON'T LOVE ME. THIS ISN'T THE SITUATION. I'M BEING A BABY AS USUAL. THERE ARE COMPLICATIONS. ARE SHADES, HUES, NEVER EITHER-OR, THE SHADES ARE MEANINGS, COME OUT, YOU ROTTEN COCKSUCKER

1
TO THE DOOR

CYNTHIA: (*The whore.*) Why aren't you grabbing my cunt every chance you get? I love fucking in public streets and why are you telling me you want to be friends and work with me more than you care about sex with me, but you don't want FOR ANY REASONS to cut out the sex? Do you want to own me without owning me? (*Cynthia leaves to search for Propertius, her boyfriend. It's night. She finds him.*) Why don't you take me? I've only got five minutes. Why does it have to least beyond these grabbing actions. Oh I believe in love that thing that is impossible to happen. (*A bones-sticking-out cow drags a cart of glittering religious objects past a dead murderer over the bumpy street.*) And you're fat and ugly and I'm more beautiful than you and I've got more money and I can earn more in five minutes in this world: you should be taking ME out to dinner. Here's a hole the window we can climb through to where we can fuck.

PROPERTIUS: (*Rubs his cock.*) When I was a kid, I used to use a bottle with something in it. Now I've got cunts, but cunts have women attached to them. By Augustus's nose! I'm a man! The best wet dream I had was in highschool, I was fucking this girl I desperately wanted to fuck her hole disappeared I still kept shoving rubbing up against her. I woke up and I was pounding into the bed. Actually I don't want you to have anything to do with me. I just want split open red and black pussy.

CYNTHIA: Why don't you let me go? I want to go back to that non-existing where I can do what I want.

PROPERTIUS: I like you a lot. (*Cynthia pisses on Propertius.*)

CYNTHIA: That doesn't work. If I let you make all the decisions, you'll be my father.

PROPERTIUS: I don't want to make any decisions. People tell me what to do very easily and I won't stand being told what to do, so I avoid people.

CYNTHIA: (*Deciding in herself.*) He's never going to give me what I want, but I'll still fuck him. (*They're standing in front of a huge partly opened window behind which is black space.*)

CYNTHIA: O.K. baby. Jump. What's the matter with you, are you too fat to jump? I've got five minutes. You're going be a creep and not do anything, I'm scared too, I want it. Flesh is it. Your lips are it.

PROPERTIUS: Isn't that guy on the corner waiting for you?

CYNTHIA: That's why we've got only five minutes.

2
AT A DOOR'S EDGE

(*During the night, these streets very narrow dirty uneven rocks no way to be sure of your footing much less direction as for safety all sorts of criminals or rather people who have to survive hiding under one level of stone or behind an arcade you can't even see just standing there. No way to tell the difference between alive and dead. Criminalities which are understandable mix with religious practices, for people have to do anything to satisfy that which can no longer be satisfied*

We shall define sexuality as all that which can't be satisfied

[Simultaneous contrasts, extravagances, incoherences, half-formed misshapen thoughts, lousy spellings.]

Elegance and completely filthy sex fit together. Expectations which can't be satiated.)

CYNTHIA: Just why are you fucking me? You've got a girlfriend named Trick and you love her. According to you, she's satisfied with you and you with her. (*Propertius is staring blankly at the door.*) I'm sick of being nice to you. So what if you want a girl who'll consider you her top priority and yet'll never ask you for anything? I can't be her. (*Propertius is staring blankly at the door and scratching his head.*) DON'T FUCK ME CAUSE YOU LIKE MY WORK. LEAVE ME ALONE. This is the only way I can directly speak to you cause you're autistic.

PROPERTIUS:
Oh little cunt door

I love you so very very much.

CYNTHIA: Well, everyone wants to fuck me so I tell you I'm sick of this life. Who cares if you're another person waiting at my door. You're just another man and you don't mean shit to me.

PROPERTIUS: Please, cunt, I'm cold and I'll be the best man for you. I know you're fucking someone else that's why you won't let me near you. You cheap rags stinking fish who wants anything to do with corpses anyway? (*To himself.*) And thus I tried to drown my mourning.

CYNTHIA: This is the door out I want, goddamn you. Now I'm dead:

I want

One. My mother father and grandmother are dead. Fuck that.

Two. When my mother popped off, afterwards, she lay in this highly polished wood coffin in the most expensive funeral house in New York City—where all the society die after they're dead—FAKE, everything was real but there are times real is fake, flowers, tons of smells, wood halls polished like fingernails, rabbi or preacher asks me, "Do you know anything good I can say (you have to say something: SAY SOMETHING!) over your mother's mutilating body?" (it being understood that all society people are such pigs that . . .) and I tell him how beautiful she is; no one cries they're there to stare at me as I make my blind way through the narrow aisle to number how hysterical I am did I really love her? The beginning of the funeral: the family lawyer, having walked over to me, shakes my lapels, "Where are the 800 IBM shares?" "What 800 IBM shares?" "There are 800 missing IBM shares and no one knows how your mother died. I thought she might have given them to you." "She never gave me a penny."

Three. I do everything for sexual love. What a life it's like I no longer exist cause no one loves me. So *when I die*, I'll die because you'll know *that you caused me to die* and you'll be responsible. That's what my death'll do to you and you'll learn to love. I'm teaching you by killing myself.

Four. You're gonna have to die too. You'll be like me. You'll be where I now am. Your cock-bone will lie in my cunt-bone.

Five. This is why life shits: because you're gonna love me the second I leave you flat. Sexuality comes from repression. In the long run, nothing matters. This is the one sentiment that makes me happy.

Please be nice to me.

BARBARELLA: You've got to own a man who has money.

DANIELLE: I want money and power.

CYNTHIA & BARBARELLA: (*Agreeing.*) Money and sex are definitely the main criteria.

DANIELLE: Sex?

CYNTHIA: I think I want a wife who has a cock. You understand what I mean. I don't understand why men even try to deal with me like I can be a wife, and then bitch at me and hurt me as much as possible cause I'm not. Who'd ever think I'm a wife? Do you think I'm a wife? (*Barbarella giggles.*) But when

I'm sexually open, I totally change and this real fem part comes out.

BARBARELLA: I want a husband. No. I take that back. I want someone who'll support me.

CYNTHIA: Good luck.

BARBARELLA: I'm both the husband and wife. Even though none of us is getting anything right now, except for Danielle who's getting everything, our desires are totally volatile.

DANIELLE: I can't be a wife. I can be a hostess. If I've got lots of money.

CYNTHIA: I think if you really worship sex, you don't fuck around. Danielle fucks around more than any of us and she's the one who doesn't care about sex.

BARBARELLA: Most men don't like sex. They like being powerful and when you have good sex you lose all power.

CYNTHIA: I need sex to stay alive.

(*A street in Rome. The sky's color is deep dark blue. One star can be seen. Very little can be seen on this street—just different shades of black.*)

3
INSIDE

Now we're fucking:

I don't have any finesse I'm all over you like a raging blonde leopard and I want to go more raging I want to go snarling and poisoning and teasing eek eek, curl around your hind leg pee, that twig over there, I want your specific piss shuddering out of your cock. I want you to help me. I need help.

Take off your clothes. Clothes imprison. Clothes imprison legs and mouths and red teeth still shudder want too much, taking off our clothes,

Why can't you ever once do something that's not allowable? I mean goddamnit.

Hit me.

Do anything.

Do something.

Sow this hideousness opposition blood to everyone proud I want to knock Ken over with a green glass I want to hire a punk to beat up Pam I will poison your milk if you don't leave your girlfriend.

Sex is public The streets made themselves for us to walk naked down them Take out your cock and piss over me.

The threshold is here. Commit yourself to not-knowing. Legs lie against legs. Hairs mixing hairs and here, a fingerpad, a space, a hand, a space, hairs mixed with hairs.

Go over this threshold with me.

Thumb, your two fingers pinch my nipples while your master bears down on me. Red eyes, stare down on the top of my eyes. Cock, my eyes are staring at you pull out of the brown hairs. Red eyes, now you're watching your cock pull out of the strange brown hairs. Thumb, your two fingers pinch my nipples while your master bears down on me.

Now you've gone away:

Joel whom I thought hated me saw me every other day and Rudy whom I thought the worst that is the meanest of my boyfriends always called me every other day or let me call him and I don't know reality. Peter who lives with another girl three thousand miles away from me and he *adores* her phones me at least once a month.

This guy obviously doesn't care about me.

But when he looks at me, I know there's a hole in him he loves me. No he doesn't. I can't do anything in the world until I know whether he loves me or not. I have to learn whether he loves me or not.

You might just as well accept you're in love with him because if you give him up just cause he doesn't adore you enough, you'll have nothing. In the other case, there's a one percent chance you'll keep touching his flesh.

CYNTHIA, sitting at her dressing-table in her little apartment overlooking the middleclass Roman whores' section, is dressing her hair: That goddamn son-of-a-bitch I hope he goes to hell I hope he gets POISONED wild city DOGS should drive their thousands of TEETH-FANGS through his flesh a twelve-year-old syphilitic named Janey Smith should wrap her cunt around that prick I hate that prick those fingers I hate black hair I want his teeth to rip themselves out in total agony I want his lips to dry up in Grand Canyon gulfs I want him PARALYZED never to be able to move again and to be conscious of it:

Now, louse, you'll learn. You'll learn what it is not to know. I want you to learn what it is to want like fire. The driest and coldest dry ice: the top of your head will burn and the rest of your body will freeze shake muscles will cramp as they do when they're not yet used to the bedless floor, at night, you will know agony.

You must learn what it is to want.

I'm a whore who's unable to hold in and repress her emotions.

Propertius decides he doesn't want to fuck Cynthia again: How can such a stinking fish, a cunt who has experienced what it is to be the wish-fulfillment of many men, hordes of men, more men than promote the Great Caesar, be innocent? Moreover she's had such a poverty-regulated life, she can't have the life in her to give me the female elegance and beauty I deserve.

My girlfriend on the other hand, if anyone ever hurts me, is going to have to murder him. For me. When I'm dying from a worn-out liver punctured guts three punches in the face and dirty track marks because I've lived life to the hilt, my girlfriend will commit suicide.

As a whore, Cynthia goes from man to man because she's no man's possession. So there's no possibility I'm going to love her and, if I fuck her, it's just
cause she's an open cunt. Women's libbers are right when they want to get rid
of all you whores by locking you up.

CYNTHIA: I've been waiting for you.
PROPERTIUS: What the he . . . (*Grabbing the other girl into him.*) Oh, hello. I'm
  busy now.
CYNTHIA: I just wanted to see you.
PROPERTIUS: I'm busy with someone now. I'll give you a call tomorrow.
CYNTHIA: Please. (*There's nothing she can do.*) O.K. (*Propertius and his girlfriend
  walk into the house. One of the dogs on the street starts barking.*)

The street of Dogs. Two lines of houses lead to a Renaissance perspective.
These lines are seemingly-only-surface connected three-story townhouses. A
sun and a three-quarter moon hang fakely over one townhouse. Common
household objects such as lamps, a part of a table, half of a torn plastic rose
kitchen curtain take up some of the window space. Outside a townhouse, a dog
leans over her basket of laundry. Two dogs, one leaning farther out of his window than the other, open their mouths to howl. Their teeth are sharp and
white and they have very long red tongues. One dog over her basket of wash
gossips with another dog. Two young dogs are mangling each other next to the
curb. On each side of the street the tall thin windows form a long row.

CYNTHIA: (*Barks like a dog.*) I can't help myself anymore I'm just a girl I didn't
  ask God to be born a girl. If I think realistically, I know I'm an alien existant.
  I hate everyone in the world. But I can't think. You're just so cute. I have to
  get you out of my body because you're a disease. I don't want to and why
  should I? I want this sweet thing that is you. I'm going to go after you, aching
  sore, (I don't care what your reaction is to me), because why not, darling.

(*Cynthia walks up to Propertius's door and sits in front of it. The door doesn't move.*)

(*A big bald-headed man opens the door lays his palms on the doorway. Cynthia goes
away.*)

You alone born from my most beautiful carecure for grief
Shuts out since your fate "COME OFTEN HERE"
Fiction by my will will become the most popular form
Propertius, your forgiveness, peace, Peter, yours.
to redefine the realms of sex so sex
I'm crawling up the wall for you.
                        I must face facts I'm not a
female. I must face facts I can't be loved. I must

face facts I need love to live. Hello, walls.
How're you doing today? Hello, my watch. Please watch
over Propertius, you are here because I will
never get near him again. He is now forbidden
territory.

(*Cynthia lies down on the street and sticks razor blades up her arms. The bums ask her if she needs a drink.*)

CYNTHIA: Madness makes an alcoholic sober, keeps the most raging beast in an invisibly locked invisible cage, turns seething masses of smoke air calm white, takes a junky off junk as if he's having a pleasant dream, halts that need FAME that's impossible.

I am only an obsession. Don't talk to me otherwise. Don't know me. Do you think I exist?

Watch out. Madness is a reality, not a perversion.

Among these women, free yet timorous, addicted to late hours darkened rooms gambling indolence, sparing of words, all they needed was an allusion.

I reveled in the quickness of their half-spoken threats more like the violent excitement of a teenager who doesn't know what he feels. These exchanges as if once the slow-thinking male is banished every message from woman to woman is clear and overwhelming are few in kind and infallible.

The first time I dined at her place, three brown tapers dripped waxen tears in tall candlesticks without dispelling the gloom. A low table, from the Orient, offered a pell-mell of les hors d'oeurve—strips of raw fish rolled upon glass wands, foie gras, shrimps, salad seasoned with pepper and cranberry—there was a well-chosen Piper Heidsieck brut and very strong Russian Greek and Chinese alcohols. I didn't believe I'd become friends with this woman who tossed off her drink with the obliviousness with which a person in the depths of opium watches his hand burn.

The "master" is never referred to by the name of woman. We seemed to be waiting for some catastrophe to project herself into our midst, but she merely kept sending invisible messengers laden with jades, enamels, laquers, furs . . . From one marvel to another . . . Who is the dark origin of all this nonsense?

"Tell me, Renèe. Are you happy?"

Renèe blushed, smiled, then abruptly stiffened.

"Why, of course, my dear Colette. Why would you want me to be unhappy?"

"I didn't say I wanted it," I retorted.

"I'm happy," Renèe explained to me, "but the sexual ecstasy is so great, I'm going to be physically sick."

4
ON THE NATURE OF ART

PROPERTIUS: If you read every poem in every anthology of Greek poetry, you wouldn't read one poem in which the character of the woman who's loved is described or matters.

That's cause women are goddamn sluts. They're goddamn sluts because the only thing they've got going for them are their cunts.

The worse thing about women is all these emotions. Take the hole I slept with last night. Sure, she moaned hard when I stuck my dick in her. But did she have any idea that I didn't feel? Sure, I'm a macho pig. Why should I pretend I'm something I'm not I care about art. Everything but art is a second-class existent.

Art, you are the black hole of vulnerability, you take everything from me and are not human. You can take me whenever you want me. A human has to care for one thing.

I use whatever I can get from women. I maul the need they offer me. I increase their anguish or insecurity and horniness to elephantine propertions. So the ugly is left ugly and consciousness' unavoidable anguish is as it is in me.

My writing will cure you of your suffering. I teach young girls how to win the love of men who don't love them. I teach boys how to endure the lacerations of long red fingernails stuck in their face flesh and how to watch the girl they crawl under fuck another man right in front of their faces.

AUGUSTUS: (Through the lips of his literary counselor Maecenas.) You're not a poet and you're not a real man because you write about emotion. Men are people who take care of the world, who care that people get enough to eat, who stop the greedy hawks at least from seizing more power and underhanded control.

Artists who are men have to change the world. When they start paying attention to emotions, what are emotions?, they're helping the power hawks destroy the social bonds people need to live.

PROPERTIUS: Then my writing destroys social bonds so that's who I am.

MAECENAS: You're speaking stupidly, pettily, and you're too smart to take this position. Writing is not about egotism.

PROPERTIUS: One day, Maecenas, you're going to realize you're not rational and then, suddenly ignorant desperate, you'll leave your politics and run to me, (Turns away from Maecenas.)

away from anything public,

the art-world: a salon resplendent with gilding and illuminations. One has just revealed original talent and with this first portrait of his shows himself the equal of his teacher. A sculptor's chatting with one of those clever satirists who refuse to recognize merit and think they're smarter than

anyone else. The people talk either about how they earn money or who's becoming famous. All for good reason are grasping. Since the only ideas are for sale, none are mentioned. A few women are existing to maintain the sur- face that heterosexuality is still conceivable. Eyes never see
mouths faces are talking to
away from the art-world,

You can say I write stories about sex and violence, with sex and violence, and therefore my writing isn't worth considering because it uses content much less lots of content and all the middle-range people or moralists say I'm a disgusting violent sadist. Well, I tell you this:
Prickly race,
who know nothing except how to eat out your own hearts with
envy, you don't eat cunt,
writing isn't a viable phenomenon anymore. Everything has been said. All these lines aren't my writing: Philetas's Demeter far outweighs his long old woman, and of the two, it's his little pieces of shit I applaud. May the crane- who-delights-in-the-Pygmies'-blood's flight from Egypt to Thrace be so long, like me in your arms, endless endless grayness, may the death shots the Massagetae're directing against a Mede be so far: what is here: desire violence will never stop. Go die off, you, you destructive race of the Evil Eye, or learn to judge poetic appearance by art: art is the elaborating of violence. Don't look to me to want to change the world. I'm out of it.

But if there hadn't been between you the two the dark streets, the risks, and the old man you had just abandoned, had there been no danger, would you have hurried so eagerly?

5
CONVERSATIONS TO PEOPLE WHO AREN'T HERE

PROPERTIUS: (*To Cynthia who isn't in front of him.*) I know you've been going through hell because I've been refusing to speak to you.

I know the moment I stopped talking to you, you slit your wrist (you did that just cause when you were in your teens you regularly cut your arms with a razor blade to show yourself you were horror), then more seriously you got an ovarian infection because your ovaries had been rejected. You tried I know you tried you did avoid me (except when you phoned ten times a day, my girlfriend answered the phone and you hung up.)

Listen, Cynthia. I fucked so many girls I took them up to this penthouse sauna and swimming pool someone had lent me. Beautiful girls pass each other on the stairway. Limbs disappear in the shadow, and there's nothing else.

(About his new girlfriend to Cynthia who isn't in front of him.) The more I knew she was fucking every man she'd meet through me, the more I'd do anything for her—crazed because I knew every move she made was part of her leaving me. Then it stopped; she ran away with her other boyfriend.

I want you, Cynthia.

If you don't give your total flesh and everything else over to me, slimy bitch, may you drink raw oyster-like blood—you now living on your dead grandmother's capitalistic hoard—may whatever food your lips and smell come near stink of shit-filled guts, human, always always you regret everything you seem to yourself to be. Your thoughts are wild fantasies. Wild fantasies eat you, hole. Looking everywhere looking everywhere looking everywhere looking everywhere: each human is so stupid it's a ravenous wolf. Long red pointed fingernails will separate the cunt lip flesh, then dig into the soft purple, and around the protrusion of the nipple right there, another fingernail.

This is why you can't run away from me. There's only obsession.

Love will turn on the lover and gnaw.

(On his knees, to Cynthia who isn't in front of him.) Last night I had this dream, Cynthia. You stood over me. The ring I had given you, your finger, the white palm outstretched. You said these following words to me:

CYNTHIA: I didn't mean to tell you your girlfriend was fucking around, but (1) you had just told me I wasn't a female because I have a "career" and because I'm not a female no man will love me. That hurt. (2) You set up the terms of the relationship, but I was thinking about you all the time so you said STAY RATIONAL but I wasn't rational: this was confusing me. I explained my identity-desperation by telling you I had known your girlfriend was two-timing you that's why I let myself love you. But the second I mentioned the first word, explosion!, so I backed off: I just heard gossip, the gossip was old she wasn't fucking anyone else. I'm wrong to listen to gossip. Let me be hurt. (3) I said "Propertius is no more," but my body reacted: I cut a razor blade through my flesh so I could see the flesh hole revealing two thin purple-blue-gray wires which frightened and reminded me of my mother's chin three days after she committed suicide, the body gets sick. I'm not a woman who takes shit, but

Why do I like you so much? I like you you so much you're necessary to the continuing of my existence right now and I don't understand this at all, I just know it's true.

PROPERTIUS: Cynthia walked away from me, and I woke up. *(To Cynthia who isn't in front of him.)* I don't want you, slut, because desire is mad and I don't want to be mad.

ACT THREE

ALI GOES TO THE MOSQUE

(AT FIRST THERE IS ONLY LANGUAGE AND NOTHING ELSE.)

آیا بازار دور است؟ نَخَیر ,خانُم،
سُرخ نیست ولی مُرگ است

Aya bazar dur ast? Naxeir, xanom, sorx nist vali marg ast.
Is the bazaar far? No, Mrs., it's not red it's dead.

نیر میوه هست

Niz mive hast.
There's fruit too.

بازار بِسیار زیباست

Bazar besiar ziba st.
The bazaar is very beautiful.

آیا میوه سُرخ است؟

Aya mive sorx ast?
Is the fruit red?

بَلی ,خانم، خَیلی گِران است

Bali, xanom, xeili geran ast.
Yes, Mrs., it's very expensive.

مَگَر این گوشت مُرده نیست؟

Magar in gusht morde nist?
Isn't this meat dead?

نَخَیر ,خانُم، مُرده نیست

Naxeir, xanom, morde nist.
No, Mrs., it isn't dead.

آیا بانک دَر این بازار هَست؟

Aya bank dar in bazar hast?
Is there a bank in this bazaar?

بَلی, خانم, سُرخ اَست

Bali, xanom, sorx ast.
Yes, Mrs., it is red.

آیا مَردان هَست ؟

Aya mardan hast?
Are there males?

(THE ARAB WOMAN'S SONG FOR HER LOVER WHO IS FAR FROM HER.)

آیا حِسّ بِنِفِرَتِ والِدَین وَ بِتَنَفُرِ بی اِنتِهای
اِجتماع پُروَرده بی دَردهای وِدّاد هَمیشه اَست ؟

Aya hesse beneferate valedein va betanaffore bi entehae
ejtema' parvarde bi dardhae vedad hamishe ast?
Is feeling fed on parental distaste forever social disdain
always without the pangs of love?

آیا خوُد اَز سِرِشت دُشمَنِ جاوِدانِ وِداد اَم ؟

Aya xod az seresht doshmane javadane vedad am?
Am I by nature the lifelong enemy of love?

دالانها چون زِندانها وَ مَحکَمهها

Dalanha cun zendanha va mahkameha
The labyrinth

کوُیهای قاتِلاد

Kuihaye qatelan
Alleyways of murderers

آیا هَمیشه تَنها اَم ؟

Aya hamishe tanha am?
Am I always alone?

لاس

Las
Bitch

تَلخی

Talxi
Bitterness

بِتوُ هَمه چیزرا میگوُیَم

Beto hame cizra miguyuam
I tell you everything

وَلِ زَبانرا نُدارُم

vali zabanra nadaram.
but I don't have a tongue.

تَبعید خوُش اَست

Tab'id xosh ast.
Banishment is pleasant.

بروی خوُد روی مَرا بِبَند

Beruye xod ruye mara beband
Link my face to your face

فَرار اَز ظالِمان مُجاز اَست

Farar az zaleman mojaz ast.
Flight from tyrants is O.K.

ظالِمان کیست؟

Zaleman ki st?
Who are the tyrants?

سَفَر اَز وُسعَتهای گُه،

safar az vos'athaye goh,
traveling through realms of garbage,

اُتومُبیل مُرده هَست.

otumobile morde hast
"There's a car wreck."

خَرچَنگِ دَرخشان بِپُرتَقالی

Xarcange daraxshan be portoqali
A phosphorescent crab

وَ لِدَین خودرا فَرار میکُنیم.

Valedeine xodra farar mikonim.
We're fleeing our parents.

خاطِرائمان نَمیدانیم.

Xateranaman namidanim.
Our minds don't know.

تُوی کُودَن، بِتُو عاشِق نَمیباشَد.

Toye koudan, beto 'asheq namibashad.
You dummy, he doesn't love you.

تو اینقدر غریب ای : هیچکس
پتو عاشق نمیباشد.

To inqadr qarib i: hickas beto 'asheq namibashad.
You're such a freak: no one loves you.

شهرهای عربی غریبانرا دوست ندارند.

Shahrhaye 'arabi qaribanra dust nadarand.
The Arab cities don't like strangers.

غریبی عاشق مرا کشت.

Qaribi 'asheqe mara kosht.
A monster has killed my love.

جسم مرده‌ء عاشق خودرا میبینم.

Jesme morde'e 'asheqe xodra mibinam.
I see my lover's dead body.

هنوز عقب او میجویم.

Hanuz aqabe u mijuyam.
I'm still looking for him.

من در زندگی دردی می‌آیم.

Man dar zendegye dardi miayam.
I come in a life of pain.

(IT'S POSSIBLE TO SEE THE STAGE.)

خیابانها خیلی سیاه اینجاست

Xeyabanha xeili seyah inja st.
The streets here are very black.

دالانهای زندانها و محکمه‌ها

Dalanhaye zendanha va mahkameha
The labyrinth

این ارتفاع
This height

آذ فرهنگستان
That academy

برجها
Towers for exposing the dead

مُرَبَّع یا گِرد

Square or round

بی دَر

No door

بی طَرّاحان

No draughtsmen

باز تَنگ

Open closed

میل سَرکَش

Obelisk refractory

شَهر بی پایان اَست

The city's endless

نَقشه صاف نیست

The map isn't clear

این عِمارَت گُود اَست

The building is deep.

آن کوچه ساکِت اَست

An kuce saket ast.
That street is still.

سِفیدی هَرجاست

Sefidi harja st.
Whiteness is all-over.

عِمارَتها شِکلِ مُنَظَّمِ ریاضیست

'Emaratha shekle monazzame riazist.
The buildings are regular mathematical shapes.

آن عِمارَتِ آبی دادسَرائ ست

An 'emarate abi dadsara'ist.
That blue building is a courthouse.

پیچهای پَستتَر رُوشَن نیست

Pichaye pasttar roushan nist.
The lower corners aren't light.

پِلِّکان بالا میرَوَد

Pellekan bala miravad.
The steps rise.

پِلِّکانِ تاریک نیست

Pellekan tarik nist.
The steps aren't dark.

صُحنهایِ آسمان باز اَست

Sahnhaye asman baz ast.
The sky's courtyards're open.

تیز اَست

Tiz ast.
It is sharp.

این مَرد بی مُغز اَست

In mard bi maqz ast.
This man's lobotomized.

مُغز را کُشتَن خَیلی بَد اَست

Maqz ra koshtan xeili bad ast.
Lobotomy is horrible.

این مَرد عَلی اُستادیست

In mard 'Ali ostadi st.
This man, Ali, is an artist.

کوچِک و کَلیمیست

Kucek va lalimi st.
He's small and Jewish.

این یُهودیان .ی مُغزان آند

In Yahudian bi maqzan and.
These Jews have no minds.

آن جوخهٔ شَهر کَلیمیست

An juxe shahr kalimi st.
That ghetto is Jewish.

عَرَبی تَهودیست

'Arabi tahudi st.
An Arab is a Jew.

عَلیِ جَوان اَست وَلی مادَرَش پیر

'Ali javan ast vali madarash pir.
Ali is young but his mother's old.

عَلی میفَهمَد آن کوچه غَریب و
عَجیب اَست

Ali mifahmad an kuce quarib v 'ajib ast.
Ali senses, that street is strange and wonderful.

کِتابفُروشِ كَليمى قَليل اَست

Ketabforushye kalimi qalil ast.
The Jewish bookstore is small.

ایا يَهوديان اَز عَرَبان باهوشتَر اَند ؟

Aya yahudian az 'araban bahushtar and?
Are Jews more educated than Arabs?

این سؤالها ئَايرا دَرد ميكنَد

In so'alha 'Ali ra dard mikonad.
These questions pain Ali.

Ali writes a letter to his mommy,

The day of Reagan's
attempted assassination

Dear Mom,

Your guts stink. I hate your hair. You must be an Arab cause you have such a large nose. All Arabs are without intelligence. You don't understand my personality because I don't have a personality: I am shifty sneaky devious worthless anonymous wormlike and you've been looking for a real assassin. You want your son to be someone: to grow up and rip out people's guts for money or send poor people to jail for money or tell people all of whom listen what reality is. I'm just like everyone else.

Smelling your flesh when you are with me is agony because you do not love me. We are so different we should hate each other and besides you're a power-monger like all Arabs. We are so unlike each other, mom, even though we fuck, the universe must have been totally sick when it made us. The universe must be totally sick to make us, the two of us, the same blood.

We are going to have to kill each other because there is no other way out of this relationship.

I am banging open my head against my livingroom wall. Any pain helps soften the dry ice needles surrounding and stabbing my right eye swelling up the soft gush around my appendix squeeze my sex muscles into tiny steel pins your presence causes me.

I think you're a real good person and I wouldn't shoot anyone else, I only shot you cause everyone in the world hates you. I do what anyone wants me to. This is the agony. I can't be real anymore. I can't be—much less who—not even what I want. I am total powerlessness. What do you know about agony? I had to shoot you. Everyone knows everything about total agony and the whole world is writhing.

Are we supposed to have sex, mom, even though you're dead?

Your son,
Ali Warnock Hinkley, Jr.
Ali Warnock Hinkley, Jr.

علی سؤال میکُنَد مُسجَد را کُجاست ؟

'Ali so'al mikonad masjed ra koja st?
Ali asks, Where is the mosque?

کِتابفَروش پاسُخ میدِهَد، نَخَیر، پِسَرِ
مُتَقَلِّب، آن کوچه نیست، این آست.

Ketabforush pasox midehad, naxeir, pasare motaqalleb, an kuce nist, in ast.
The bookstore man replies, No, creepy boy, it is not that sidestreet, it is this sidestreet.

مُسجِد مُهِمّ آست

Masjed mohemm ast.
The mosque is important.

آنجا آزادی هُست

Anja azadi hast.
There, there is freedom.

مَگَر این آزادی خَیلی گِران نیست ؟

Magar in azadi xeili geran nist?
Isn't this freedom very expensive?

عَلی توِ بازارِ گوشت میرَوَد

'Ali tue bazare gusht miravad.
Ali goes into the meat market.

قاچهایِ بازویان وَ پایان هست

Qachaye bazuyan va payan hast.
There are cut-off arms and legs.

قاتِلِ بازویان وَ پایان کیست ؟

Qatele bazuyan va payan kist?
Who is the cutter-off of arms and legs?

ایا این خِیابان بالا میرَوَد ؟

Aya in xeyaban bala miravad?
Is this street climbing upwards?

بَلی، وَ زَرد آست

Bali, va zard ast.
Yes, and it is pale.

ایا یَهودی یا عَرَبی یا قاتِلِ سیاس هَستید؟

Aya yahudi ya 'Arabi ya qatele siasi hastid?
Are you a Jew, an Arab, or a terrorist?

اینجا چیزهایِ خالی فَقَط هُست

Inja cizhaye xali faqat hast.
Here is just emptiness.

ابا این عِمار'ت مَسجِد اَست؟

Aya in 'emarat masjed ast?
Is this building the mosque?

این عِمار'ت باز نیست

In 'emrat baz nist.
This building is closed.

مُرکزیَت نیست. فِکرها نیست. عاقِبَتها
نیست. اِنتِظارِها نیست.

Markaziat nist. Fekrha nist. 'Aqebatha nist. Entezarha nist.
There is no centralization. There are no thoughts. There are no goals. There
aren't expectations.

هُرج و مُرج قِسمَتِ جَنگ اَست

Harj o marj qesmate jang ast.
Anarchy is part of war.

این بُچّه د'زدیست

In bacce dozdi st.
The child is a blackmailer.

این بُچِّگان سیاه آند

In baccegan siah and.
These children are black.

د'زدانِ بُخیلُوحَریص 'و د'ارازد'ست آز
تَو'لُد و حِقار'تِ تَمام مُرد'مِ بِیرون و'
خِلافِ حُکومَت

Dozdane baxil or haris o darazdast az tavallod va heqarate tamame mardome
birun va xelafe hokumat
Avaricious, rapacious, predatory, born free-booters, hate strangers, intolerant
of restraint

During the days following the assassination of the Archduke Ferdinand at
Sarajevo, people evolved new—because everything is being destroyed every
second—usable languages including noise distortion lies destruction no
language. So today, humans are at the point of being catatonic and evolving
new languages.

Just as post World War I humans had Lenin and Freud, we have people who are making the most basic processes of human mentality and we don't need anything old.

We are no longer hierarchical. We no longer need men. We prefer deviation anomie anomaly shift fiction to rules and names. The repeating noise-making ridiculous functions of language are more pleasurable when mixed with the expressing ones.

A. In times of war all times we are warriors.

هَرج 'وُ مَرج قِسمَتِ جَنگ اَست

Harj o marj qesmate jang ast.
Anarchy is part of war.

این بالاخانۀ بُلَندیست

In balaxane'e bolandi st.
This is a high grating.

اینجا د'خترِ عَرَبی ایستاد

Inja doxtare 'Arabi istad.
An Arab woman stood here.

پائین د'مِ مَردی نِگاه کَرد

Pa'in dame mardi naqah kard.
She looked down at a man.

شَوهَرِ عَرَبیَش اورا کُشت

Shouhare 'Arabiash ura kosht.
Her Arab husband stabbed her.

حَوضِ بُزُرگِی خون هَست

Houze bozorgye xuni hast.
There was a large pool of blood.

ایا د'خترِ عَرَبی زِنده است

Aya doxtare 'Arabi zende ast?
Is the Arab woman alive?

د'ختر مَرده نیست، وَ'لی حَسَد زِنده

Doxtar morde nist vali hasad zende.
The woman isn't dead, but jealousy is alive.

زیار'تّی ته مَسجِد

Ziaati te masjed
A VISIT TO THE MOSQUE

عَلی د'رِ مَسجِدرا ز'د

'Ali dare masjedra zad.
Ali knocked on the door of the mosque.

رَنجِ خو'دْرا تَسْلیم کَرْد

Ranje xodra taslim kard.
He brought his anguish.

داخِلِ مَسجِدِ چای و، شیرینی را

میخُو'رَند

Daxele masjed cay va shirini ra mixorand.
In the mosque they drink tea and sweets.

عَلی گُفت

'Ali goft
Ali said

اینجا سَگ هَست

Inja sagi hast.
Here is a dog.

اینجا گُربهٔ هَست

Inja gorbe' hast.
Here is a cat.

اینجا زِندِگی نیست

Inja zendegi nist.
Here there is no life.

هیچ چیز را نَمیکُنی

Hic ciz ra namikoni
You don't do anything.

تَنبَل ای

Tanbal i.
You're lazy.

به هیچ چیز عَقیده دارْم

Be hic ciz 'aqide daram.
I don't believe anything.

دَر جَهانِ عَقیدِگان نَمیزیَم

Dar jahanye 'aquidegan namiziam.
I don't live in a world of beliefs.

بَشَری از جَهان هیچ چیز را کَی یافت ؟

Bashari az jahan hic ciz ra kay yaft?
When has a human gotten anything from the world?

شاه و' پدر را نُدارُم و اَز هَمه کَس نِفرَت

دارُم و مُن خِلافِ خوُد میجَنگَم

Shah o pedar ra nadaram v az hame kas nefrat daram va man xelafe xod mijangam.

I have no king no father I hate everyone and I'm in continuous war against the self.

هَرچیز را میگوُیَم : هیچکَس دَر هَر صوُرَت

این زُبان را نُدانَد

Har ciz ra miguyam: hickas dar har surat in zaban ra nadanad.

I say anything no one knows this language anyway.

جِنسِ موُّنَثَّم بِتوُ باز اَست

Jense mo'annasam beto baz ast.

My vagina is open to you.

جِنسِ موُّنَثَّم دَم دَّستَت اَست

Jense mo'annasam dame dastat ast.

My vagina is at your hand.

موُیَم دَّم دَّستَت اَست

Muyam dame dastat ast.

My hair is at your hand.

نِفرَت تو جِنسِ مُذَکَّرُم نیستید

Nefrat to jense mozakkaram nistid.

You are not my cock, hatred.

جِنسِ موُّنَثَّم دَر بازار تازِتَرین گوُشت

اَست و دَّستی

Jense mo'annasam dar bazar tazetarin gusht ast va dasti.

My vagina is the freshest meat in the market and a hand.

جِنسِ موُّنَثَّم دَر جَهان سیاهتَرین گُه اَست

Jense mo'annasam dar jahan siahtarin goh ast.

My vagina is the blackest shit in the world.

مَغزِ مَن آتِشیست

Maqze man ateshi st.

My brain is a fire.

فَریاد میکنُم

Faryad mikonam.

I'm screaming.

مَسجِد تِکّهٔ گُهٔ اَست

Masjed tekke'e goh' ast.
The mosque is a piece of shit.

زَبانِ فَقَط مُمکِنَم عَهیرٗاهایهیست

Zabane faqate momkenam 'ahirrahaiiiii st.
My only possible speech is 'ahirrahaiiiii.

تُو خُودکُشیَم اى

To xodkoshyam i.
You're my suicide.

الله بُد بو دار'د

___ bad bu darad.
Allah stinks.

ALI GOES TO A WITCH

دَر یأُس و جاهِل عَلى بِوَسیلهٔ کِتابِ لُغَتِ
تِلِفون عَقَبِ زَنِ جادوئى میگرَد'د.

Dar ya's va jahel 'Ali be vasileye ketabe loqate telefun aqabe zane jadu'i
migradad.
In desperation because not knowing anything, Ali looks through the phone
director for a witch.

زَنِ جادو بَرادَرِ خُود را میجَوید.

Zane jadu baradare xodra mijavid.
The witch was gnawing on her brother.

عَلى بِزَنِ جادو گُفت،

'Ali bezane jadu goft,
Ali said to the witch,

تَنها، مُعَلِّم، تَنها و مُست به نِفرَتُ خُنَک؛

Tanha, mo'allem, tanha va mast be nefrat o xonak;
Alone, Mistress, alone, drunk on disgust and boring;

تَنها: پِسَر با آیَنده بالا زُخم طُلوع نَکَرده
اَست؛

Tanha: pesar ba ayande bala zaxm tolu' nakarde ast;
Alone: the son with expectation hasn't risen above the wound;

تَنها، وَلی فَروَردین اَز دَریایِ تاریکِ نورِ
خُودرا میدَرَخشَد

Tanha, vali farvardin az daryaye tarik nure xod ra midaraxshad
Alone, but Farvardin is glowing its light through the dark sea

وَ وُسعَتِ آبی موسیقیِ خون اَست ظُهرِ
سوزِش اَست

Va vos'ate abi musiqye xun ast zohre suzesh ast
And blue space is rock-n-roll is burning noon

وُسعَتِ آویزان کَرده با نَبضهایِ گُلهایِ
اَندوخته هَمه جا.

Vos'ate avizan karde ba nabzhaye golhaye anduxte hame ja.
Space all around hung with pulsating, heaped-up roses.

دَر باغها بَر باغها بَر رویِ باغها

Dar baqha bar baqha bar ruye baqha.
Gardens upon gardens upon gardens.

بِیَک گُل نِشان بِده

Beyak gol neshan bedeh
Point to one rose

گُل جِنسِ مؤَنَّث اَست. گُل تَریاک اَست.

Gol jense mo'annas ast. Gol taryak ast.
The rose is a cunt. The rose is opium.

تَنها، زِمِستان مُعَلِّم، به یَکدیگَر وَحشَتِ
سَرد فَقَط را زیارَت کَرده

Tanha, zamestan mo'allem, be yakdigar vahshate sard faqat ra ziarat karde
Alone, Winter Mistress, having visited only cold horror on each other

یا پِدَر یا بَرادَر را نَدارُم.

Ya pedar ya baradar ra nadaram.
I have no father no brother.

مَن مالِ یا هیچ حَسَد یا هیچ غَضَب
یا هیچ صَندوق نیستَم؛

Man male ya hic hasad ya hic qazab ya hic sanduq nistam;
I don't belong to any envy or anger or box;

هَر کَس مَرا تَرک کَرده اَست : داخِلِ

مَملُوتِ خوابِها زِندِگی میکنَم،

Har kas mara tark karde ast; daxele mamlovvye xabha zendegi mikonam,
Everyone has left me: I'm living in the fullness of dreams,

میانِ خُود وَ جِنسِ مُؤَنَّثِ خویشِ وَ

عِشق را خِدمَت کَرده آم.

Miane xod va jense mo'annasi xishi va 'eshq ra xedmat karde am.
I've served kinship and love between me and a twat.

زَنِ جادو پاسُخ داد،

Zane jadu dad,
The witch replied,

شاشِ پَروین کَثیف اَست. شاشِ حَسَن

کَثیف اَست. اینجا دَرمانِ اِحتِیاجَتان اَست.

بِمَن دَه بَراترا بِدِهید وَ وِداع بِکُنید.

Shashe Parvin kasif ast. Shashe Hasan kasif ast. Inja darmane ehteyajatan ast.
Beman dah barat ra bedehid va veda' beknoid.
Parvin's piss is dirty. Hasan's piss is dirty. Here's the curse you want. Give me
ten dollars and leave.

عَلی بِه او دَه بَراترا داد وَ وِداع کَرد.

'Ali be u dah baratra dad va veda' kard.
Ali gave her ten dollars and left.

(THE STAGE IS LEFT WITH THE CRIES OF PEACOCKS.)

END

AUTHORS' BIOGRAPHIES

James Strahs wrote *North Atlantic* for the Wooster Group which also performed his *Oil Rig* as part of *Point Judith*. His novel *Wrong Guys* was adapted for the Mabou Mines production of the same name. Strahs wrote a Vietnam book, *Seed Journal*, and is currently completing a novel, *Queer and Alone*.

Des McAnuff is Artistic Director of the La Jolla Playhouse, one of America's most innovative regional theatres. He also directed *Big River* on Broadway. His plays, *The Death of von Richthofen as Witnessed from Earth* and *Leave It To Beaver is Dead* have been produced at the Public Theatre. McAnuff was previously part of The Dodger Company producing team.

James Lapine is a playwright and director who received the 1985 Pulitzer Prize for Drama in collaboration with Stephen Sondheim for *Sunday in the Park with George*. Lapine is also the author of *Twelve Dreams* and *Table Settings*. He had directed *March of the Falsettos* at Playwrights Horizons and *A Midsummer Night's Dream* at the New York Shakespeare Festival.

Stephen Sondheim wrote the scores for *Merrily We Roll Along*, *Sweeney Todd*, *Pacific Overtures*, *A Little Night Music*, *The Frogs*, *Follies*, *Company*, *Anyone Can Whistle* and *A Funny Thing Happened on the Way to the Forum*, and wrote the lyrics for *West Side Story*, *Gypsy*, and *Do I Hear a Waltz?*.

Kathy Acker is the author of several novels, including *Blood and Guts in High School*, *My Death*, *My Life by Pier Paolo Pasolini*, and most recently, *Don Quixote*. She is also the author of the film *Variety*, directed by Betty Gordon.

John Jesurun has written and staged several works which include *White Water*, *Shatterhand Massacree*, and *Chang in a Void Moon*. As a filmmaker he has made *Where are My Legs* and *Last Days of Pompeii*. *Deep Sleep* received an Obie Award in 1986.